Incontinent on the Continent

Jane Christmas

INCONTINENT

ON THE

CONTINENT

My Mother, Her Walker, and
Our Grand Tour of Italy

GREYSTONE BOOKS

D&M PUBLISHERS INC.

Vancouver/Toronto/Berkeley

Greystone Books
An imprint of D&M Publishers Inc.
2323 Quebec Street, Suite 201
Vancouver BC Canada V5T 4S7
www.greystonebooks.com

Library and Archives Canada Cataloguing in Publication
Christmas, Jane
Incontinent on the continent : my mother, her walker,
and our grand tour of Italy / Jane Christmas.

ISBN 978-1-55365-400-1

1. Christmas, Jane—Travel—Italy. 2. Italy—Description and travel.
3. Mothers and daughters. I. Title.

DG430.2.C57 2009   914.504'93   C2009-903507-3

Editing by Nancy Flight
Copyediting by Eve Rickert
Cover design by Peter Cocking
Text design by Naomi MacDougall
Cover photograph by R. Ian Lloyd/Masterfile
Map by Stuart Daniel
Printed and bound in Canada by Friesens
Printed on acid-free paper that is forest friendly (100% post-consumer recycled paper) and has been processed chlorine free
Distributed in the U.S. by Publishers Group West

We gratefully acknowledge the financial support of the Canada Council for the Arts, the British Columbia Arts Council, the Province of British Columbia through the Book Publishing Tax Credit, and the Government of Canada through the Book Publishing Industry Development Program (BPIDP) for our publishing activities.

For my mother, Valerie, of course

Contents

OUR ROAD TRIP THROUGH ITALY

AUSTRIA
HUNGARY
SWITZERLAND
SLOVENIA
CROATIA
Treviso
Venice
BOSNIA
Pisa Florence
Ligurian Sea
Siena Foligno
Rome
CORSICA
Naples Bari Alberobello
Sorrento Potenza Taranto
Tyrrhenian Sea
Ionian Sea
SARDINIA
San Mango d'Aquino
Reggio di Calabria
SICILY Taormina
Agrigento Racalmuto
Mediterranean Sea
TUNISIA

0   100   200   300   400   500
kilometres

1

Extending the Olive Branch

"Now, what are you going to do about that hair?" This was my mother's immediate reaction when I broached the idea of our going to Italy. Just her and me. For six weeks.

"Nothing," I replied. I picked up a magazine from the coffee table and began to leaf through it, pretending not to be bothered by her comment. "I'm not doing anything about my hair."

Even with my eyes averted I knew Mom's jaw was tightening and her head was shaking with disapproval. She is convinced that if she could just fix my hair she could fix my life. As if it were that easy.

Mom is five feet two inches short with a soft, plump body and a round face that exudes a charming, effervescent sweetness. Beneath that sugary exterior, however, is a tough cookie.

Imagine, if you will, a cross between Queen Victoria and Hyacinth Bucket ("It's pronounced 'bouquet,' dear," the fussy, social-climbing character on the Britcom *Keeping Up Appearances* constantly reminds people).

She has a thoroughly determined personality, my mom. Her opinions and beliefs are so entrenched that a tidal wave of evidence to the contrary cannot dissuade her. Her faith in God is as unwavering as her certainty that she will win the Publishers Clearing House Sweepstakes. She pooh-poohs the notion that man ever set foot on the moon: according to my mother, the lunar landing was staged in a movie studio.

Mom's hair is blond—ash blond, according to the product description—and she has maintained the same hairstyle for as long as I can remember: short, frothy, and layered. She likes it shorter at the back of her neck because she complains that that area gets hot. The front is swept off her face to reveal a smooth forehead; the sides are slightly curled.

To my mom, a tidy hairstyle signifies order, control, maturity (the very qualities, coincidentally, she feels I lack), and she trots out her theory like religious dogma at every opportunity.

Whether watching TV, stopped at a traffic light, sitting in a church pew, reading the newspaper, or getting groceries, my mother monitors the world's hairstyles. No one escapes her appraisal: the Queen ("A bit too severe"), Adolph Hitler ("I hope he shot his barber"), the Woman in the Street ("That style does nothing for her"), Robert Redford ("Perfect"). Wander into my mother's range of vision and you'll get an immediate, no-charge assessment.

Men I have dated and introduced to my mother have been accepted or rejected—mostly rejected—on the basis of their hair: "I didn't know whether to let him in or sweep him off the doorstep. That hair!" Or, "You tell him that he's not sitting at my dining room table unless he gets a haircut." Or, "He'd look much better if he parted his hair on the side." Or, "His hair is his best feature, and that's not saying much." On rare occasions, she has confided: "Oh, I do like his hair." The guy could be a serial killer but that would only register as a minor concern.

To my mom, hair is the yardstick by which civilized 3 people are measured—and that includes me. She scolds me if my hair drifts into my eyes ("Get it off your face"), for not getting it cut short enough ("I hope the hairdresser paid *you* for that cut"), or for not having age-appropriate hair ("A woman your age should have a neat, smart hairstyle").

When she spots an agreeable style in a magazine or in a shopping mall she shoots me a baleful look and says: "There's a nice style for you." A tight smile or a nod indicating total agreement from me is usually sufficient to end the conversation—until she hones in on another passing hairstyle. Lately, she's been pushing a short streaky blond bob as the elixir to happiness. The fact that such a hairstyle would not work with my face shape, my personality, or my impossibly fine, unpredictable dark hair is inconsequential.

If I have learned anything in life, it is that my one-day-limp, next-day-curly hair is best left alone. Over the years, I have made peace with my hair, but I have not done so with my mother. I wanted us to go to Italy to see if I could finally fall in love with her. This trip was my olive branch.

I wasn't going to allow her question about my hair to bug me. Not one bit.

I looked up nonchalantly from the magazine I was perusing and flashed a calm smile to mask the emotional maelstrom that was swirling and slopping inside me like the contents of the boiling cauldron being stirred by the Three Witches.

"Dishevelled is my look," I said playfully, tousling my hair as I prepared to shift the conversation to our travel itinerary.

"Your hair looks like your life," she said.

WHAT WOULD possess anyone to go to Italy, the Land of Love, with a sparring partner?

The answer: it was part détente, part deathbed request.

It has been a source of sadness and perplexity that my mother and I have not been able to get along. Don't get me wrong: it's not always a battle. The wary coolness between us has evaporated during moments of laughter or when we have weathered loss together. She never turned down a request to look after my children when I was struggling to adapt to single parenthood; she has always been a kind and generous grandparent. I, too, have been there for her: when she falls ill or when she needs my help around her home. She has even been known to seek my opinion.

Still, the tectonic plates of our relationship have never stopped shifting, and the fault lines—there's an interesting metaphor—have, according to my mom, been entirely my creations. She also thinks I am too sensitive—and there is no question that I am—but she doesn't think she needs to modify her tact when dealing with me.

"You take my words too seriously," she scolds impatiently.

"Really?" I reply. "So when you say that my hair looks like a rat's nest I should just laugh it off?"

"No," she answers thoughtfully. "You should go to a hairdresser and do something about it."

It's that sort of no-win bickering.

Then there is the matter of the deathbed request:

"Make friends with your mother," my father had instructed as I sat on the edge of his hospital bed a few weeks before he died.

I had wanted to scream, "CAN'T YOU JUST ASK ME TO WIN THE NOBEL PRIZE IN MEDICINE? THAT WOULD BE EASIER!"

When my father died in 1999, Mom and I lost our mediator and our buffer. We were left to soldier on through the minefield of our relationship as best we could. We maintained an awkward truce while marching to the beat of old drums.

Now, with life ebbing away and my mother's health issues mounting, I decided to be proactive and use what time we had left to set things right—if that were at all possible. So I came up with this ingenious idea of a trip to Italy. I wanted to see whether my mother and I could spend six weeks together without biting off each other's head, six weeks so distracted by art and antiquity that we could see each other as the individual works of art—flaws and all—that we are. I wanted to get to know this woman I call Mom, a woman I'm pretty certain, deep down, I love—but have had trouble liking. I hoped that in Italy the conversations I've always wanted to have with my mother would bubble up and help ease, if not resolve, decades of discontent.

I believe we take two trips when we embark on a journey of almost any duration: there's the physical trip, with its attendant need for schedules, accommodations, maps, and fretting about what to pack, how much money to bring, where to go and what to see, all the while anticipating possible calamities. Then there's the parallel journey, the internal journey. We talk about "leaving it all behind," but in reality a lot of emotional and primal baggage accompanies us on our travels. Trips are as much about testing ourselves or seeing how we adapt to a new place or to unfamiliar circumstances as they are about exploring new territory. Removing ourselves from our daily routines, from day-to-day relationships, from regimentation, allows us to see ourselves and others more clearly in new surroundings. Sometimes it allows us to resolve a gnawing problem or to find clarity about a situation or event from our present or our past. In this, I was no different: I wanted to resolve the mother-daughter dilemma.

6

Most daughters have an uneasy or tempestuous relationship with their moms. Just ask them, and stand by for a torrent of venting. It's usually a one-sided complaint—most mothers will rarely admit to difficulties with their daughters (and being the mother of a daughter I know of what I speak). Show me a mother who claims to have a great relationship with her daughter, and I'll show you a daughter in therapy.

Privately, many mothers fret about their relationships with their daughters. Maybe that's because mothers see themselves most clearly in their daughters. When they are successful we feel a shared sense of accomplishment; when an argument flares between mother and daughter it is like arguing with ourselves. I gleaned this handy bit of insight from Don the electrician. An electrician. How apropos.

One morning, while Don was fishing wires through a wall in my home, my daughter's fuse blew. I can't remember what the issue was, but I do clearly recall trying to keep the argument quiet because, well, I really dislike public displays of aggression. Zoë had no such reservations, and our quarrel regrettably escalated to the point where the electrician felt it prudent to intervene.

"You know why you two are arguing, don't you?" Don interrupted, straining to be heard above our raised voices.

Zoë and I froze, a bit shocked by the intrusion but none-theless curious about what he had to say.

"Because you're both exactly the same!" he said with exasperation.

Zoë stormed off, horrified by the verdict. My reaction was quite different: The Little Voice Inside let out a victory cry of "Yes!" Deep down, mothers yearn for their daughters to be mirror images of themselves. For daughters, it's different. There's nothing worse for a woman than to be told, "You're just like your mother." Not even when it is said in a nice way.

I'll admit: I sometimes live vicariously through my daughter. Zoë is the type of young woman I wanted to be at her age: smart, confident, unafraid to push back against authority. (She also does amazing, twisty things with her hair, a knack I can't even begin to learn). I was very much a late bloomer when it came to finding my groove. Seriously late: like, in my forties. Some of that emotional growth spurt occurred while Zoë was flexing her teenage spirit, and her newfound feisti-ness occasionally clashed with mine. It was a marked contrast to my teenage rebellion and my own mother's midlife awaken-ing. Whereas I let the reins on my daughter slacken slightly, my mother gripped them tighter and yanked on them. She was often strict and sharp with me and never short on advice about how to improve my life or my appearance. Handwritten notes accompanied by pertinent newspaper clippings or reli-gious homilies frequently appeared in my mailbox.

I just knew that another side of my mother existed, a fun-loving character with an intrepid nature. I wanted to spend time with that person.

Like me, my mother found her voice late in life. Her boundless creativity and can-do spirit was out of step with the times. The 1960s, for all the psychedelic talk of freedom and "doing your own thing," were still a time of repression, not least for women. Proper women stayed home to raise their children and do volunteer work; they didn't make waves, and those who defied convention would have their husbands' masculinity called into question. My mother managed to maintain the status quo on the home and volunteer fronts, but she also wrote a newspaper column and cultivated hobbies that weren't typical of a suburban mother in those days. She was different from any other mother I knew.

Along with my father, she developed a passion for preserving old homes. When no one could be found to assume old ruins slated for demolition, our family would move in. No house was deemed too run-down to save—not even if the place lacked running water. It bears reminding that in the early 1960s, the term "home renovation" was not in the lexicon.

Mom also had an insatiable appetite for antiques and was adept at scouring the back rooms and basements of dusty antique shops in parts of downtown Toronto where no other mother dared to tread. She cared not that the rest of civilized North America was swooning over the Swedish Modern look or that the color palate of the '60s favored hot-pink and fluorescent green: Our family lived in a 19th-century time warp of ball-and-claw-footed chairs, brocade and damask upholstery, inlaid walnut tables, and mahogany dining room suites that could seat twelve people. Our home resembled the set of *The Addams Family*. I was the only eight-year-old who knew that crewel work was not a reference to torture. Frequently my mom would drag me into shop after shop on her endless but unspecified quest for "a piece." When something caught her eye—a china platter or a carved medallion, for instance—she would lovingly examine it, running a delicate finger slowly and reverently around its detailed scalloped edges while marvelling at its beauty. It made me flush with jealousy; I craved for her to touch, admire, and notice me in the same way.

We operate differently as parents, my mother and I, and yet—and it pains me to admit this—there are undeniable similarities, just like Don the electrician said about Zoë and me. In an effort to be our own people we will deny any similarities and even try to make them look like differences.

Later in life, when I had children of my own, some of my mother's criticism waned, but the wounds never healed. All it took was one comment about my hair, my housekeeping standards, or my parenting skills to reopen the scars. I adopted unconsciously her insistence on perfection in everything and everyone around me, including her.

I also inherited my mother's penchant for busyness. Single parenting for much of my adult life was a frightening juggling act of keeping my head above water financially while maintaining the facade that the lack of a husband/father was but a minor inconvenience. I tossed more balls in the air just to prove my point. I enlisted my children to help out so we could all appear productive, respectable, and on our toes. I subscribe to the belief that chores and responsibilities are important to a child's development, but the memory of my own chore-filled childhood was a reminder to go easy on them and to cultivate within them, and within me, gentleness, helpfulness, and forgiveness. I didn't always succeed but I tried.

Somehow, I could not bring myself to be gentle with my mother.

Not that it was all miserable between my mom and me. We're white Anglo-Saxons after all; we are able to hide vast amounts of emotional damage behind stiff upper lips, fake smiles, and forced laughter. Still, an awkward detachment exists.

The question that has always bedevilled me—besides, Was I adopted?—is, How did my mother and I fall off the rails so early in our relationship and why was there no attempt to mend our rift? Instead, we let things drift and accepted dysfunction as the status quo. Whenever we locked eyes it was like the bell had been struck to begin another round. Still, no matter how bitter things got we never left the ring. We kept swinging and bouncing off the ropes till we all but exhausted ourselves.

A trip to Italy was the reward for two old prizefighters.

What better place to hash out mother-daughter matters than in Italy? The country positively invented motherhood—worships it, in fact. It is the backbone of Italy's dominant religion; it is woven into the social fabric; it is an iconic feature of the culture. You cannot picture Italy without visualizing a robust mother smiling at the head of the family dinner table or smacking the head of a misbehaving adult son or pinching his cheeks with her chubby fingers out of love and pride.

Italy seemed like the best place to view our relationship from a safe, therapeutic distance; a place where we could assess the past as if it had been some kind of psychosocial experiment whose results had been submitted for peer review, and where we could regard the hurt, the rage, the what-ifs, the sharp words, the crushing disappointments with breezy dispassion.

Who was I kidding?

Still, nothing can silence my mother like the sight of a faded tapestry or an ancient ruin, and that was another reason I thought Italy would be perfect for us: When we ooh and ahh over stone follies, pastoral views, oil paintings, and antiques, we give voice to a common denominator that confirms our familial tie, a tie frayed by too many years of tugging.

Our shared interest in antiquity was the reason we gave when well-meaning friends, aware of our contentious history, carefully inquired as to why we were going on holiday together. But the unspoken reason—one that my mom and I could barely admit to one another—was that we were going to use the background of the Italian Renaissance to spark a renaissance of our own.

I WAS stretched out on my tummy on the living room carpet like a teenager, legs bent at ninety-degree angles and crossed at the ankles, elbows propping me up as I pressed the phone's receiver to my ear. My favorite book, the *National Geographic Atlas of the World,* was open in front of me. My index finger was languorously following the contours of Italy's curvaceous coastline while my mind dallied with fantasies involving stiletto heels and a swarthy hunk named Giancarlo. Then Mom's voice spoke sharply across the phone line.

"And make sure you tell them I need a wheelchair. Those airports are too big, and I can't make it from the check-in counter to the plane without one."

Poof! Giancarlo and the stilettos vanished.

The words "wheelchair" and "Italy" seemed incompatible, almost as incompatible as my mother and I. The mere mention of a wheelchair caused my chest to tighten and brought my vocal chords to the brink of a scream. I had only considered pushing my mother around Italy in a purely metaphorical sense.

"And I'm bringing my walker. The red one."

I hate the walker. It makes me feel seriously old, even though I'm not the one using it. I do not like to think of myself as being old enough to have a mother who uses a walker. And of course when you walk with someone who is pushing a walker, you unconsciously adopt the walker shuffle: a slow, deliberate one-step, the type of gait you use when you're recovering from a C-section or hysterectomy.

The wheelchair was but one consideration in planning this trip.

My mother is at an age where myriad health issues are gradually clipping her wings. (She has threatened to cut me out of her will if I divulge her exact age, so let's just say that she is younger than one hundred and older than sixty-five.)

Seating on the plane had to be near a washroom: my mom is incontinent.

The hotel rooms had to have ensuites for the same reason.

The hotel could not have too many stairs: my mom has osteoarthritis in her knees.

The distance from the lobby to the hotel room could not be too far: my mom has asthma and heart problems.

Food to nibble on needed to be packed: my mom has diabetes.

No-fish meals had to be requested: my mom is allergic to seafood.

Rental cars had to have enough storage space to stow the walker.

Mom also has two canes: a fold-up cane for travelling and a non-folding cane in case she loses the fold-up one. (She only brought one to Italy.)

Did I mention that she's hard of hearing? (At times I think this affliction is selective.)

"Other than that I'm perfectly healthy," Mom cheerfully told me.

"Are you sure?" I asked as we discussed our trip.

"Absolutely," she said.

Most women my age planning a six-week holiday to Italy would be conducting forensic online research into the precise location of every Ferragamo or Prada outlet in the country. My research consisted of figuring out how much room a package of incontinence diapers would take up in a suitcase and whether a smorgasbord of medication and asthma puffers would be an issue at customs.

Travelling with a senior is not much different from travelling with a small child. Same preparation time, same cargo-ship's worth of paraphernalia in anticipation of every manner of disaster, same dashing-back-into-the-house routine to retrieve a forgotten item. The gear is essentially the same; a pale blue or pink carrying bag is replaced by one in a more dignified sage or black. Walkers or wheelchairs replace strollers, books and magazines replace toys, peppermint candies replace cookies, sweaters and shawls replace blankies, eyeglasses and hearing aids replace pacifiers—and diapers are replaced by, well, bigger diapers.

Then there is the medication.

I dropped in one day to help Mom with her packing. Her bed was heaped with bottles and jars and crinkly packages. It looked as if she and her neighbors had taken the contents of their medicine cabinets and dumped them.

"What's all this?" I said with mild horror.

"My medication," she replied matter-of-factly.

I'll admit, not proudly either, that whenever Mom launched into a description of her health problems and prescriptions the information waltzed in one ear and out the other. As soon as she uttered the words "I was at the doctor's the other day," I would politely say, "Keep talking," and leave the room to pour myself a large glass of wine.

That behavior ended when I became the person who would be carrying her luggage to, through, and back from Italy.

14   I looked down at the array of pills on her bed and shook my head. There was a prescription for everything short of leprosy.

"Don't worry," said Mom. "The pharmacist is making up dose-ettes for me."

"What?"

"Like this." She held out a cardboard platform with small plastic bubblelike compartments arranged in a grid, containing all the pills to be consumed that day. Across the top row was marked, in large type, the days of the week; down the left side was the time of day—morning, noon, evening—the medication was to be taken.

"Why do you need a prescription for vitamins?" I asked, peering at the label of one medicine bottle I had picked up at random.

"Because the doctor gave it to me," she said in a tone of voice reserved for addressing morons.

"You should check whether your doctor isn't getting a kickback from the pharmacist," I said. "You can buy this stuff over the counter and save yourself the dispensing fee."

"Don't interfere," she said petulantly. "I know what I'm doing. Besides, it's hard to get a doctor these days."

My packing required less attention to health concerns; I am, touch wood, in good health. I don't believe in taking medication of any sort—not even vitamins—except when something like sudden depression or a freak infection hits me, and then I am all for prescription drugs.

Without the worry of drugs and walking aids, I loaded my suitcase with clothes and makeup. And shoes. I seem to require a lot of shoes whenever I travel. I also cannot leave home without a small arsenal of face creams, cleansers, shower gels, hair conditioners, and body lotions to fend off dry weather. Whenever I pack and review my heaving case of toiletries, I realize with a heavy heart that I was born in the wrong part of the world. My skin and hair are at their best in tropical climates.

All the guidebooks and Web sites I had perused before heading to Italy mentioned that during the winter months the weather was moderate and mostly warm, especially in the south. I happily packed light skirts, sandals, T-shirts, and—because there would be a pool at one place we had booked—bathing suits and silky pareos.

Mom left all the arrangements and decisions about the trip in my hands ("Wherever you want to go is fine with me") and then insisted on seeing a printed itinerary of the sort found in travel brochures or issued by tour operators.

Rarely do I travel with a plan. I'm like Robert Louis Stevenson, who once said, "I travel not to go anywhere, but to go." But since Mom was expecting something more than "Get on plane; fly to London, then to Bari. Rent car," I cobbled together a basic plan to keep her happy.

This was it: We would fly from Toronto to London, transfer to a flight to Bari, rent a car, and drive from Bari to Alberobello, where we would stay for two weeks. From there we would drive to Sorrento and stay for four days, then drive from Sorrento to Viterbo, our base for three weeks. Our flight home would begin in Rome, with a connecting flight in London.

I was especially proud of the accommodations I had booked.

In Alberobello we would be staying in a renovated *trullo*. *Trulli* are the traditional small shelters built about eight hundred years ago by field workers in Italy's Apulia region. They look like little white stucco beehives with conical slate roofs. As a field worker's family grew, so did the *trullo*, and more beehive-shaped units were added. Eventually some *trulli* consisted of three or four buildings, each cone serving as a room. *Trulli* are the latest real-estate craze, especially among the Brits, who are flocking to the area and snapping them up as income properties. One of those Brits happens to be the brother of my beau, Colin. Mom and I would be his first clients.

In Sorrento we had booked a family-run hotel that had been recommended by an acquaintance.

Our Viterbo digs consisted of a medieval town house I came across on the Internet. It was located in the center of the old quarter, and its Web site promised antique stores and cafés right outside the front door. It would be perfect for my antique-loving mom, and for me since I love soaking up the historical atmosphere in out-of-the-way places.

"And of course we're going to Tuscany and Venice," said Mom as she scrupulously reviewed my itinerary.

Neither of those places was part of my plan. I was so sick of clichés about Tuscany and its amber-colored, manufactured romanticism that I had lost interest in the place long before preparing for this trip to Italy. As for Venice, a friend who had recently returned from a visit had told me it was dirty and dismal. I nixed Venice, too.

"We're not going to Tuscany or Venice?" Mom asked loudly. "What's Italy without Tuscany or Venice?"

"Exactly," I replied firmly. "We are not going near the tourist traps."

"Look," she said, fixing me with a dark, penetrating stare. "I've never been to Italy, and this is the one and only time I'll be there. This is my last trip to Europe. Make no mistake: We are going to Tuscany *and* Venice!"

"Well, we might go into Tuscany a bit," I allowed.

"And Florence," she said emphatically, not quite grabbing me with both hands by the lapels, but you get the picture. "We have to go to Florence."

"Yes, of course," I sputtered.

I felt myself shrinking into a ten-year-old version of myself, so I squared my shoulders, straightened what remained of my backbone, and said, "Listen here. This isn't going to be one of those holidays where we're rushing from one end of the country to the other. I am not going to be forced to drive like a lunatic all over the place. Do you understand?"

"I know," she said, her eyes refusing to meet my gaze. "That won't happen."

2

En Route to Italy

It was a bitterly cold late afternoon in February when we arrived at Toronto's Pearson International Airport. Minus twenty-two degrees Fahrenheit, according to an electronic billboard we passed on the highway. It was so cold that when I inhaled, the tiny hairs inside my nasal passages turned to icicles, and I felt the onset of hypothermia around the frontal lobes of my brain.

Certain things in this world test my Christian soul—cell phones, airports, the United Nations, the spattering, ear-splitting rev of motorcycles, Brad Pitt and Angelina Jolie—but nothing tests it more than winter. It was no coincidence that I planned our trip so that we would be out of Canada for as much of the winter as possible. It's not just the snow; it's the cold, the dry air, the feeling that every drop of moisture is being sucked out of me. I could hardly wait to be in sunny, warm Italy. The weather forecasts there, which I had been monitoring multiple times a day, listed temperatures around seventy-five degrees Fahrenheit. I imagined myself attired in an outfit of gauzy fabric, strolling down narrow lanes bordered by tall, blindingly bright white stucco walls and occasionally darting into a sliver of shade to escape a searing noon sun.

At the entrance to the airport terminal I wrestled with a luggage cart from the trolley stand, and was piling on our suitcases when I glanced around and saw Mom hailing nonwhite travellers, assuming they were porters.

I was caught for a split second between screaming *"No!"* and melting in a puddle of shame on the sidewalk.

I watched her for a moment as she waddled unsteadily along the sidewalk before stopping, with a somewhat bewildered look on her face, and raising her hand for attention. There was a frailty and vulnerability to her that I had never noticed before. At that precise moment I knew that the balance of our parent-child relationship had completely shifted.

"Where are the porters?" Mom demanded imperiously, pounding her cane. A black man in a very smart tan suit was walking briskly in her direction; she started to raise her hand in a gesture to hail him, and he shot her a disapproving look.

"Come on, Mom," I said gently, catching her by the fold in her jacket sleeve. "They don't have them anymore, or not many of them. They're for special cases."

"Aren't I special?" she pouted.

"Of course you are," I soothed. "C'mon. Let's get our tickets, shall we?"

With one hand on the luggage trolley and the other on her shoulder I slowly turned her around and aimed her toward the check-in counter. I placed one of her hands on the cart's push bars and then covered it with one of my own hands. It was something I had done countless times with my children to keep them from wandering off. Gosh, was that really more than twenty years ago? The memory of it had all but fizzled out.

At the airline check-in counter a wheelchair was promptly summoned. It arrived with a porter—an efficient, older Indian man.

Mom regarded him with a moment of suspicion before letting him assist her into the wheelchair.

He left us on the other side of the security cordon, and thank goodness, because that's when my cringe-o-meter went into overdrive.

"Look at all the immigrants!" Mom exclaimed with childish awe when she surveyed the security workers.

Being of a certain generation, my mom figures that if you are not white then you are automatically an immigrant. Yet this is a woman who reads books and newspapers and who watches TV. Had she mistaken the nightly news for serialized episodes of *National Geographic*?

Italy's Silvio Berlusconi, during one of his many election campaigns, commented that all incoming immigrants should be shot in their boats. I decided not to share that with her.

I did consider jerking her hand and telling her sharply to hush, but people have a tendency to react differently when you do that to a senior than to a child. I did not want to be cited for elder abuse.

Of course, it works the opposite way for seniors. They can apparently abuse their caregivers and make demands with impunity.

Mom's worldview aside, there was the issue about her physical ability. Based on the few hours we spent in the airport lounge, it was clear she could not do anything without my help. When she dropped something on the floor, I had to pick it up; when I was reading a book or working on a Sudoku puzzle, she would mew about being thirsty, so I would fetch her a drink. Then she would spill some of it and I would have to jump up and get a cloth to mop it up.

The upside of flying with a senior, as I pleasantly dis-
covered, was priority boarding and lots of fussing-over by normally ice-queen flight attendants.

We settled into our seats, and I arranged my little conve-
niences in the pouch in front of me. Through the small oval window beside my seat I watched the ground crew, huge puffs of frosty breath emanating through the scarves lashed around their faces, finish deicing the plane's wings. It gives me no comfort to know that a plane that I am sitting in is being deiced.

I turned to my mother. Her tongue was curled around her upper lip as she struggled for a small eternity with the cello-
phane wrapping on a candy. A thought began to weave and wind itself through my mind: This could be the longest six weeks of my life. I had seriously miscalculated her ability to do anything without assistance, a miscalculation largely borne of her cheerful insistence, "I'm capable of doing anything!"

Her endless stream of questions began on the tarmac and continued thirty thousand feet into the air, regardless of whether I was reading or listening through headphones to the in-flight movie. "Why was the plane delayed?" "Why do so many people travel at the same time?" "Why are there so many immigrants working at airports?" "What's 'deicing' mean?"

After a handful of hours in the air, during which I looked longingly at the emergency exit, she drifted off to sleep. When she awoke, she denied having ever slept and proceeded to

21

complain about everything from the airline food to the too-busy stewards to the location of her seat (I had purposely selected her upgraded seat for its legroom and proximity to the bathroom).

By the time we reached London's Gatwick Airport, I was wound up tighter than a yo-yo and began second-guessing my staunch refusal to take mood-enhancing medication. I was considering cashing in our tickets and taking the next flight back to Canada when a heavyset porter wearing a turban approached us with a wheelchair. Mom shot me a worried look.

"God, Mom," I groaned wearily under my breath as I eased her into the chair. "I don't think he's with the Taliban."

"HE'S WITH THE TALIBAN?" she shouted.

Something to remember: There is only one speaking volume used by the hearing impaired.

I gave a sideways glance to the glowering porter and mouthed the word "sorry," then raised my index finger to my ear and made a few circular motions before pointing to the back of Mom's head. He accepted this with grudging understanding, gripped the handles of the wheelchair tightly, and led us through customs.

Our flight to Bari was not leaving from Gatwick Airport; it was leaving from Stansted Airport, a fair distance away.

Luckily my beau lives in London. He was only too happy to be our taxi.

As I wheeled Mom out the door of customs, I spied Colin's lanky frame leaning on the metal barricade, an ever-present newspaper rolled up in his hands. Colin waved and beamed at us. I returned a look that was all rolled eyes and grim face.

"She's grouchy; lousy flight," I muttered as Colin and I kissed.

He pulled gently away from me and crouched down in front of my mother.

"Hello there, Val." Colin spoke kindly, slightly upping the volume of his soft voice for Mom's benefit. "How was your flight?"

"It was lovely, absolutely perfect," she chirped, flashing a multiwatt smile.   23

He looked at me questioningly.

I shrugged. What can I say? The woman lies.

"I'll get the car and bring it round to the front of the terminal," he said. "Then we'll go for lunch."

Then he repeated this a bit louder for my mother's benefit: "Are you hungry, Val? I know a nice little pub on the way to Stansted that I think you'll like."

"Wonderful!" she beamed.

He looked at me for confirmation. I smiled and nodded.

"Oh, he's a nice man, Jane," she said approvingly as Colin hurried away. "So cheerful. And tidy looking. I do like his hair."

In the forty years I have been on and off the dating circuit, Colin is the only man my mother has liked. Well, there was another guy she sort of liked, way back when I was a teenager. He was a drug user and a groper. She didn't know that, of course.

"Is Colin coming to Italy with us?" she asked.

"No, but he's coming in a few weeks when we get to Viterbo," I said, wheeling her outside the terminal and scanning the sidewalk for a wheelchair ramp. I tried to channel Colin's patience. "Remember? We've discussed that a few times now."

She stared ahead, and I could see the cogs in her brain churning to retrieve the information.

Colin's pale silvery-green car pulled up to the curb. I immediately pulled the luggage off the cart and began to stuff it into the hatchback. With an air of slight annoyance I stuck my head around the back end of the car to see why Colin was taking so long to help me. There he was, carefully helping my mother into the front seat of his car and ensuring that she was comfortable and that her arms and legs were safely tucked inside before he closed the car door. This is one reason why I love this man: He has his priorities straight.

"I didn't think she'd be able to get into the backseat," he said, joining me at the back of the car. "Sorry."

He stole another kiss. I ran a hand through his gray-flecked ginger hair.

"Nice to see you," he smiled. "You look stressed. Everything OK?"

"It's my first time travelling with a disabled person," I said. "Plus she's my mother, and she's crazy. I don't know how I'm going to handle this."

"She seems fine to me," he said. "Really chipper and lucid. C'mon. Let's get some lunch."

I squeezed into the backseat, and off we drove.

It was a relief to be in the backseat. It meant I could relinquish my responsibilities for a while. Colin and Mom were bantering between themselves, and I was about to nod off when...

"But all the immigrants! I've never seen so many. Where would we be without them!"

"*Mom!* Stop it!"

"She's so sensitive about this," Mom said, shaking her head and confiding to Colin as if I weren't there. "I just don't understand her. Anyway, there were immigrants *everywhere*."

"You're an immigrant, too," I said, smiling through clenched teeth.

"I'm different," she snorted.

Naturally. It is the considered opinion of all immigrants that the immigration door should have been bolted after they were let in.

"What do you think of all the colored people at airports?" she pressed Colin.   25

I emitted a painful groan.

"Mom, Colin travels a lot. And he lives in London, which, believe it or not, has 'colored' people."

"I don't believe I was talking to you, dear," she said in a singsong cadence as she cast me a Hyacinth Bucket smile— the one that is part pity, part shut the hell up.

Colin gripped the steering wheel tighter—I could see the whites of his knuckles—and from the slight rev of the engine I knew he was surreptitiously pressing down on the accelerator pedal.

AFTER A cozy lunch at the Goose and Turd—or something like that—Colin delivered us to Stansted Airport and kissed us good-bye before we handed ourselves over once again to the indignities of an airport security check.

I had booked our flight from London to Bari over the Internet for the astonishingly low price of thirty-nine pence per person. The cost didn't include taxes or luggage premiums but it did, I'm happy to report, include the wings for the plane.

It also included a chance to engage with a swarm of humanity the likes of which I hope never to experience again.

By the time we arrived in the departure lounge, our fellow Ryanair passengers were straining the flimsy fabric barrier of the preboarding corral. Some were practically crouched in a starting position, ready to make a mad dash across the tarmac to the plane as soon as the boarding announcement was made.

A steward noticed my wheelchair-bound mom, and then me, cowering in the midst of the foaming-mouthed horde.

"Might wanna move 'er over 'ere, luv," the steward said. She bulldozed a path for us to the front of the line and, with a grim nod, added, "You get priority boarding."

The horde seemed to take great umbrage with this concession.

Priority boarding among this group was a dubious advantage. It basically granted you a head start and a count of ten.

"I suggest you move smartly, luv," said the steward, lowering her voice and giving me a knowing look of raised eyebrows and pursed lips. She unhooked the fabric barricade and let us through. The other passengers surged forward. The last I heard from the steward was a loud thwacking sound and her booming voice. "'Ere! Get back you lot!"

I pushed the wheelchair onto the tarmac and began walking briskly toward the plane. I looked back nervously several times to make sure the other passengers were still securely held in place. We were halfway to the plane when it became apparent that permission to board had been granted to one and all. It looked like a prison break.

I stepped up my pace. OK, I won't mince words: I was running for dear life. Mom clutched our purses to her breast.

As we neared the plane, two ground crew workers intercepted us and hustled us into a wheelchair elevator. It lifted off and raised us to the airplane door just as the mob arrived, out of breath with their ties flopped over their shoulders and their hair and eyeglasses wildly askew.

26

"Ha, ha! Suckers!" I chuckled to myself in a victorious James Bond sort of way.

We grabbed our seats aboard the plane, and soon the silver beast was roaring down the runway toward a late afternoon sky streaked with the fading light of day.

I took a deep breath and exhaled slowly. We were on our way to Italy. Finally.

There have been times in my life when I have felt Italian to the depths of my soul, where the cells belonging to heritage reside. I do not possess a smidgen of Italian blood, yet whenever I hear Italian spoken on the street, my heart catches; whenever I hear Puccini's *La Bohème* or *Gianni Schicchi,* I am overwhelmed to the point of tears; whenever I observe Italian families walking arm in arm or huddled in serious discussion around the meat counter debating the merits of one brand of prosciutto over another, my soul swells with happiness knowing that all is right with the world and that Italy is the last line of defense between those whose passion is political and religious fanaticism and those whose passion is living.

When I would hit the valleys of a roller-coaster life and wonder what, aside from my children, there was worth living for, my mind would default to a series of clichéd images of Italy that shuddered into action like an old film reel—boisterous families gathered beneath a pergola of grape vines around a table laden with baskets of home-baked bread and bowls of fresh pasta, tomatoes, leafy greens, and fruit; a searing band of sunlight slashing through olive branches; red wine in raffia-wrapped bottles; an aerial view of a sports car zipping along a narrow, winding seawall road on a bright, clear day.

"Yes," I would sigh to myself as I quietly put away the razor blades. "There's still Italy."

After five decades of pining, this was a long-awaited visit to my true homeland. I wanted to experience what Stendhal meant when he said, "The charm of Italy is akin to that of being in love."

Through one of the plane's windows I saw the twinkling lights along the Adriatic coast come into view. I was on the verge of slipping into a state of profound contentment when...

"Did you ask about a wheelchair?" Mom asked as the plane's wheels bounced on the tarmac of Bari's airport.

Christ. The wheelchair again.

"Yes," I assured her with a forced smile.

"I don't see one out there," she clucked, peering through the window to scan the runway.

"Well, it is nighttime so it would be difficult to see a wheelchair," I said. "Just be patient." I bit back the urge to add, "Your Majesty."

Portable stairs were wheeled up to the plane, and the able-bodied passengers shoved, elbowed, swore, and kicked their way off the plane as if someone had shouted "SARS!"

Mom and I remained in our seats. A few rows ahead sat a woman with her leg in a cast.

Four airport workers appeared onboard with a single wheelchair. Mom struggled to her feet and was about to make a hasty beeline for them when I grabbed the back of her pants and pulled her back in her seat.

"If you do that they'll think that you really don't need a wheelchair," I whispered sternly.

"But what about...?"

"Just. Wait."

The crew gingerly moved the young woman from her seat to the wheelchair, then proceeded to discuss her injury (a broken knee) and how they were going to get her off the plane. The woman was accompanied by an older man who might have been her father, though you can never tell these days. She explained in Italian to the crew that her injury—a fall— had occurred in England. A vociferous discussion ensued. I did not understand everything but gathered they were talking about the English medical system and whether English sur- geons were capable of properly resetting a broken bone.

There were lots of furrowed brows, flailing arms, gestur- ing hands, shaking heads, and pointing fingers aimed at the young woman's cast. It was like performance art.

Italians love problems and puzzles. Everyone is a closet Galileo who believes he or she alone holds the key to enlight- enment on any subject. If you are brave enough to dispute someone's solution or opinion, he (or she) will shrug his shoulders as if to say, "Suit yourself, but don't say I didn't warn you."

Ah, the utter loveliness of hearing people converse in Ital- ian, I thought.

Mom, meanwhile, was getting impatient. She gave a little cough to get their attention.

"*Momento,*" a crew member replied tersely, and the group resumed their discussion.

About ten minutes later, having exhausted the subject and any possible solutions, the crew turned their eyes to my mother.

They finally twigged to the bigger problem—two disabled women, one wheelchair. Another heated discussion arose. Finally, the fellow who seemed to be in charge of the crew said something to one of his coworkers, a tall, dark-haired, strap- ping young man, and gestured to my mother.

The woman in the cast was wheeled into a portable elevator that had materialized at the cabin door while the young
man strode over to my mother and, with great gentleness and
purpose, took her hand and walked her to the lift. He held her
hand during the descent in the elevator, he held her hand as
he walked her into a second portable lift that lowered her to
the tarmac, and he continued to hold her hand as he patiently
and slowly walked her across the tarmac to the terminal. I
suppose they had decided that as long as someone was holding her hand, my mother could magically walk better.

A baggage handler had spotted my mother's metallic-
red walker in the luggage compartment of the plane and had
placed it on the tarmac.

The young man left my mother's side and joined the baggage handler. Together they valiantly struggled with the
packing tape and a shoulder strap from an old carry-on bag,
which had held the walker tightly throughout our journey.

"I did a good job tying that, didn't I?" Mom whispered to
me proudly.

Suddenly, the walker sprang from its bounds and into
position. Mom toddled unsteadily toward it like a child who
suddenly spies a favorite toy.

The young man placed his hand under my mother's elbow
while she pushed her walker. He took us through passport
control and to our waiting luggage.

"Do you think he'll stay with us for the entire holiday?"
Mom tittered. "He's very handsome, isn't he? I like his hair.
Should I give him a little something? He seems to be waiting
for a tip."

While the young man sat impassively with my mother it
was left to me to heave our luggage off the baggage carousel,

drag it over to the rental car counter, and haul it all through the parking lot while trying to locate our rental car.

"Really, someone should be helping you," admonished Mom when she caught up to me, having finally bid *ciao* to her handsome attendant. She had managed to find time to touch up her lipstick and face powder.

"Unfortunately, airports do not offer Italian stallions to single, able-bodied, middle-aged women," I grumbled.

I loaded our two large, heavy suitcases, our two carry-on bags, and my mother's red walker into the backseat of the rental car, a silver Ford Focus station wagon that shone under the glare of a nearby street lamp. Three men stood nearby, idly watching me, dragging on their cigarettes.

I slid in behind the wheel and started up the car. I placed Mom's disabled parking permit, which she had brought with her from Canada, onto the dashboard, and also retrieved from my purse the directions to Alberobello, about an hour and a half from the airport.

Two weeks before we left for Italy I had awakened in the middle of the night in a sweat-soaked panic, overcome with fear about the prospect of driving in Italy. I had sprung out of bed, dashed downstairs, and Googled "driving in Italy," which led to sites that either described the experience as insane (confirming my fears) or not so bad (confirming Google's unreliability). I focused on the former and perused information about petrol stations, how to pump gas, horror stories about dealing with masses of directional signs, Kafkaesque roundabouts, and the nuances of Italian highway etiquette. None of what I found put my mind at ease.

I telephoned a friend who had rented a car in Italy a few years earlier.

"Are you an aggressive driver?" he asked.

I was unsure whether it was wise to ask him to define "aggressive."

A survey by Britain's Automobile Association ranked Italy as the second-worst country for bad drivers (the honor of first place goes to Spain). There was also the worrying fact that nearly 5,500 people had been killed in Italy the previous year in traffic accidents. That's the sort of statistic that makes you wonder whether a travel advisory ought to be issued.

It was bad enough that I was driving in Italy, but to do so after a transatlantic flight *and* late at night was exceedingly reckless. It took three attempts to locate the on-ramp to the highway, but after that, to my surprise and relief, driving in Italy proved no different than driving at home. Within minutes of hitting the autostrada I was passing other vehicles with confidence.

Then we got lost.

"Where's the map?" I asked.

Mom began to slowly and delicately unfold the road map we had been given at the car rental kiosk.

"You're supposed to be my copilot. Don't you think your first duty should be to unfold the map?"

"Don't snap at me," she retorted. "Why don't you stop at this gas station and ask directions?"

"First, it's closed. Second, in case you haven't noticed, we're in Italy. They speak Italian; we don't."

"I'm sure they understand English," she said. "My friends told me everyone speaks English in Italy."

"Your friends were on a seniors' coach tour," I reminded her. "They only visited places that get a deluge of English-speaking tourists."

The farther we drove, the less sure I was of where we were. We followed signs to a five-star resort that was deserted except for a suspicious-looking man who was wandering the grounds. I collared him nonetheless. He spoke less English than I speak Italian, but I got the gist of what he was saying, and in short order we arrived at a road that got us on the right track.

Then we got lost again.

"There's a place that's open. Ask directions," said Mom.

"No. I don't like the look of that place."

"Look, there's a gas station that's open. Just pull in there, and I'll ask."

"No!"

"Honestly, I've never met anyone so stubborn! You're just like your father."

"Put on your bloody seat belt."

"I'm not going to wear it; it's uncomfortable."

"It's the law, Mother. Put it on."

"Fine. It's on."

"No, it isn't. Can't you hear that beeping noise? It tells you the seat belt is not buckled. Do it up now!"

And so it continued for many, many miles. Jet lag and exhaustion had pushed aside any semblance of civility.

We eventually found the correct turnoff and then travelled an interminable distance in silence to the town of Locorotondo. In a small square with four or five roads emanating from it, I stopped another lone wolf wandering the darkened streets and asked for directions. He grabbed my map and proceeded to weave uncontrollably until a whiff of alcohol invaded my senses. I snatched back the map.

"See? This is what happens when you ask strangers," I barked at Mom.

"Why don't you just call someone?" Mom suggested.

"On what?"

"Your cell phone."

"I don't have a cell phone."

"You seem to have money for everything else, why wouldn't you buy a cell phone?" she huffed.

I dislike cell phones—their omnipresence, their tinny rings, the tyranny of their billing plans, the lack of etiquette they encourage in their users. I am distressed by how quickly they have been gobbled up by a culture too afraid to be caught alone and silent for ten minutes. And those claims of benign electromagnetic activity? Nonsense.

It was well past midnight when we found the town hall, the prearranged rendezvous point with a property manager who would guide us to our accommodation.

Mom and I were barely on speaking terms.

"Give him hell for not meeting us at the airport," Mom demanded as our car jerked to a stop in the parking lot and a tall man, who I assumed was the property manager, approached us. "What kind of an outfit is this, anyway?"

I had no energy left to berate anyone. Besides, it is one thing to rant like a lunatic to my mother, and quite another to do so to a complete stranger. Not that I haven't, but I wisely bit my lip now. And a good thing: the very tall, muscular guy walking toward us looked like he was in a bad mood, too.

I rolled down the window and murmured a greeting. This man's name was Chris, and he was a transplanted Brit. On Chris's instructions we followed him in our car out of the dimly lit town into a black countryside of narrow, winding, bumpy roads. This went on for quite some time, long enough for me to wonder whether we were being taken somewhere to be murdered.

The road wound around low walls of stucco and stone that almost grazed our car. By North American standards our rented car would be considered a small-to-midsize vehicle, but by Italian standards it was a boat. My murder fantasy was replaced by a more practical concern: Had I read the damages clause of our car rental agreement?

The car stalled several times as we ascended a steep, curving driveway that led up to the *trullo* we had rented. I spit out a few expletives. Mom said nothing, but from the set of her jaw it was clear that her annoyance was inching up. It was hard to imagine two grumpier visitors to Italy.

We parked the car and struggled out of our seats.

"How do you undo this damn thing?" said Mom, yanking with mighty irritation at her seat belt.

Chris was already at the front door of the *trullo,* fumbling in the dark with a large ring of door keys.

"You'll find that these are a bit of a pain," he said with a frustrated sigh as he made several attempts at the keyhole.

Finally, one of the keys did the trick, and Chris pushed open the door.

With a flick of a light switch our mood changed. The *trullo* was truly gorgeous, even better than the Web site photos had indicated. Whitewashed stone interior walls soared to domed ceilings; shiny terra-cotta tiles lay on the diagonal; niches of varying sizes and shapes—some used as windows, others to store knickknacks, books, and DVDs—were cut into the wall. Broad archways marked the passageways to rooms. The wood trims around the doors and window frames were stained a dark brown. The living room, in which we stood, was furnished with black leather sofas and natural pine tables and dressers. I noticed a fireplace in a small alcove off the living room.

"You can't use that, I'm afraid," said Chris, following my eyes. "Not sure whether it works all that well."

Instead, he gave me a quick rundown of the heating system and the locking mechanisms of the shuttered doors, and then incredibly convoluted instructions for operating the VCR/DVD/ satellite TV console, instructions that evaporated in my jet-lagged brain. Even in an alert and rested state, I am unable to retain information when it involves mastering more than the basics of modern electronics.

He deposited a superintendent's quantity of keys into my palm—every door in the place had two locks, and the front door had three—then he bade us good-night and disappeared into the blackness.

I watched the taillights of his little car recede down the driveway and then reappear on the opposite hill. A wave of panic shot through me when I realized that not only did I not have his phone number in case of an emergency, the *trullo* itself did not have a phone.

Mom had headed off to inspect the washroom facilities, and I wandered around to check out the rest of the *trullo*.

I found a small bedroom with twin beds off the front room, part of the original structure. The back section of the *trullo,* however, was a completely modern addition consisting of two bedrooms—each with a queen-sized bed, and one (which Mom had claimed) with an ensuite—a kitchen with a small laundry room, and a second bathroom, all connected by a hall. Doors opened from the bedrooms and kitchen to the rear patio and an hourglass-shaped inground pool.

I poked around the kitchen, opening cupboard doors and drawers. Provisions had thoughtfully been left for us—pasta, tomato sauce, fresh cheese, crusty Italian bread, olive oil, salad greens, tomatoes, beer. And two bottles of wine, one of which—the red—I opened and immediately drained by half.

Mom and I sank into the black leather sofas in the front room.

"Well, here's to Italy and our adventure," she said, jubilantly raising her glass to mine.

No mention was made of our tempers—mine in particular—and I could not bring myself to apologize.

3

Alberobello, Martina Franca, Locorotondo

RAIN WAS hammering the slate tiles of the *trullo*'s roof when my eyes opened the next morning.

I threw off the bedcovers, scrambled out of bed, pulled open the heavy wooden shuttered doors, and peeked through the glass. Fat drops were pinging, staccato-like, off the patio and the pool.

I unlocked then opened the door to embrace the warm Italian air, and a bitter blast of cold—colder than I had experienced over a lifetime of Canadian winters—shot into the room. I gasped and slammed the door shut.

I glanced at the floor, where the contents of my opened suitcase flopped over the edges, exposing their unsuitability: two bathing suits, capri pants, long gauzy skirts, sleeveless tops, strappy sandals. What was lacking were thick sweaters, wool socks, hip waders, mittens, and a hot water bottle.

I pulled on the only sweater I had packed—an oversized, sickly pale green garment with a deep V-neck, which I had thrown in at the last minute—and wandered down the hall to the living room. Peering out a small window past the rain and the dissipating fog, I was alarmed at how high up on a hill we actually were. The driveway wound frighteningly into an abyss and then rose up a sharply steep, rut-infested incline. It looked impossible to scale by foot, much less car. I could not believe I had driven that road in the dark without screaming in fear.

I padded off to Mom's room.

"Well, it's not the best day to start a holiday, is it?" said Mom as she peeked out from under a thick layer of bedcovers. "Has the rain stopped?"

"I'm sure it'll clear up soon," I said with assurance. "This is southern Italy, after all. Let's go into town."

She did not seem pleased by this suggestion.

"Why?" she pouted.

"Because we just arrived in Italy," I said impatiently. "Aren't you curious to see the area? I'll put on the kettle."

She didn't say another word and gamely struggled out of bed.

As we chowed down slices of a toasted baguette and tea in the kitchen, we could hear the low rumble of distant thunder.

"What time did you want to leave?" asked Mom.

"Now," I answered. "Is that OK?"

"Well, no," she replied primly. "It takes me a bit of time to get moving."

"OK, how about five minutes?"

She winced.

"A bit longer than that. What I meant is that it takes me a while to *get moving*."

"Oh, right," I said, catching the euphemism.

"I'll let you know," she said, and toddled unsteadily toward the bathroom.

I waited. And waited. Her morning ablutions took longer than my teenage daughter's. I passed the time flipping through an English-Italian phrasebook.

My absolute favorite Italian word is *"andiamo!"* which translates into "let's go!" It has such energy, enthusiasm, and optimism. When I am feeling full of vigor and anticipation I will say, *"Andiamo!"* I just love the sound of that word. I had the feeling that I would be using it a lot on this trip, but not in a good way.

An hour later Mom emerged from her bedroom, startling me out of a nap.

"ok, I think I'm ready," she said. "Now, where did I put my glasses?"

Four more minutes.

She located her glasses and began rummaging through her purse.

"I was sure I had some Kleenex in my purse. Oh, where is it? Would you mind grabbing me some from the bathroom?"

One minute.

"I need my puffer. Let's see. Maybe it's in my purse."

She conducted a forensic audit of the contents of her purse.

"Yes, I think it's there. Yes. There it is. I really should clean out my purse."

Two minutes.

"Now, do you think I should bring my cane or my walker? Well, the walker is in the car anyway, isn't it? I'll bring both. What else am I forgetting?"

"That I am impatient, perhaps?" I ventured.

She paused in the middle of the room, put a finger to her lips, and stared at the floor as her brain scanned the possibilities.

Two more minutes.

She suddenly straightened up and beamed, "Well, whatever it is, it can't be that important."

She shuffled to the front door and continued through it out onto the patio and toward the car. This all took another three minutes.

I followed her and paused at the door to find the right key to lock up. Three more minutes.

"What's keeping you?!" Mom hollered from the car.

Once in the car, I turned the ignition. The seat belt signal promptly began to beep.

"Seat belt," I said to Mom.

"Oh come on," she tutted. "We don't need seat belts here."

"Yes, we do."

"But it's so uncomfortable."

Her body stiffened as I leaned over her, wrenched the buckle and sash from the passenger side, and drew it across her chest, theatrically snapping the buckle into its mate and adjusting it for comfort, though, according to my mother, a seat belt can never be adjusted for comfort. Years ago, she once seriously considered cutting the seat belts completely out of her car because, in addition to being a nuisance—they kept getting caught in the door, she claimed—they were not esthetically pleasing.

My mind drifted back some twenty years to when I routinely strapped my toddlers into their car seats. Their bodies never stiffened; gosh, they were such compliant and agreeable little tykes, accepting without question the necessity of seat belt use.

I loved hovering over my kids in those days, inhaling the sweet smell of their fresh-washed hair and clothing or catching the twinkle in their eyes. Occasionally they would grab my hair with their chubby, clumsy hands and pull my face close for a kiss, then erupt into shy but victorious giggles.

But this was my mother, not my children. I smelled the familiar scent of her makeup, but it was not a moment that inspired playfulness.

I can't say I felt entirely comfortable mothering my mother. What comes naturally to me as a mother does not come naturally to me as a daughter. The emotional distance that had been allowed to grow between us over the years had seen to that.

"You don't have to baby me, you know," said Mom sternly. "I'm quite capable of putting on my own seat belt, thank you very much."

She let out a sniff of disapproval as I double-checked that the buckle was secured. Like a practiced parent, I ignored the pout.

We drove in silence toward Alberobello along rain-soaked, narrow, winding country roads and rolling landscape for about five miles. We could barely see anything through the rain-splattered windshield.

I made a left turn at what appeared to be a main thoroughfare, and within seconds the sorts of buildings that signal the approach of civilization began to appear: a garden center, a few restaurants, a store selling ceramic tiles and flooring. Nothing looked remotely open.

We pulled into a gas station, but no one approached us at the pumps. I got out of the car and wandered into the gas station's café.

"Chiusa oggi. Tutto," a young man behind the counter said brusquely, with a wave of his hand. Closed today. Everything. No reason was given. Italians take their closings very seriously.

"The town's closed today," I said to Mom when I returned to the car.

"Why?"

"Beats me," I shrugged.

"But it's Thursday!"

We drove up and down the empty streets of Alberobello. There's something unsettling about a town without any activity. Eventually, with a sigh of surrender, we returned to our *trullo*.

We retreated to our individual rooms and the warmth of our beds. I put my pajamas back on and added socks and the snot-green sweater. I scoured the cupboards and drawers for more blankets but came up empty-handed. How was it possible for Italy—my beloved, hot Italy!—to feel colder than Canada?

"Are you warm enough?" I asked Mom when I peeked into her room.

But her eyes were already shut.

THE NEXT day we took another stab at checking out the area.

Culture shock was no match for how utterly blindsided I was by a lack of all sense of direction. A road map was of no help because it did not show the numerous small country lanes that shot off in various directions from the main road. At least I assumed it was a main road.

We dutifully followed the road signs to the nearby town of Locorotondo but, despite our efforts, ended up in another town, Martina Franca. Dumbfounded, I glanced down at the map in my lap. I had no idea how we ended up there, much less how we would find our way back.

At least there was some action in Martina Franca. We inched through the busy streets filled with small cars. Elderly men and women wandered in and out of traffic.

"Oh look!" cried Mom. "A church! Stop! I want to go in!"

"It's hard to stop here, Mom," I stammered, checking my rearview mirror and swerving to avoid an oncoming car. "There's traffic piling up behind me. You get out and go in. I'll try to find a parking spot."

"You just passed a parking spot," she said. "Why didn't you park there?"

"What spot?" I said, turning my head just as a small car deftly slipped into the vacant space. "How am I supposed to look for parking spaces *and* concentrate on driving in a foreign country?"

"You'd notice them if you stopped being so grumpy," she replied flatly. "Now stop the car."

In the middle of the street I jammed the car's gear into neutral and pulled on the emergency brake.

Mom flung open the passenger door (without looking first to see if another car or someone on a bicycle was approaching; luckily, neither was) and laboriously maneuvered herself out of the car. Meanwhile I sprinted to the rear of the car, lifted the hatch, and unloaded her walker. I could feel the impatience of Italy boring into my back as horns tooted their irritation at this nervy pit stop.

Normally when this happens, and I am possessed by the moral superiority of knowing that there is a very good reason why I have stopped the car, I launch into a small rage that involves certain fingers and unladylike language. But something prevented me this time. Perhaps it was the old man behind the wheel of the car that was nosing my rear bumper. I did not have the words to fire at him—well, not Italian words.

Instead, I watched Mom persevere to the sidewalk, slowly raise her walker over the curb, and set off with great effort for the church.

"Dear God," I muttered. "Please shoot me before I reach that stage of life."

I got back into the car and began searching for a parking space, creeping along a dense labyrinth of streets. Upon circling the block I spotted—aha!—an empty spot close to the church where I had dropped off Mom. I pulled in—and it took all my skills to shoehorn the car into the space without scraping off the paint on my car or the cars on either side, I might add. After congratulating myself I squeezed out of the driver's side, locked the car, double-checked that the car doors were indeed locked, and then turned toward the church, just in time to see Mom walking toward me.

"I thought you wanted to see the church," I said.

"I saw it, said a prayer; it's a lovely church," she said. "Let's go."

Gee, when I pray I feel obliged to tell God that He might want to pour Himself a large coffee and settle into a comfortable chair. My prayers are rarely brief.

Low stone walls lined both sides of the two-lane highway back to Alberobello. Ahead, a hilltop town came into view. An impressively ancient white stone church dome and bell tower hovered behind a whitewashed stone wall bordering terraced fields. The town was Locorotondo.

We followed the signs to the *centro storico* and by some

fluke wound up in front of the same town hall where we had first rendezvoused with Chris a few nights earlier. Across the street, people were milling around tables and stalls arrayed with brightly colored goods.

"I'll bet that's the market," I said to Mom. "I'll let you out here, and once I find a parking spot I'll catch up with you."

I stopped the car to let her out, then jumped out myself to unpack her walker from the back of the station wagon, set it up, and help her and the walker mount the curb. Then I got back into the car and drove off in search of a parking spot.

We had only been in Italy a couple of days, and already I was resenting the responsibility of driving and parking. Usually when I travel, I am free as a butterfly. I am more likely to be on foot and can stop and start, linger or jet off when the mood strikes. Not on this trip. I was responsible not only for my mother and her walker but also for our rental car, for finding our way around, for negotiating things in Italian, for deciding the itinerary, for, hell, even when and where to eat. I have on occasion been characterized as a control freak (usually by an ex-husband), and my reasonable response was always, "Well, someone has to be!" But truthfully, the accusation was patently unfair. I would kill—*kill*—to be led around by the nose for at least a week or so and have someone else take control of the day-to-day responsibilities.

By the time I caught up to Mom, she had already scuttled halfway through the market. She and that red walker of hers can really fly.

The market was crammed with vendors selling every conceivable item: clothing of questionable style and vintage, plastic bins, small appliances, leather or leather-looking purses (I was not tempted to take a closer look), duvets and comforters sporting large, unattractive floral patterns in faded pastels, and various household gadgets that, while likely useful, lacked esthetic charm.

Mom and I stood out like greenhorns among the legion of local women, some who were weathered of face, with kerchiefs tied under their chins and dressed in Italy's national color— black, others who were younger and wore smart-looking jeans but who, if such facial expressions as narrowed eyes and furrowed brows offer a window on a person's lifestyle, endured hardworking lives and scant resources. They wandered by the stalls, casting looks of profound indifference at the wares displayed, occasionally poking and prodding an item as if taunting the vendors, who would then leap to their feet and launch into their sales pitch, which most certainly included the phrase, "Today, everything is 30 percent off."

In this crowd my mother was easy to spot. She wore beige slacks with a matching zip-front jacket. She was the only blonde in the crowd—Italian women dye their hair dark until their dying day—and she was pushing a metallic-red walker, a rare and novel contraption in these parts judging by the number of turned heads.

Picking up the scent of fresh ignorant tourists, the vendors upped their volume and come-ons. Some made endearing attempts to speak English in the hope of coaxing Mom and me closer. I was tempted to try out what small amount of Italian I knew, but any skills I possessed (or even thought I possessed) now seemed patently inadequate.

We were making our way along the narrow concourse of stalls when we came upon a small medieval church in the middle of a small piazza. We were about to enter it when my ears pricked up at the sound of two women speaking English. I sidled closer to them to be certain my ears hadn't deceived me and then dove onto them as if they were long-lost relatives.

"You speak English!" I said, with perhaps a tad too much enthusiasm. A raft of questions tumbled from my mouth. "Can you explain this place to us? Why do entire towns shut down midweek? How do we find our way around?"

The women were from Scotland but had been holidaying in these parts for many years, the jolly one with dark hair, protruding teeth, and a chubby smile told me. The other, of slight build with spiky, gray hair and a severe expression, never spoke.

"We've just purchased a *trullo*," the chubby one gushed in a thick brogue. "We're getting ready to renovate. We saw the plans yesterday."

I congratulated them. Buying and renovating property in a foreign country requires a definite leap of faith.

"You must be very good with the language," I said, privately entertaining fantasies of their taking Mom and me under their wing for the duration of our stay in Alberobello.

"Oh, we've been coming here for fifteen years and we still can't speak Italian," the chubby one giggled. "Just say to them, '*Il mio italiano è poco e male.*' It means, literally, 'My Italian is small and bad.'"

She sounded the phrase out slowly and deliberately and prompted me to repeat it. She must have been a schoolteacher.

"What's with the weather?" I asked. "I thought southern Italy was warmer than this."

"It is chilly today, isn't it?" she said, pulling her sweater tightly around her big bosom. "You should have been here last week. It was seventy-five degrees and beautiful."

That sentence would be repeated many times during our trip. I wished the women well and headed off to find Mom, who had wandered away at some point during the conversation.

When I located her, she was poking around a stall that sold kitchenware, and was holding a plastic spatula as if considering its purchase. I gently pried it out of her hand and placed it back on the table.

"How on earth were you able to converse with those women?" Mom asked.

"They spoke English, so it wasn't too difficult for me," I answered.

"That didn't sound like English to me."

We walked a little more, but Mom was now tiring.

"Had enough?"

She nodded.

"Then let's go home."

I steered her toward a rendezvous point and accompanied her across the street. Then I took off to get the car. In my absence, the parking lot had devolved into a hodgepodge of vehicles parked at random angles. There was nothing remotely organized about the arrangement. It looked like someone had given Stevie Wonder the authority to park cars.

I located my car, boxed in by an old, faded-red Fiat, and before I had time to react, an elderly man came hobbling quickly toward me, got into the Fiat, and moved it out of the way. I gave him a wave of thanks, but he had already scooted off to find another car to block.

I eased out of the lot—how I managed not to scrape every vehicle in the vicinity remains a mystery—and drove to the prearranged corner of the market area to pick up Mom. I threw the car into park, pushed a button to pop the trunk, jumped out, opened the passenger-side door for Mom, grabbed her walker, and folded it up and wedged it carefully into the trunk, then returned to the driver's seat, did up my seat belt, and prepared to drive off. In the amount of time it took me to accomplish all those small tasks, Mom had managed to lift one leg into the car.

Adjusting to the pace of someone at least ten times slower than normal speed made me feel as if I were in a perpetual state of slow motion. It drove me mad. I held back the urge to snap, *"Andiamo!"*

Leaving Locorotondo, we slipped out onto the rural roads and headed toward our *trullo,* relying solely on instinct and vaguely familiar landmarks as we sailed through a sweep of empty pastures, ancient olive groves, vineyards, and farmland. In a distant field a lone, bent figure with a scythe methodically thwacked around the edges of his property while a small brush fire burned. Smoke curled from the chimney of a modest home. Those were the only signs that anyone was about. It was an eerily empty countryside.

Then a movement indicating life materialized on the road ahead. Coming toward us was a man on horseback. I eased up on the gas pedal.

He was a handsome fellow—I'm referring to the man, not the horse—well into middle age and elegantly attired in the chaps and fitted tweed jacket favored by lords of the manor. He looked not to have a care in the world as he swayed confidently and languorously on his steed. One of his brown-leather-gloved hands clutched the reins, and the other was raised to his ear: He was chatting merrily on his cell phone.

As we passed he gave us a smile and a wink.

"See?" harrumphed Mom. "Even he has a cell phone."

THE RAIN and cold persisted, and within days Mom had developed a worrisome bronchial cough. It was so bad that I wasn't sure whether to be concerned that she would develop pneumonia or that she would have a stroke brought on by her constant hacking. The worry and the hacking kept me awake at night.

Early one morning, shivering from cold and heavy with sleep deprivation, I peeled off one of the blankets on my bed and took it to Mom.

Knock, knock. No answer. I rapped again a bit louder. Still no answer. Finally I opened the door a crack. Mom was lying on her back, staring happily at the ceiling, occasionally coughing. She had obviously not heard me enter. I gave a little cough, but again she didn't hear.

"For God's sake, get a hearing aid, woman," I said. Still she didn't hear me.

So I shut the door quietly, then knocked quite loudly and opened it noisily.

"Hi there!" she said, turning her head toward me.

"I couldn't sleep," I said. "I brought you another blanket. Your coughing kept me awake."

"How did you sleep? I bet my coughing kept you awake."

"Yes," I replied wearily.

"I'm so sorry," she said. "I didn't sleep well either."

"Can I get you anything?"

"Well, I need to take my blood-sugar reading. The diabetes, you know."

I fetched her kit from the bathroom.

"Can you help me up?" she asked, extending an arm.

I pulled her five-foot-two-inch frame up and helped her swing her legs around to the edge of the bed. When she was seated, her feet just grazed the floor and swung slightly, like a child's. A surge of protectiveness welled up in me.

"Let me show you how I do it," she said, eagerly opening her diabetes kit.

It has come to this, I thought, as I took a seat beside her on the bed. Watching my mother prick her finger to extract blood for a diabetes reading was now passing for entertainment on my Italian holiday.

She pricked her finger with a tiny needle, which automatically drew a small amount of blood and registered the reading on the kit's LCD display.

"Five point four?" she gasped, taking a closer look at the results.

"Is that bad?" I asked with concern.

"It's incredible!" she said. "It's never been that low. I wonder what I'm doing right!"

"You should get back into bed," I said. "So you don't get cold. We won't go out today. I'll bring you some tea."

I sauntered into the kitchen and put on the kettle. As I waited for it to boil, I spied Chris, the property manager, by the pool. It didn't matter that it was freezing outside or raining; Chris kept the pool in pristine condition. I was aching to use it.

"The weather's an aberration," he said, anticipating my question when I joined him on the patio later. His brown, short-spiked hair was damp. "You should have been here a week ago."

"So I've heard," I said.

"How's your mum doing?"

"Not so well," I said. "She has a really bad cough. The *trullo* is freezing."

"Did you crank up the heat?" he asked.

"I wasn't sure whether that was something I should tinker with," I said. "Are there any more blankets?"

"Loads more," he said. "I'll show you where they are. And let's get the heat going."

I received an unnecessary primer on the workings of the thermostat—honestly, I know how they operate—and was shown the stash of blankets piled in the cupboard that was under lock and key—a key that was, incidentally, not among the half-dozen or so Chris had given me.

The sound of Mom's coughing came from behind the bedroom door.

Chris looked at me with alarm.

"I really should get her some cough medicine," I said. "Is there a pharmacy nearby?"

"Let me drive you," he said. "I'll show you a shortcut."

I was grateful to be a passenger for once and let someone else do the thinking.

As for shortcuts, well, call me a pessimist, but they do not exist in Italy. Chris's "shortcut" turned out to be a more circuitous and convoluted route than I could imagine. By the time we reached the pharmacy—and I could not tell whether we were in Martina Franca or Locorotondo or even Italy for that matter—I was thoroughly confused and disoriented. Had Chris asked me to find my own way home, I might still be driving.

The *farmacia* was a snug, rather precious shop with a white marble counter that spanned the width of the premises. Behind it small glass bottles and boxes and jars of every size and shape were neatly arranged on a wall of white shelving. A brass scale and a white marble mortar and pestle sat on the counter. I wasn't sure whether those items were there for show or for actual use, but it was all charming nonetheless.

In front of the counter there was just enough space to accommodate a handful of people, and several were there when we walked in, waiting impatiently for their prescriptions to be filled. They hurriedly shuffled closer to close the gaps in the queue. Judging by the looks on their faces I would say they all had something terminal.

When our turn came, Chris spoke softly in Italian to the pharmacist, asking for cough syrup. I nudged Chris and asked him to add some Vicks VapoRub to the bill, but the pharmacist appeared to understand, because he produced a jar immediately. I paid the bill and we left.

"I've got to stop off and get some nappies for our baby," said Chris as we exited the *farmacia*. "Do you mind?"

"Absolutely not," I said. It would give me a chance to pick up some groceries. I hastily assembled a list in my head, beginning with wine.

Once the errand was accomplished, we left the town and drove back to the *trullo*, passing dozens of these adorable abodes along the country road. There were stucco-clad *trulli* and *tufo* stone *trulli;* some domes sported finials in the shape of a ball, while others had a more fluted shape. Some *trulli* were close to the road; others were situated in distant fields.

Thousands of these adorable buildings dot the countryside of Apulia (it's actually called Puglia now, but I prefer the more historic appellation), and they have been under UNESCO's protection since 1996. Recently, some of the restrictions governing *trullo* restoration and renovation have been lifted. I thought back to the Scottish women we had met in Locorotondo, and wondered how they would fare with their Italian *trullo*.

I asked Chris about the hobbitlike homes.

"Oh, they're popular with the Italians, too," Chris said. "They're just waking up to the fact that *trulli* are a part of their heritage. Nobody ever takes their history seriously until people from another country come and snap up the real estate.

"In fact," he continued, "people in this area tend to use the *trulli* as holiday homes. Believe it or not, some people have a holiday home only a few miles from their regular home. If you see a lot of *trulli* boarded up, it's only because it's early in the season. Even the locals find them damp and cold at this time of year. But by summer—and believe me, the heat is hellish around here—a *trullo* is the coolest place to be."

Chris returned me to our frigid *trullo,* which was looking more like an igloo to me than a Mediterranean home.

"I brought you a treat," I said to Mom when I returned to her bedside.

"Oh goody! What?"

I placed the Vicks and the cough syrup on her pine bedside table. With a jazz-hand flourish I gave a little "ta-da!"

She looked profoundly disappointed.

"Did you have fun?" she asked.

"Well, as much fun as you can have buying cough syrup and Vicks VapoRub in an Italian pharmacy," I said.

She sat up in bed, and I plumped the cushions for her.

"I'm amazed how you go out and just get things," she said.

"Well, I didn't this time," I said. "Chris drove me. And he spoke Italian in the pharmacy on my behalf."

"Tell me about the pharmacy. What was it like?" she gushed excitedly, as if I had just returned from an expedition to Katmandu.

"It was what you'd expect. It was small and had lots of bottles and potions. It wasn't like our drugstores in Canada."

"Oh," she said blankly. I got the impression that she was hoping it might have provided a potential shopping excursion for her later in the week.

"Did you have a sleep while I was gone?"

"Not really; I was lying here thinking about when I was a little girl, about when I was a rebel."

"A rebel? You?"

My mother's idea of rebellion is wearing white before May 24 or having a shot of sherry before noon.

"Once upon a time I was," she said. "As a teenager. Oh, I was a bad girl."

This should be interesting, I thought.

"Being a rebel doesn't make you bad," I offered as I sat on the edge of her bed. "What made you a rebel?"

"Well, I rebelled about joining Hungarian social activities and about dating Hungarian men," she said. "I refused to date a Hungarian, and my parents got so upset with me."

Mom had immigrated to Canada from Hungary with her parents when she was a youngster. By the time she hit her teens, her mind was made up that she was going to be part of WASP society, and that meant marrying a WASP. All her friends were Anglo-Saxons; she had no time for the marriageable sons of her parents' friends.

"One day, a Hungarian couple dropped by—they were friends of my parents—and they demanded that my parents force me to date or at least talk to their son, who was about my age. I was so angry and I refused to go out with him."

"What did Granny and Grandpa do?" I asked.

"My dad, luckily, forgave me, but my mother wasn't so easy," said Mom. "But I didn't care—that was her problem. I was set on marrying a Canadian."

At age eighteen, she had moved to Toronto and begun working as a reporter for the Canadian Press, quickly catching the eye of a blond, blue-eyed fellow reporter.

In 1952 the union of a Canadian-born Anglican and a Hungarian-born Roman Catholic was considered a mixed marriage. My parents were not allowed to marry in a church, and instead were wed in the modest clergy office of Saint

Gregory's Roman Catholic Church in Oshawa. I was born a few years later, and my brother eighteen months after that.

I was fascinated by my mother's Hungarian Catholic heritage, but it was a subject that was not discussed outside our home. My young and fertile imagination determined that this was because my mother was a spy, a thought that was amplified whenever I heard her and her kin speaking Hungarian.

57

I was amazed, proud in fact, at how my mother could toggle effortlessly between English and Hungarian. To the average North American in those days, Hungary was a vaguely gray, heavily shelled Eastern Bloc country of people who used paprika when they cooked. To me, it was exotic, mysterious, and dangerous. At family gatherings, one of my mother's cousins would roll up his pant leg to show off the bullet wounds he received from the Russian soldiers in 1956 when he and his young bride were escaping on their bellies through a farmer's field during the Hungarian Revolution. A little thrill would rise up in me whenever he recounted that story, and I would sit on the floor, my arms clasped around my knees, and beg for more details.

On rare occasions my mother would allude to her heritage proudly. "Don't forget the definition of a Hungarian," she would remind me. "A Hungarian is someone who goes into a revolving door behind you and comes out ahead."

My mother rarely talked about her past, either because there had never been time to do so or because she didn't think it was interesting enough to share with me. But her anecdote about refusing to date the Hungarian couple's son was an eye-opener for me. When I was growing up, she would despair at my single-mindedness, and yet here she was relating an episode that illustrated a much stronger will than mine. Why don't parents ever notice themselves in their children, and why do they have such a hard time cutting their kids some slack? Perhaps for the same reasons we have such a hard time cutting our parents some slack.

I was about to voice this observation, but she interrupted.

"Now you, you are too permissive a parent," she said, pointing a crooked finger at me. "You need to drill into your children about not getting involved [that's Mom code for "not having sex"] with nonwhites. I can be flexible now—they can marry Europeans, but they have to be white Europeans."

I imagined sharing this news flash with my children. When they were much younger—long before they were near dating age—they would return home from a visit to their grandparents and inform me of their Nana's strict rule about dating nonwhites.

"She said she would cut us out of her will if we did," they would say in earnest little voices.

Still, my mother is entitled to her opinions and prejudices like everyone else. Not wanting to get into a heated argument about it, I replied, "My children's preference for a mate is really none of my business. I know you think it should be but it isn't, nor will it ever be. I do not control their sex lives."

"I DON'T WANT TO IMAGINE ANYONE HAVING SEX!" Mom shouted. Then, in a softer voice, "Has it stopped raining?"

4

Alberobello

"How are you feeling today?" I asked, poking my head into Mom's bedroom the next morning. Her pine bed was festooned with a pretty white lace canopy that suited her often queenly demeanor.

"I feel OK," she mewed, pulling the covers closer to her. "But I just want to sleep."

In the planning stages of our trip I had fantasized about Mom and me lounging poolside in our swimsuits on the sun-soaked patio of our *trullo,* sipping wine and amiably chatting about our dysfunctional relationship. We would raise a thorny subject, discuss it with civilized, WASPlike, faux nonchalance, and then laugh hysterically at the folly of our past foolishness. With a clink of our wine glasses we would bury the hatchet, take another sip, and stare dreamily into the distance as the toll of a church bell and the light rustle of olive leaves provided a soothing soundtrack. When we weren't sipping *vino* by the pool we would be off on day trips exploring towns and cities in the vicinity.

The reality was that we stayed cocooned in our separate rooms, warding off the cold and trying to ignore the rain pounding incessantly on the windows. Mom would sleep or read; I would study a road map of Italy, work my way through a book of Sudoku puzzles, or practice Italian from the little phrase book my daughter had slipped into my stocking the previous Christmas.

The phrase book turned out to be a small delight. It carried the curious warning that travellers to Italy should steer clear of three topics of conversation: the Mafia, Mussolini, and the Vatican. That just made me want to raise those topics with someone immediately. The book also contained a number of rather salacious offerings, which I read and reread with intense interest. What else was there to do?

Curled up in bed, I sounded out such provocative sentences as: *Non lo farò senza protezione* (I won't do it without protection); *Toccami qui* (Touch me here); *Andiamo a letto* (Let's go to bed); *O dio mio!* (Oh my god!); and the ever-handy *Calma!* (Easy, tiger!)

In the evenings, Mom and I fell into a lazy routine. We made our own dinner—usually pasta and salad followed by yogurt or an orange—then watched the BBC's *World News* or a movie from the small video library stacked in a corner niche of the living room.

"Watched" was a bit of a misnomer: My mother didn't actually listen to the movie; she more or less conducted a running commentary that began before the DVD was loaded into the player.

Here's an example.

"What shall we watch tonight?" she asked one evening.

"Have you seen *Bridget Jones's Diary*? It's a comedy," I said.

"No I haven't," she replied. "Who's in it?"

"Renée Zellweger and Hugh Grant."

"Oh, I can't stand Hugh Grant," she said. "What an awful, disgusting creature."

"You don't have to like him—in fact, he plays a jerk in the movie anyway, so it'll make it easier for you to watch," I offered.

The movie began.

"Who's that nice young man with the dark hair?" Mom asked about five minutes into the action.

"Colin Firth."

"He's a handsome one, isn't he?" Mom said admiringly. "He'd be nice for you, Jane. I do like his hair. Oh, now look at that dreadful Hugh Grant. Ewww! Look at him. I don't see what anyone sees in him. Don't you agree?"

I nodded eagerly so as not to prolong the discussion.

When she wasn't critiquing the actors' off-screen life-styles or on-screen hairstyles she insisted I recap the plot for her—every five minutes. A volume setting of one hundred is apparently not loud enough for her to glean comprehension on her own.

"HE'S SLEEPING WITH HER BUT HE'S ACTUALLY ENGAGED TO SOMEONE ELSE!" I yelled over the TV volume and into her deaf ear.

"I don't like it when people sleep around like that," she replied with much tutting and shaking of her head, as if it were my fault that Hugh Grant was bonking Renée Zellweger, or as if I somehow had the moral authority to call a halt to the action and redirect the players to a more appropriate pastime, such as antiquing in the Cotswolds.

The movie ended happily, not because Renée Zellweger wound up with Colin Firth, but because Mom had the pleasure of seeing Hugh Grant get his comeuppance.

As I removed the DVD from the player and returned it to its case, Mom studied her watch.

"Is it really 7:45?" she gasped. "Where *does* the day go?"

"I wouldn't say 'dago' too quickly in these parts," I muttered.

"Pardon?"

"Yes, it is 7:45," I said louder. "The rest of Italy is just getting dressed to go out for dinner."

"Well, those Italians can do what they want," said Mom with the vigor of someone rallying the troops before a battle. "Because we Canadians are going to bed!"

And with that, she hauled herself upright, paused to get her balance, and then inched her way toward her bedroom. The click of her cane on the terra-cotta tiles was the last I heard of her for the night.

After three days of this I had had all I could stand.

"I'm going out," I announced to Mom between naps one afternoon. "Will you be OK without me?"

"You're going out in the rain?"

"It's let up a bit. Do you need me to pick up anything?"

"Where are you going?" she asked. "And why are you going?

The interrogation had begun.

"Just into Alberobello. I'm getting cabin fever. I shouldn't be long."

"But we were there the other day. Why are you going?"

"I need a bit of air and a change of scenery," I said evenly, holding back an urge to explode into a weeping tirade of how utterly bored I had become. Bored, in Italy! I had dreamed of Italy for about forty years, had pined for everything Italian— the music, the language, the architecture, the art of the great masters. During my university days I had taken courses in conversational Italian and in art history in an attempt to forge a deeper connection to the Italy of my dreams. In those days I sought out Italian men in the hopes that I could become their girlfriend and they would whisk me off to their parents' villa and introduce me to a large and boisterous family of apple-cheeked aunts and swarthy cousins. I never did find an Italian boyfriend, but that didn't stop me from craving all things Italian. I frequented small Italian grocery stores, pausing to eavesdrop on Italian conversations, and gravitated toward Italian recipes. I gave clothing with a "Made in Italy" label top priority in the dressing room and in purchasing decisions. Without having stepped on Italian soil, I could close my eyes and summon smells and sensations connected to Italy—the thrashing sea against the coast, the aroma of homemade tomato sauce, the notes of an uncorked bottle of wine, a smoky café; or even the haughty indifference of a Milanese store clerk. With such a vast repertoire to explore, how was it possible that I was already bored in Italy? As I saw it, precious time was being wasted holed up in a cute but remote home with Ms. Lazy Bones.

I unlocked and opened up the solid wooden front door of the *trullo,* struggled to find the right key to unlock the double wrought-iron screen doors beyond it—getting in and out of the place was like coming and going from Fort Knox—and then sprinted to the car, splashing through puddles that had accumulated on the pale stone patio.

63

Safely in the car, I was about to turn the key in the ignition when I was seized by panic. I was about to go for a drive with only the vaguest idea of my destination. Once there, would I be able to find my way back? What if the car broke down? What if I had an accident? I spoke no Italian. I had no cell phone. No map of the region. If I made a wrong turn it could catapult me to the far reaches of Apulia and beyond, and I might never find my way back. Despite the few forays Mom and I had made in and around Alberobello since our arrival, I did not feel confident venturing out on my own.

When I encounter situations in which it is clear that I have bitten off more than I can chew, my mind defaults to an intense longing for home and familiarity. Six weeks in Italy no longer sounded as idyllic as it had during the six months in which I planned the trip and spoke excitedly of it to friends. Now it sounded daunting and reckless.

I'm the type of person who gives herself over to suggestibility and impulse. When an idea launches in my brain I am off to the races, and there is no stopping me. I am propelled by my own enthusiasm. I become a one-person cheering section while those around me aren't sure whether to humor me and wish me well or alert the nearest mental institution. It was the sort of reaction that greeted me when I took up rollerblading in my forties and when I decided to sell almost everything I owned and move to small, remote Pelee Island, Ontario, one winter to embrace the simple life.

So it was one day about six months earlier when Frank, the Italian owner of a café I frequent in my hometown, suggested I go to Italy. I don't know whether it was the way he said it, with tears glistening in his eyes—he had emigrated from Italy to Canada about fifty years before and had never been back—or whether I had worn myself out with unfulfilled promises to visit Italy. Whatever. As soon as I realized that there was no logical reason preventing me from going to Italy I began packing my bags. It seemed like the most sensible course of action.

I have intermittent bouts of confidence. I give the impression of being a blithe and brave spirit when it comes to travelling, but there is a part of me that is a total scaredy-cat. Rationality flies out the window—not in the planning stages, but only when my two feet are firmly planted at my destination. In other words, at the point of no return. There I stand, stockstill and dumbfounded, as the tap of common sense suddenly turns on and begins to course through me. The question that should have been asked much, much earlier sputters to life in my right brain: "What the hell were you thinking when you came up with this bright idea?" Like the time I stood at the base of the Pyrenees and realized I was going to spend the next eight hours of my life climbing them. God, that was hard. Oddly enough, I continue to put myself in the same predicament time and time again.

The thought of returning to Mom's bedside and telling her I was too frightened to go out on my own was simply out of the question. So I did the only logical thing: I turned the key in the ignition.

I drove tentatively down the long steep driveway and then carefully up the insanely steep road opposite the *trullo,* stalling the car half a dozen times in the process. I inched my way along a lane that was no more than six inches wider than my car and oppressively bordered by stone fences and *trulli* whose walls abutted the road. I took a deep breath, foolishly thinking that by inhaling I might somehow shrink the width of the car by an inch or two and make the passage easier.

Upon reaching the main road, with the rolling Apulia countryside stretching out on either side of me, I turned left and steered the car toward Alberobello.

The steady sweep-and-thump of the windshield wipers and the low rumble of distant thunder provided an ominous soundtrack. Fog drifted like wispy ghosts in front of my car and encircled the twisted, gnarled trunks of the olive trees with their weary branches stretched out like Christ on the cross.

"At least there's no snow," I murmured to myself, trying to find the bright side in the soggy scene and buoy my resolve.

Distant brush fires burned and smoldered on a couple of farms. A tradition occurs around mid-March in southern Italy when vines, limbs of olive trees, and other bits of vegetation from the previous harvest are collected, piled into huge mounds, and lit as a sign of rebirth and renewal for the coming season.

Yes, rebirth and renewal: Wasn't that the reason for this trip to Italy? At least I'm in sync with the spirit of the season, I told myself, desperately clutching at any straw that might make sense of my being here.

I pressed the accelerator pedal down a bit more firmly. The forces of coincidence or happenstance are, for me, like stars aligning, and when this occurs a feeling of confidence returns. I began to feel more like an adventurer and less like an impulsive idiot.

Low, ivy-draped drystone walls built from the abundant local *tufo* stone were everywhere. They were weathered to an ancient patina, but in spots you could tell by the lighter coloring where new sections had been built or recently patched. This stone border lined the narrow roads and formed gray ribbons across trapezoids of farms, olive groves, and vineyards. The landscape looked a lot like rural England, and the resemblance is no coincidence. About fifty years before they launched their famous conquest of England, the Normans were checking out some Italian real estate. A group of them, fed up with being mercenary Crusaders, left the grinding poverty of their French homeland and trundled off to southern Italy. One day, one of them likely said something along the lines of, "Hey, you know that crossroads we reach on our way to Palestine—the one where we always go straight rather than hanging a right? Let's check out that other route." And off they went.

Once the Normans had heaved themselves over the Apennines, the formidable range that runs like a spine from the north of Italy to the tip of its boot, they discovered, to their great delight, à largely wild but culturally prosperous and diverse frontier populated by Byzantines, Lombards, and Carolingians.

One of the many gifts the Normans brought to southern Italy was order—a paradoxical commodity given Italy's sterling reputation as the epicenter of chaos. In addition to their neat and tidy Norman rules, the Normans introduced their neat and tidy stone fences. The Normans were big on boundaries.

I had told Mom that I was going into Alberobello just to get more familiar with the region, but my real purpose was to hunt for an Internet café. It had been several days since I had last logged on. I hated being out of contact with people, especially my children—something my mother could not comprehend. When I was growing up and left my parents for an extended period of time, we never checked in with one another. We operated under the assumption that everything was fine and dandy unless we heard otherwise.

Those days are long gone, and as much as I like being off the grid, an innate sense of wanting to know, just to be sure, seizes me until it can be assuaged.

I was sure my little family was fine, but we have a habit of staying in contact with each other every few days. I was curious to know what was new in their lives. My boys were in their early twenties—Adam in his first year of college, Matt taking a year off college to work, and sixteen-year-old Zoë was on a three-month exchange program in France. Likewise, they would want to know what I was up to. At the very least they would want to know that their Nana and I had arrived safely.

Now, you would think an Internet café would be fairly easy to find in Europe, but finding one in southern Italy became a grail-like quest. I parked the car and set off under gray skies to troll the streets and lanes of Alberobello, which were slick with rain. I did this for a long time, until I got cold and returned to the car.

I drove to Locorotondo, where I also came up empty-handed. I approached a couple of girls—they were probably about fourteen years of age—with long, straight hair and the teenage uniform of hoodies and jeans. They were holding hands, an endearing cultural affectation.

With my trusty phrase book in hand, I asked if they knew of an Internet café. They looked at each other and seemed confused by the question. I tried speaking to them in French, with marginally better success.

The girls took me on a long walk through town, down a steep set of stairs, and along an unpopulated street—a walk of about fifteen minutes—but once we reached our destination it became clear that they had misinterpreted my request and had taken me to a computer store, which was closed anyway.

I thanked them graciously, but as I retraced my steps I muttered unkind things about their intelligence. Really, how many teens these days don't know about the Internet? Were these girls still playing with dolls?

I wandered into a few hotels and asked about Internet availability, but they either did not have it or did not know what I was talking about.

I headed back to Alberobello. (That I even found my way back to Alberobello says a lot about intuitive driving and the power of prayer.) Motoring slowly through a tangle of narrow roads and lanes, resolutely determined to find an Internet café, I passed the oddly named Twin Pub. In the window sat a computer terminal.

I parked the car and dashed inside. The place was empty save for the old owner/barista. Did he, by chance, have Internet access?

"*Sì*," he said, cocking his head toward the computer. He extended his hand for identification; I handed over my passport. He had me sign a form that was written in Italian but that I gathered was a promise I would not launch porn or terrorist activity onto his system.

The formalities concluded, I sat down and logged on. Within seconds I was greeted with fifty-five messages in my inbox. Nothing says you belong to the world more than dozens of messages in your inbox.

After deleting the solicitations to buy Viagra, the heartfelt pleas to help princes spirit money out of Nigeria, and the well-intentioned but thoroughly annoying jokes, cute-animal photos, and homilies forwarded by friends from friends of friends, I was left with five real messages.

Adam announced he had a girlfriend who was so pretty

he wasn't entirely certain he deserved her. Matthew's message was a simple "'Sup?" I keep telling that boy that I am his mother, not a rap artist, but he clearly sees no distinction between the two. Zoë excitedly reported that she was having a blast on her French exchange. She loved her host family, her new friends, school, and life in France in general. A couple of messages from Colin inquired how Mom and I were faring and how it felt to feel the warm sun on our faces. (I hastily corrected his weather assumptions.) I answered all of them.

Immensely satisfied that all was right with the world and my loved ones, I logged off. Before leaving, I asked the barista for a cappuccino, savored every drop, then drove contentedly back to the *trullo*.

THE NEXT day, having found my sea legs for travelling in unfamiliar places, I returned to Alberobello and followed the signs to the *centro storico*. I arrived in front of the imposing neoclassical basilica just as Mass had ended. The grand Piazza Antonio Curri was swarming with people, mostly older men and women strolling leisurely in small groups down Corso Vittorio Emanuele, every one of them dressed in black.

Judging by the alarmed looks on their faces, I had obviously missed a sign informing me that vehicular traffic was prohibited, at least at this time of day. I pulled off into the small Piazza XXVII Maggio and grabbed the last available parking spot.

I got out of the car and took a short stroll. My eyes settled on a small terrace next to a church, and I walked to the edge of it to check out the view. An incredible sight greeted me: a hillside crammed and cascading with hundreds and hundreds of white stucco *trulli*. This was Rione Monti, a UNESCO World Heritage site.

Small, conical-shaped stone dwellings are unique to this area of Italy, though not to the world. They can be found in Egypt, Turkey, Malta, Syria, Spain, France, and even Ireland. But the sheer proliferation of these buildings in the southern part of Apulia makes Alberobello the *trulli* headquarters.

Initially constructed using the drystone method, they served as seasonal or daily shelters for farmers and shepherds, and also housed livestock and farm equipment. When the region came under the feudal system, the ruling counts of Conversano permitted farmers to build their little stone homes as long as they didn't use mortar. What the cunning counts were trying to do was evade taxation. A law had been established forbidding the creation of large urban areas without the consent of the emperor's tribunal. The counts reckoned that if they could keep their little growing fiefdoms under the radar they could pocket the taxes from their tenant farmers and avoid paying taxes to the Crown. Whenever word got out that a royal inspector was in the vicinity, the counts ordered their farmers to dismantle their homes and make themselves scarce. Once the inspector had left—likely curious as to why there were so many little rock piles dotting the fields—the counts called their farmers back to work and let them reconstruct their *trulli*. You can imagine the scale of such an operation, with three thousand inhabitants in a "non-existent" village. And you can also imagine the farmers' resentment.

In 1797 a couple of them had had enough. Risking the wrath of the counts, they successfully petitioned King Ferdinand IV of Bourbon to be liberated from their feudal restraints, including the silly no-mortar rule.

Looking out onto the sea of these adorable and enchanting dwellings—I half expected the Seven Dwarfs to march out of them—it occurred to me that Mom might enjoy this sight. As

I walked quickly back to the car I passed a museum devoted to *trullo* history. A sign indicated it was open until 4:00 PM. I looked at my watch—1:00 PM. There was still time to dash back home and get Mom.

"This is ridiculous," I said half aloud as I started up the car. "We've been in Italy for nearly five days, and all I've become acquainted with is the inside of this car."

By the time I returned to the *trullo* I had made up my mind about a few things.

"C'mon," I said to Mom as I stood at her bedside. "Get dressed, and let's go out. I found something you'd like."

"But I'm so comfortable here," she squeaked, pulling the covers close to her chin.

"No really, this is crazy. We're in Italy. You're not seeing anything, and by extension neither am I. We'll be back in an hour."

She propped herself up and gave me an imploring look, hoping I'd change my mind.

"I'm serious," I said as patiently as I could.

"Do I get a cup of tea first?" she asked.

"A quick one then. I'll put on the kettle."

Fifteen minutes later, after she had put on her beige pant-suit and running shoes and applied her coral lipstick, we began what was becoming a routine drive—descending the long driveway and then ascending the steep hill on the opposite side of the valley. This time I managed not to stall the car.

We returned to the square and the museum in Alberobello. The little church that had taken me twenty seconds to walk to took Mom ten painful minutes to reach, and once there all she seemed to care about was locating a bench so she could sit down to catch her breath.

"I've got a surprise for you," I said. "Come here and look at this view. You won't believe it."

She raised herself reluctantly from the bench, hobbled unsteadily toward where I stood, and gazed out at the masses of *trulli* before her. I looked at her, waiting for an excited reaction.

"That's nice, dear," she said vacantly. "Now can I sit down?"

She turned around and returned to the bench.

I stared at her in disbelief. "That's nice"? What had happened to her? She loves this sort of stuff!

Suddenly, an older version of my mother materialized before me. Over the years I had ignored the fact that she was aging. Even when she had hip surgery and a knee replacement, I had considered them merely tune-ups to return her to full mobility. It had never occurred to me that her condition would worsen.

Now, with clarity and shock, I saw her frailty and her stoic determination to maintain her independence and spirits while coping with a debilitating disability. She always denied having pain in her legs, but her eyes now betrayed her practiced optimism.

There were other signs. I had noticed how she fumbled with the simplest items as if she were holding them for the first time. And she was becoming increasingly absentminded. At first I thought I had forgotten to relay information to her, but the lapses were occurring with regularity. She claimed I never told her things, such as the fact that we were going to Viterbo in a few weeks. Yet we had talked about that part of our trip numerous times. In new surroundings I was seeing a different version of my mother.

I sat down on the bench with her. "There's an antique store across the street. Do you want to go in?"

When I was growing up, she could sniff out antique stores a mile away, and nothing could get her moving faster than the knowledge that one was in the vicinity. It had become something of a family joke.

74

"No, it's OK. You go over if you like," she said. "I'm happy to stay here."

She did not want to walk up the piazza to the basilica or stroll over to the gelato shop or even window-shop. She was content to see Italy from the passenger seat of a car.

"There's a museum about the *trulli* just up there," I said. "You like museums. Would you like to see it?"

It was obvious from her expression that she would not. Nevertheless, she got up from the bench and wobbled for a moment. I took her hand as she steadied herself on her cane, and carefully led her to the Museo del Territorio.

We paid our entry fee and wandered from room to room looking at shards of pottery and ancient farm implements, diagrams explaining the construction of a *trullo,* and historical photos of the area. Nothing held Mom's attention for long.

"I want to go back to bed," she said finally.

On the drive back to the *trullo* we commiserated about the cold, rainy weather. I was certain that warmth and sun would improve her health and our holiday.

"Maybe we should head down south to Sicily," I suggested. "The weather might be better there."

"Yes, let's do that," she said dreamily. "When were you thinking of going?"

"First thing tomorrow morning."

5

San Mango d'Aquino, Reggio di Calabria, Taormina

I WASN'T ENTIRELY certain how to get to Sicily, but I had a map. Based on my quick calculation it looked to be a day's drive. Early the next morning I bundled Mom into the car and drove away from our chilly *trullo*. Naturally, because we were trying to escape the rain, the sun popped out.

Our first stop was an Agip gas station in Martina Franca.

"*Il pieno, per favore,*" I said confidently to the gas jockey. It was one of the less salacious phrases I had managed to memorize from my little Italian phrase book.

The gas jockey inserted the hose from the gas pump into the tank of my car, and while the euros turned over briskly on the pump's display panel he proceeded to rattle on about, I think, whether I wanted the windshield cleaned or the engine checked.

Although I have a very limited knowledge of Italian, I have been told that I have a convincing Italian accent. The danger is that Italians then assume that I speak the language fluently. I have also been told that I look Italian, probably because of my dark hair.

"*Grazie, solo il pieno, per favore,*" I answered with a firm nod, hoping that would be the end of it. Then I could not help adding, "*Signor? Dov'è la strada a Sicilia?*" I asked.

I recognized phrases in his response such as *a sinistra* (to the left), *a destra* (to the right), and *sempre diritto* (straight ahead). That was all I needed to get me started.

Within a few minutes we were sailing along the ss172, through orange groves and the rolling hills of Apulia. I tried to channel the spirit of Francesco da Mosto, the puckish and exuberant host of a TV series of Italian travelogues, who scoots about the country in a little red convertible. Hmm, a little red convertible, I mused; perhaps we should have rented one.

Less than an hour later, the *trullo*-dotted landscape came to an abrupt end, and the road began a lazy descent. The sun was burning off the morning haze, and directly in front of us was the sparking Gulf of Taranto.

Returning my attention to the road—and since I was driving, this seemed a fairly smart move—the coastal plain revealed Taranto, an industrial city with a smell to match. Its factory stacks were already belching smoke and steam, fouling the air of a new day. Not exactly what I expected from the city whose claim to fame is the tarantella.

The terrain levelled out, and we turned onto the E90. The road ran close to the coast but, sadly, did not afford a view of the Gulf of Taranto. We caught the occasional glimpse of sparkling blue sea or an olive grove surrounding a tidy farm, but generally speaking, the route did not serve up anything but a bland and desolate landscape of lumbering truck traffic and dust-choked road construction.

Although we kept our eyes peeled for the E940 turn off at Sybaris, we missed it, and I pulled into a gas station/café to verify directions. I was about to get into the car to resume our journey when Apollo of the E90 roared into the parking lot on his motorcycle. He was dressed head to toe in metallic-blue, skintight leather, under which rippled a gazillion taut muscles. He alighted gracefully from his matching blue hog and walked with long purposeful strides, as if in slow-motion, toward the café, running his fingers through shoulder-length, dark hair that he shook free, the curls obediently falling into place. Cradled under his right arm was a metallic-blue helmet in a design that Mercury himself might have favored.

He had such a dazzling combination of confidence and vanity. There was nothing to do but stand helplessly with my mouth wide open, which I did for too long a time.

"Now, what would you do with him?" snapped my mother disapprovingly. "Get in the car and let's go."

"Actually, I was wondering what he would do with me," I mumbled as I slipped behind the steering wheel of our station wagon.

"Pardon?"

"Nothing," I said, letting the sound of the ignition drown my reply.

Our journey along the A3 Autostrada del Sol was leisurely, toll free, and not nearly as harrowing as I had expected. There were no cars shooting past like rocket launchers (well, not many), the directional signs were pretty straightforward and understandable even to a non-Italian, and the scenery became more arresting the farther south we drove.

Dark clouds gathered and followed us through the coastal plains of Basilicata and then to mountainous Calabria, where the Pollino range merges with the Sila mountains. We found ourselves entering a terrain of immense forested mountains and plunging valleys. The only evidence of civilization was the road on which our car zipped around gasp-inducing bends and through black tunnels of blasted rock. The rock face was so close that in places you could stretch your hand out of the car window and touch it. Every so often, the sort of scenery that lands on the cover of a tourist brochure of Italy would pop into view: a villa perched on a hilltop surrounded by a stand of cypress, or clusters of homes and tidy vineyards and orchards scattered around the base of a valley.

But the scene-stealer for me was the autostrada.

Civil engineering is an art form in Italy. When it comes to roads and road design, the Italians are, in my humble opinion, the hands-down world champions. Italian engineers approach their construction projects without disturbing the land or its natural contours. They don't bully the landscape into submission; they caress it.

For someone who is not particularly fond of driving and who had such misgivings about driving in Italy, I felt exhilarated behind the wheel, taking curves that hugged a mountain bend, barrelling through dark tunnels, and crossing bridges that soared above precipitous valleys. It was pure scenery— not an advertising billboard in sight. Had we so desired, we could have pulled into one of the numerous rest stops thoughtfully provided along the road for travellers seeking a place to pause and admire the view or to munch on their lunch.

Speaking of lunch, someone was getting hungry.

"It's twelve o'clock," said Mom. "I need to eat. My diabetes, you know."

"OK, the next exit we reach, we'll turn off," I replied.

Just past Cosenza I veered onto an off-ramp with a sign announcing San Mango d'Aquino. I figured it would produce a restaurant. This was Italy, after all.

The road wound steeply up a mountain and continued this way for some time. Nothing resembling a restaurant (or rather, an open one) presented itself. The route was lined with bland buildings that appeared to be boarded up or abandoned. Still, we continued to follow the road upward. I considered turning around, but by now we were half intrigued, half amused by our choice of exit.

"If you see people wearing wings then we can safely assume that we've gone too far," I said.

Up and up we continued. When we finally arrived at the summit, we were too afraid to look down. Homes were hung over the lip of a cliff, giving literal meaning to "living on the edge."

"Can you imagine waking up each morning in a place like this?" gasped Mom. She is not a fan of heights. "I'd die."

The grade of the road levelled off, and we inched our way along a cobblestone street in search of a restaurant. Finding nothing that fit that description, we broadened our criteria to include a grocery store.

"There's one," I said, bringing the car to a stop alongside a small store. Beside it was a small fenced courtyard that over-looked the abyss. "Maybe we can get sandwiches made up."

The sound of a *signora* humming happily greeted us when we entered the grocery store. *"Buongiorno,"* she called out in a singsong voice from behind the deli counter.

She was a petite woman with short, curly, dark hair and

thick dark eyebrows. She wore a crewneck black top printed with red, stylized flowers, over which was a red vest of boiled wool, whose placket edges were embroidered with small colorful flowers. Topping it was a crisp white bibbed apron. Simple gold hoop earrings adorned her ears; a small but substantial diamond-studded cross on a fine gold chain hung carefully around her neck. Her face, devoid of makeup, was the most contented I have seen on anyone.

"*Buongiorno,*" I smiled. "*Vorrei due panini con prosciutto e provolone per favore.*"

"*Sì. Inglese?*" she asked in a thoroughly friendly manner. Perhaps my accent wasn't that good after all.

"*Sì.* Yes," I replied humbly.

"My husband, he speak some English," she said as she selected two fresh rolls.

She called out to him, and he emerged from the end of an aisle where he had been stocking the shelves with packages of toilet paper.

He was a bit taller than his wife, with salt-and-pepper hair and gray-flecked eyebrows and stubble. Tortoiseshell-rimmed, square glasses sat on the bridge of his nose, and he pushed them slightly as he approached. His black ski jacket was partially open, revealing a fawn-colored scarf that had been expertly folded and furled in a cravat style.

"You speak a bit of English, *un po' di inglese?*" I asked in that unfortunate tone people reserve for imbeciles and those who do not speak their language.

"I sure hope so," he deadpanned in a flawless American accent. "I spent almost twenty years in Pittsburgh."

Relieved that I could revert to a language that didn't require me to keep flipping through a phrase book, I asked

Federico—for he had introduced himself—how he had ended up in an American city and what drew him back to this remote town in the sky. His happy wife began preparing our sandwiches, and Federico was only too pleased to indulge my question. He had left this town, San Mango d'Aquino, the place of his birth, as a young engineer, he said.

"Professional jobs in Calabria were few and far between at the time," he explained. "If I wanted to practice engineering I had to move, and Pittsburgh gave me that opportunity.

"After eighteen years, I packed it in. I'd had enough," he said, leaning against the glass case of the deli counter. "So I came back to marry her." He shot a smile and a wink at his wife, who giggled shyly. "That's my Marisa. We have two kids now, both of them away at Cosenza—you would have passed it on your way here. Our son is at university studying computer engineering; our daughter is studying to be a hairdresser."

He gave us the *Reader's Digest* version of San Mango, telling us that it was settled in the 15th century and now has a population of about eighteen hundred. Sure, he agreed with a slight shrug, it was a sleepy place compared with the bustle of Pittsburgh, but the trade-off suited him. He shot another smile at Marisa, who beamed back at him.

A good and happy marriage, I decided.

Marisa handed us our sandwiches and popped some complimentary pastries into the bag as we paid the bill.

"You know," said Federico as we prepared to leave, "my son's trying to learn English. Can I give him your e-mail address so he can practice with you?"

"Of course," I replied, though I privately doubted a twenty-year-old guy would want to correspond with a fifty-something woman. I gave Federico the date we would be back in Canada.

Sure enough, the day after we returned home, I received an e-mail from Federico and Marisa's son. We have been corresponding sporadically ever since.

"What are the odds of us travelling through a country we barely know, taking a random exit, winding up in this town, and meeting those two?" I asked Mom as we drove out of San Mango. I put the car in neutral and let it coast down the sixteen-hundred-foot descent.

"It's like a little miracle, isn't it?" said Mom. "What a lovely couple."

Within minutes we had left the quiet simplicity of San Mango and found ourselves back in the warp-speed world of the A3.

"They looked very much in love, didn't they?" I said, still smiling at the memory of this lovely couple. "Why didn't you and Dad ever show affection to one another? I don't think I ever heard you say 'I love you' to each other—or to me, for that matter."

In my own household, "I love you" tends to be as common a phrase as "shut up!"

"To say 'I love you' is meaningless," Mom said with a practical clip to her voice. "When you think about it, what does 'I love you' mean? I'd rather have someone show me than say it."

"Show it how?"

"By respect and honesty, an occasional little gift," she said.

"That's where we're different," I replied. "Respect and honesty are the baseline in any relationship, but I also need physical intimacy and verbal reinforcement. I want it all."

Out of the corner of my eye I could see Mom twitch at the words "physical intimacy."

"Your father and I showed you and your brother enough love when you were little," she said defensively.

But had they? Certainly my brother and I lacked nothing growing up. We had a lovely warm place to live, good clothes, firm values to model, and no shortage of food on the table. But the many chores (from polishing silver to planting trees) and strict routines (from curfews to regimented homework and piano-practice times) imposed by my parents never allowed for relaxed interactions. By the time the chores were done and the routine had been followed to the letter, everyone was too worn out and too resentful to care about bonding.

My mother—she must have been Norman in a former life—ensured that order reigned when it came to me. My posture, my hairstyle and color, my personality, my clothing, came under her microscopic scrutiny. She wanted a neat, compliant, gregarious, and happy child; I was none of those things. The more she insisted, the more I resisted. She was not gentle with me, and I retaliated by not being gentle with her.

Talk of "feelings" was not encouraged in our family. It was the '60s after all. I picked up by nuance what I had to know, and that made me anxious because I was always looking for clues or anticipating disasters, afraid of messing up. There was a tension in our home, an anticipatory sense that something was about to happen or that someone was going to be asked to do something productive. When I came home after playing with my friends, I would tiptoe in the door, gauging the tenor of the household before shouting out a wary "Hello?"

I would intently watch TV sitcoms and privately wonder what ingredient, aside from product sponsorship, our family needed in order to become just like the TV family. What made other families so easygoing and good natured?

My parents seldom laughed around my brother and me. Certainly not on weekdays. There wasn't a formal decree or anything about this, but if memory serves, Monday to Friday was a sober, almost monastic time of schoolwork, green vegetables, and early bedtimes. On the weekends we did chores during the day and were allowed to eat hamburgers and french fries on Saturday night while watching *Hockey Night in Canada*. Our bedtime was extended to 10:00 PM, when the game ended.

84

But when my parents had a dinner party, which they occasionally did on Saturday nights, they unleashed their fun-loving, witty natures among an eclectic, colorful cast of friends—artists, academics, businesspeople, writers, and engineers. The women were always glamorous in their cocktail dresses, high heels, and glittering bijoux, the men exuding elegance in their dark suits with starched white shirts and polished shoes.

A steady din of chatter and tinkling glasses would pervade our home on these nights, frequently punctuated by an outbreak of riotous laughter. These were giddy, relaxed affairs. My father would croon along with Frank Sinatra on the hi-fi while shaking a batch of his signature martinis; my mother would lay out a remarkable buffet and be the consummate hostess of grace and ease.

I would loiter in the shadows upstairs, trying to catch a glimpse of the guests, but more importantly to watch my parents laugh and let loose. I felt hurt that they didn't act this way in front of me.

When the guests were gone, our household settled back into its somnolent, orderly state. My father would retreat behind a book or the *Globe and Mail;* my restless mother would keep the activity level and routines running like clockwork.

My parents were not big on showing physical affection. I have no memory of ever being cuddled or hugged by either of them when I was growing up, aside from the occasional stiff embrace, and yet I don't recall ever being worried about the lack of hugging. This changed when I had children of my own. The presence of little tykes softened my parents, and from then on, they were all about hugging.

As our car zoomed along the autostrada, I began to drift into a zone of self-pity, wishing that we had been a cuddling family, wondering why my parents had felt more comfortable with rigidity and remoteness.

It was the sort of intense, forthright conversation I wanted to have with my mother during our trip. But discussions with her require the kind of checklist preparation that Batman undertakes when he climbs into the Batmobile and races off to face his wily opponent: "Guilt deflector up, hostility radar activated, I-told-you-so shields engaged, self-esteem force field on standby." In other words, I need to be psychologically armed when I face my mother. A stiff drink doesn't hurt, either.

I wanted that conversation with my mother desperately, and I wanted it to be meaningful and cleansing for us both. But a car is never the ideal place for an intense talk, especially if I'm behind the wheel. Besides, I was holding out for something more from Mom, something more than her predictable response, "You only seem capable of remembering the unhappy events in your childhood," which she had started to chant in the car. Memory, like hearing, can be selective.

THE RAIN caught up to us and accompanied us through most of Calabria. Pewter clouds hung low and heavy as our tires swished through sprawling puddles, and the thwap-thwap of windshield wipers dodged a staccato fire of rain pellets.

Would we have been better off staying in Alberobello? I had a suspicion bad weather was following us.

Still, there was a prehistoric beauty to what we could glimpse through the rain-splattered windshield of this new landscape. The vegetation in these parts was fecund, moist, sexy, and oversized. Huge swollen aloe limbs thrashed wildly like octopus tentacles; massive prickly pear with pancake-shaped pads the size of brontosaurus footprints sprouted tomato-sized red buds that looked ready to burst. Glossy new growth was evident everywhere in this richly saturated green landscape.

We had not yet seen northern Italy to make an informed comparison, but based on what we were glimpsing of southern Italy I couldn't help but jump to conclusions. Aside from Taranto—and to be fair, it was a modest size—we did not encounter any explosively large cities on the scale of, say, Milan or Naples. In fact, once you are south of Naples, there isn't anything that could be called a booming metropolis. There is a refreshing absence of glossy shopping malls, skyscrapers, and tourist attractions, though, sadly, those fixtures seem to be the measure of a boom economy these days.

A wide socioeconomic chasm has existed between northern and southern Italy for centuries, a disparity that is particularly pronounced nowadays. Although Italy has boomed economically since the Second World War, the spoils have not been equally distributed. The country might very well be united under one government, but it is starkly divided between the prosperous North and the poor South.

In 2006 a referendum was held on whether the North and South should separate. Despite all the bickering from the North about how their hard-earned cash is being used to prop up the South—or maybe because the Northerners were too lazy to get out of their café chairs to vote (only half of them cast ballots)—Italians overwhelmingly agreed to remain united. That might very well change: Silvio Berlusconi, who bounces in and out of the presidential job, has campaigned on a promise to split Italy in two.

According to 2006 statistics, unemployment in the South sits at more than 12 percent, compared with 3.6 percent in the North. More disturbing is the exodus of young people from the South: more than 34 percent are fleeing small towns in the South such as San Mango d'Aquino, compared with 13 percent of their Northern counterparts.

Italy's government is trying to reverse the trend by sending loads of cash to tart up the South for international tourists. Still, the question remains, Why has action been so slow in coming?

This was a question raised in 1969 by H.V. Morton in *A Traveller in Southern Italy.* Morton bemoaned the state of some of southern Italy's treasures: castles neglected to the point of being regularly pillaged, fortresses left to the mercy of the elements, important ruins overgrown by brush, towns unable to afford gatekeepers to protect their artifacts. Much of what Morton described then was still in evidence during our trip nearly forty years later.

Still, the South is not entirely disadvantaged, as I learned while leafing through *La Repubblica* one day. Southerners work fewer hours, have more holidays, and enjoy a lower cost of living than their frenetic-living northern counterparts.

The South also has a more ancient pedigree. You can see it in the robust and gnarly trunks of the olive trees.

Here's my advice: If you want to experience Old Italy, don't go to Tuscany; go to Calabria. It is the sole and the soul of Italy.

NEARLY THREE hundred miles and about five hours after leaving Alberobello, we arrived just after 1:00 PM in Reggio di Calabria, the tip of the toe of Italy's boot.

"Keep your eyes out for the word *traghetti*," I said to Mom. "That's the word for ferries."

"Did you say spaghetti?" she asked. "I'm not really hungry."

"No, *tra-ghetti*," I said, louder. "Just look for signs with a boat symbol."

It wasn't long before we arrived on an industrial-looking quay stacked with rust-colored cargo containers. I stopped at a small building inside a raised gate barrier to ask for directions to the ferry. A big swarthy man with a cigarette dangling from his mouth pointed to the far end of the quay.

I got back into the car and drove farther along, through a graveyard of rusting metal, but could not find the ferry's ticket booth. We circled around, and on our second loop spied a tiny, nondescript kiosk.

I got out of the car and approached the window. A young, jaundice-skinned fellow with a cigarette hanging from his mouth was absorbed in the task of counting a wad of euros.

As I waited for him to finish, glancing down at the phrase book I held in my hand to make sure I was going to ask my question correctly, one of the lenses in my (new, I might add) eyeglasses inexplicably popped out and fell to the pavement.

"What the hell?"

I dropped to my knees and groped madly around. I located the lost lens inches from my foot—it had not broken, thankfully—then fumbled to replace it in the empty frame. My eyesight had declined rapidly in the last year, and without glasses I was hopeless.

The young man stopped counting his money and regarded

me with amused curiosity, as if I were some odd species he had not encountered before.

"Mi scusi," I smiled. *"Dove posso comprare un biglietto per Messina? Due biglietto... biglietti?"*

"Qui. Venti euros," the man in the booth said in a gruff voice.

"Per due? Con macchina?" I asked, trying to clarify whether the cheap ticket price included passage for our car.

89

"Sì," he answered.

"A che ora..."

"Le tre e mezza," he replied quickly.

I looked puzzled. He held up three fingers and slowly with emphasis said *"e mezza."*

I pretended to understand and then remembered that *mezzo* meant half, so, of course, half past three.

"That was cheap," I said to Mom returning to the car. "Only twenty euros, about twenty-eight dollars."

"With the car?" she asked with surprise.

"Yup."

We waited in the car for an hour and a half, not wanting to risk leaving the dock in case we could not find our way back. We were hungry, but the lone café on the dock was, naturally, closed.

Two truck drivers loitering nearby—one large and shy; the other thin and uncertain looking—edged their way toward us. Mom's hands tightened around her purse.

"You go there?" said the larger of the two in halting English, pointing across the Strait of Messina to Sicily. Both men maintained a respectful distance from our car.

"Yes," I replied. "Does the boat dock right here?"

"Yes," he replied. "It will come. Three-thirty. Stay here. I tell you when to drive on."

He had short, strawlike hair and round features, and was dressed in worn black sweatpants, dusty black plastic beach sandals, and a loose, dirty navy T-shirt. His stocky build and quiet, almost shy demeanor reminded me of someone, but I could not place my finger on who.

They were from Germany, they said. Yes, they agreed, nodding their heads vigorously, they were a long way from home, but they had made this journey many times before and were used to it.

They asked where we were from. I answered "Canada," and they stared with slight incomprehension, as if trying to fix the location of Canada in their minds. Or maybe they expected us to be attired in parkas and mukluks.

The conversation was quickly exhausted. The larger of the two gave us a slight smile and a polite nod of his head, and they both sauntered back to their respective vehicles to await the ferry's arrival.

Several sleek white ferries were docked along the quay, so I was somewhat taken aback when ours arrived. It wasn't a glamorous ferry—not that I cared—but I was expecting something a bit more polished than what chugged up to the dock. It looked more like a barge, with a large open deck for transporting vehicles or cargo and a third of the vessel dedicated to passengers. My first impression when I saw it was that it could do with a paint job. I looked at the large shy trucker inquiringly, and with a firm nod he indicated that this was indeed the ferry for Messina. We drove our car onto the open deck and parked it alongside a number of bulky transport trucks, including those of our new German friends.

Mom and I got out of the car, and I guided her through the mass of vehicles and up a flight of metal stairs to the passenger deck. The crew was hardened and rough-looking, with dirty hands and black grime outlining their fingernails. Their navy-blue uniforms were frayed at the cuffs and stained with dirt. Sweaty stubble, greasy hair, and dark circles under their eyes gave their gaunt faces a shifty, desperate look, the sort that conjures visions of *The Rime of the Ancient Mariner.*

We took our seats facing the bow of the ferry so we could enjoy a good view of our approach to Sicily. The rain had paused, and it was warm enough for us to spend the half-hour voyage on the outer deck. I longed to feel the sea air on my face and to compare the receding Italian mainland with the approaching island of Sicily, but given our scruffy surroundings I decided to stay with Mom. Besides, she had taken to calling my name loudly and repeatedly whenever I drifted out of her sight, prompting the same response in me as someone yelling "GRENADE!"—the urge to dive for cover.

A crew member approached us and beckoned me to follow. At the stairwell he pointed to the distressed wooden door of the women's washroom and offered to unlock it for me. I glanced past the crewman's shoulder and saw the large shy German trucker leaning against a wall, his arms crossed in front of him and his eyes fixed sternly on us. Catching my eye he quietly shook his head as a silent warning.

"No, grazie," I smiled politely to the crew member.

The sailor was insistent, but I repeated "No" more emphatically this time and walked away. Mom never turns down a chance to use a washroom, but I had the feeling that this one would not produce a pleasant experience.

"What did he want?" Mom asked when I returned to my seat.

"He was, um, just showing me the vending machines in case we wanted food," I replied quickly. "I don't think we need anything. We'll wait till we get to the hotel."

I glanced around the passenger deck and realized we were the only women onboard. It all seemed rather weird.

"I don't think many people go to Sicily," I whispered to Mom.

We sat it in our seats and stared straight ahead as the ferry chugged across the Strait of Messina. The sun had begun to dip, and its reflected rays looked like a million brilliant diamonds cast upon the water.

Out of the corner of my eye I noticed Mom looking at me.

"I was thinking of the conversation we had on the way down. The one about showing love," she said. "Since you apparently like being touched so much, why don't you let me do your hair? It needs a good brushing."

"I don't think so, but thanks anyway," I said, and took a sudden interest in the road map in my hand.

Several minutes later I turned in my seat slightly and saw the stocky German trucker again. This time he was lost in thought as he gazed at Sicily's coastline. Was he pining for someone he loved back home? Was he was thinking about the long-distance drives and how much he hated them? Was he casting about, as we all do from time to time, for ways to secure an easier future? Or was he replaying the what-ifs of his life?

Then it dawned on me why he looked familiar. He reminded me of a neighbor I once had—same round features and stocky build, same quiet sadness. I've often wondered at the significance of meeting people on holiday who resemble or in some way remind me of people back home. Are doppelgängers sent to reassure us when we find ourselves in unfamiliar situations, or are they a cosmic nudge to be friendlier to the person back home?

The ferry slid alongside the dock in Messina just after 4:00 PM. In March, night falls quickly in Italy; in another hour the sky would be pitch. With another thirty miles between Messina and Taormina, our destination, it was likely we would be arriving after dark.

I don't like arriving in an unfamiliar city in the dark. By midafternoon the cogs in my brain are grinding to a halt, along with any special powers of observation I need to locate and secure a place to lay my head for the night. This is especially true when I have driven over three hundred miles basically nonstop in one day.

"Why are we going to Taormina?" asked Mom.

"I was told it was worth checking out," I said. A recommendation from someone I know is often all the encouragement I need to visit a place.

We bade *auf Wiedersehen* to the German truckers, found our car, and drove off the ferry and onto the autostrada.

By the time we reached the exit for Taormina, the only thing visible was the fluorescent glow from the road signs. We dutifully followed the arrows and began a circular ascent reminiscent of our experience in San Mango earlier that day.

My preference is always to find a charming place to spend the night, and I usually conduct a dogged search upon arrival in a town I have never visited. It is a habit that irritates others, except Mom, who can't imagine why someone would stay in a boring hotel when you could get a room that oozes history and architectural interest.

But driving the skinny streets of Taormina, with its hairpin turns and gridlocked traffic—everyone seemed to be reversing his car on this particular night—I was too worn out to care. I would take any place that might have a bed to spare.

93

After passing it twice during my initial pursuit of more appetizing fare, we pulled up in front of the Hotel Continental.

"Stay here," I said to Mom. "I'll see if they have a room." I said a quick prayer to myself that there would be one.

I strode into the time warp of a yellowed 1970s-era lobby with swag lamps and tall plateglass windows hung with dull orange curtains. The furniture was Swedish Modern and upholstered in that indestructible but hideously bland, nubby, mustard-colored fabric that was popular once upon a time. It was the sort of establishment where a Clairtone TV would not have been out of place. In its day, this lobby was probably considered breathtakingly stylish.

A well-groomed young man and woman in crisp navy-blue uniforms greeted me with smiles.

"Good evening," I smiled back, with a hint of pleading in my voice. "Do you have a room?"

They did, and they offered to show it to me.

The room had zero personality: two twin beds with faded green bedspreads and a claustrophobically small bathroom that was slightly elevated from the rest of the room and required a step up, which would be difficult for Mom's arthritically heavy legs. "They are all like this," apologized the front desk clerk who showed me the room. Orange, heavily lined drapes skimmed the windowsill. It was too dark outside to see what the view offered; all I could see was my own reflection, which showed the strain of a day spent on the road.

"It's perfect," I said, turning to the desk clerk. "We'll take it."

Mom has always been a conscientious student of design. She is self-taught, knows every architectural style, and has an uncanny knack with color and fabric. Every house we have ever lived in—and some of them were real dumps when my parents purchased them—was perfectly renovated and decorated and appointed all by her hand. Sometimes our homes ended up in magazine spreads. I've always wondered why she never pursued interior design as an occupation. To this day, she will arrive in a place and immediately start rearranging the furniture while critiquing the fabric choices and the placement of the artwork. She does this on occasion in my home.

So after leading her through the shabby-retro lobby, then along a corridor with lighting that cast a puke-green glow and made everyone look like zombies, I flicked on the dim light in our hotel room and was shocked when she gushed, "This is lovely!"

I looked at her as if she were joking.

"Oh really, stop being so picky," she said with irritation. "At my age all you care about is that the room has a bed and a toilet that flushes. And a dining room. When's dinner?"

Our dinner and service, I'm happy to report, were excellent. The dining room itself was down-at-the-heels—the same drab orange curtains hung on the patio doors, and another set acted as a barrier between the dining area and the kitchen. The ceilings were high and the lighting was dim, but no one seemed to mind. We tucked into a delicious meal of roast pork, potatoes, and salad.

The room was bustling and buzzing with a newly arrived coach tour of American seniors. All of them were trim and fit. The men looked slightly grizzled of face in a handsome, almost academic sort of way, and they wore solid-colored corduroy trousers with plaid shirts. The women were nicely coiffed—some with hairstyles that were sleek and chin length, others that were short and a bit trendy, with streaks and gelled ends—and many were attired in casual, sporty ensembles that invariably consisted of those dressy versions of track pants and matching jacket. It wasn't a style that appealed to me, but for that age group it seemed practical. There wasn't a cane or a walker among them.

Some looked older than my mother, and I wondered why my mother, who had led such an active life—it wasn't that long ago, really, that she was playing tennis—had physically deteriorated so much. This is going to sound irrational, but I was beginning to resent my mother's physical condition. Perhaps if she had tried harder to keep her weight down, I thought, she would have staved off many of her infirmities.

On a more superficial level, Mom's hairstyle and clothing had not changed in decades. She had never taken an interest in fashion; her interests were restricted to art and architecture from a bygone era. She did not hold back on her suggestions that others—well, me at least—make changes, yet she never made changes to herself.

"I need a new wardrobe," Mom said out of the blue. "I was rather hoping the airline would lose my luggage."

She, too, was watching the American seniors.

"Yes, you do need a bit of an update," I ventured. "You spent your life renovating old homes and yet you never spent time or money maintaining yourself. Why was that?"

"I couldn't just go out and spend money on myself," she replied, as if that were the most preposterous idea she had ever heard. "We had a family to raise. It wasn't like you kids today going out and getting manicures and pedicures every week."

"But your generation used to go out and get their hair done every week," I countered. "Isn't that the same thing?"

"When it came to clothes, no one ever offered to help me," she shrugged, ignoring my question.

Here it comes, I thought. The guilt. "No one" meant "you."

"I'd be happy to help you chose a wardrobe," I said. "But I don't think you're willing to take my advice. Besides, you're cheap when it comes to clothes and spending money on yourself."

"See that gal over there," Mom said, zeroing in on a willowy woman with chin-length, side-parted hair that was hooked behind an ear on one side and hung freely on the other. "That's a hairstyle I'd like. What do you think? Would it suit me?"

"Sure, it would look great," I said with slight exasperation at her inability to stick to a train of thought. "But you have to be prepared to let your hair grow to achieve that style."

"Oh, I have no patience for that," she said, then turning to me: "It would be a good style for you, though. Why don't you try that one?"

"Why are you suggesting hairstyles for me that are worn by old women?" I asked pointedly.

"Those people aren't that old," she said, taken aback. "I bet they're your age!"

I had to get out of there before I did something that might prompt a call to security.

A pretty courtyard garden with an orange tree beckoned beyond the patio doors of the dining room.

"I'm going for a walk after dinner," I announced stiffly.

"You can't go out alone. You never know who's out there," she said.

"I'm sure it's safe," I answered curtly. "It's a small town."

The maître d', whom I recognized from the front desk when we first arrived, came by to refill our water glasses. I rolled my eyes as Mom pressed him for his opinion of this madcap idea of mine.

"Can you guarantee that she'll be safe?" Mom asked him warily. "In writing? She's the only daughter I have."

"Your daughter will be fine," he assured her with a firm smile, giving me a paternalistic nod.

The man was less than half my age. Honestly, my mother treats me like a ten-year-old.

"I promise I won't be long," I told her as she poured her tea. She looked unconvinced.

Was it my safety that she was worried about, or was she envious of my mobility? I was getting the sense that she expected me to hang back with her. Well, that wasn't going to happen.

I accompanied Mom back to our room, grabbed a jacket, gave her a peck on her forehead, and promised to be back soon.

As I pushed open the tall black wrought-iron gate that opened onto a back lane, I felt the singular pleasure that comes from being footloose—no timetable, no destination, and a landscape unseen by me just waiting to be discovered. I love darting in and out of places, exploring their deepest regions if I want or just giving them a cursory appraisal.

I trotted down four levels of stone steps and arrived on Taormina's tiny main drag, Corso Umberto 1, a charming and elegant pedestrian-only mall of chevron-patterned cobbles, black coach lamps, and wrought-iron balconies. At each end of the mall, soaring archways marked the town's pre-Roman stone walls.

The street itself was lined with fashionable, upscale boutiques. I wandered into a few of them, more out of something to do than actual interest. There was a relaxed vibe on the street. The Piazza Chiesa looked like a movie set, with its stone, cherub-topped fountain and café tables set out around the perimeter. Young, hand-holding couples strolled aimlessly along the lamplit thoroughfare, and I felt a pang of regret about not being able to share the moment with Colin.

Taormina is known for a 5,400-seat Greek amphitheater, hailed as much for its preservation as its drop-dead gorgeous setting overlooking a scalloped coastline with snowcapped Mount Etna in the background. I wanted to see the theater for myself, but my attention was suddenly distracted by the words "Internet Point" flashing on a neon sign affixed to a rough stone building halfway up a dimly lit, ancient alley.

The door to the Internet café was ajar. I stepped into a very modern space bathed in that electric cool-blue lighting that always makes me feel like I'm about to take part in some illicit activity. A young woman with the same bangs-and-bob hairstyle my mom had been pushing on me for some time whipped up a cappuccino and logged me on to a terminal.

E-mails from my family cheered me immensely, and I wrote back describing my high-tech surroundings amid a pre–Roman Empire town. By a stroke of luck, Zoë was online at the same time and tapped back a message instantly. We bantered back and forth excitedly for a few minutes, comparing our respective adventures. She was still having a fabulous time in France.

"And guess what?" she wrote. "I've already bought three pairs of shoes!" I gave a proud chuckle. Like mother, like daughter. Then I stared for a long time at her closing sentence, "I miss you so much."

I felt proud that we had such an open, un-self-conscious connection with one another, and at the same time I felt a bit wistful. I have never uttered those words to my own mother, nor has she said them to me. I could not put my finger on why

Mom and I have had such a hard time expressing our feelings to each other or why it comes so easily to my daughter and me.

The sky was spitting rain when I left the Internet café. I made my way back to the hotel and promised myself to check out the Greek amphitheater in the morning.

At the door of our hotel room I quietly turned the knob and entered.

It was the first time I had shared a room with my mother in about thirty years. I'll say this much: Seniors make strange noises when they sleep. I listened to Mom's labored breathing, the phlegmy rattle in her throat, her fitful cries and whimpers. She was curled on her side, away from me, and for the first time in my life I glimpsed her as someone other than my mother.

There is a photo of my parents that sits in my mother's living room. I love it because it is the antithesis of the people who raised me: It was taken at a dance, when they were dating in their early twenties. The photo shows my elegant father in a white dinner jacket and black, loose trousers—zoot trousers, they were called back in those days, he had told me. His blond hair and happy, confident smile make him look like a movie star. His left hand rests on my mother's tiny waist; the right one clutches her hand as they pose in mid-dance. My mother, too, is the epitome of early 1950s glamor. Her long, luxuriant raven hair tumbles with a bouncy thick curl over her shoulders; a sleek, ballet-length, shimmering polka-dot dress skims her lean figure; she stands erect in black peep-toe shoes with what look like five-inch heels.

Now here she was with short white hair, a body far from slim and crippled by osteoarthritis, her mind slightly forgetful. The delicate, soft, small hands in the photograph are now gnarled with thick, ropy blue veins running like gopher tunnels beneath a crepey surface.

I watched her sleeping: Her face looked peaceful, but I knew, as I have somehow always known, that inside churned decades of disappointment that her family—particularly her children—did not meet her ideals.

She had longed for a family like the Waltons, with its cheerful optimism and loving interactions. What she ended up with best resembled a cross between the super-regimented Banks family in *Mary Poppins* and the wacky Beverly Hillbillies (minus the money).

I stood beside Mom's bed and watched her sleep. I tried to figure out where it had gone wrong, and why we had been too afraid, or perhaps too proud, to admit that there was a rift in the first place.

I slipped into the twin bed next to hers and turned off the light.

In the black void I prayed that she would recover from every ache, pain, and infirmity—emotional and physical—that plagued her.

Then I prayed for a more graceful old age for myself—one that did not include a walker.

6

Sicily: Racalmuto, Agrigento

Morning broke, and the heavens looked ready to do likewise.

I stood at the window of our hotel room, surveying the landscape and wondering whether it was possible for it to rain every day of our trip.

"Good morning!" Mom chimed perkily as she emerged from the bathroom. She was already dressed and had her makeup bag in her hand.

"It's going to rain . . . again," I said. On cue, big drops began to splatter the pane.

"That's ok," she smiled. "We'll be in a car."

I peered at the choppy gray Ionian Sea and the red-clay-tiled rooftops of Taormina. We were so high up that vertigo began to grip me. I gave a sigh of resignation and headed into the washroom to take a shower.

In the bathroom sink, several small white pills were scattered around the drain stopper. One or two were strewn around the basin's edge. They had obviously dropped from Mom's hand as she was taking her morning dose. I glanced at the floor and found a few more.

Back at our *trullo* in Alberobello I had come across a stray pill or two beneath a loaf of bread as I was wiping down the kitchen countertop one morning, and then another on the floor of her bedroom. I had encountered the same stray pills in her home, but I had never said anything to her about it, assuming the pills had simply tumbled out of their packaging.

103

Now I saw it as a worrisome pattern, and I wondered how best to broach the subject without her feeling that her faculties were being questioned. I settled on the direct approach.

I emerged from the bathroom with a towel wrapped around my wet hair and a toothbrush in my mouth.

"Hey, I found some of your pills in the sink and on the floor," I said.

"Oh, that's where they went," Mom said absently. She was sitting on the edge of the bed drawing on her coral lipstick and pursing her lips together to evenly coat them.

"How many pills do you take a day?"

"Sixteen."

"Um, isn't it rather critical to take *all* of them?"

"I do!" she exclaimed.

"Well, actually you don't if you're dropping them in the sink and on the floor. This isn't the first time I've found your pills scattered about. Are you OK?"

"Oh for heaven's sake, of course I'm OK. I haven't died, have I?"

"You're right," I said, pausing with the toothbrush in my

mouth. "Maybe that means you don't really need to take all those pills."

"My doctor says..."

"Do you always believe everything your doctor tells you?" I cut in. Her unwavering belief in the absolute wisdom of the medical profession exasperates me to no end. "Maybe you should take me with you to your next appointment. I've got a few questions for him."

"If I took you with me I'd be blacklisted by every doctor in the city."

"Sort of like that time I came to church with you when..."

"I don't want to talk about *that*," she said abruptly and looked away. "*That* was terrible."

That was when I had accompanied my mother to her church one Sunday years earlier. I had endured a sonorous homily by the priest and was going down for a final head-nod when he said something that snapped me back to life. "The Roman Catholic Church is the only true religion in the world."

I had snorted disbelievingly—the nerve!—and twisted around in my seat to see if his words had had any effect on the congregation. But no, they sat there doe-eyed and passive. I couldn't tell whether they had accepted the priest's statements as truth or whether they were all thinking about how they were going to spend their afternoon once they were sprung from church.

After Mass we shuffled out of church in a line, everyone shaking hands with the padre. When our turn came to press the flesh I confronted the priest about his sermon.

"You're sowing the seeds of intolerance," I said brazenly.

"And you're holding up the line," the priest glowered, turning his glare from me to my red-faced mother.

She felt it best that she find a new church immediately...in another town and, just to be on the safe side, with another denomination.

"Well, he had it coming," I protested as I swished the toothbrush around my mouth.

"Your problem is that you don't know when to keep your mouth shut," she said primly.

"But..."

"ENOUGH!" she boomed. Then, smoothing out the wrinkles of her white pants, she collected herself and said softly and evenly, "Now let's get some breakfast."

AFTER BREAKFAST, I wandered out onto the hotel's upper-level patio for a panoramic survey of Taormina. I threaded my way through a gaggle of the ubiquitous white plastic patio tables and chairs, across the terra-cotta-tiled deck, toward a small black railing. I wanted to see the hotel's promised grand view of Mount Etna, the undulating coastline, beaches galore, and the Greek amphitheater. I peered into the moody, misty air and saw nothing more than a vague squiggle of coastline. Then the rain came pelting down and forced me back inside.

There was nothing left to do but check out.

Navigating your way out of Taormina requires the sort of stamina that is unreasonable to expect of someone first thing in the morning. We had been on the road just six minutes, and already I was tense and thinking of something alcoholic.

Tight, narrow laneways gave way to one twisting road after another, as if we were steering through an intestinal tract. Then, like a little miracle, a road sign appeared and pointed the way to the autostrada. Before we knew it, we were hurtling through long dark tunnels and being spit out the other end into a landscape of inexpressible beauty.

Rolling green hills surrounded us; ruins of various vintages were silhouetted against distant hilltops, soft lush meadows stretched to infinity—all this beauty despite cloudy skies. It did not matter. With wide open space in front of me, I took a deep breath and exhaled with immense satisfaction, leaned back in the driver's seat a bit, loosened the death grip on the steering wheel, and relaxed my legs where the opened road map had been permanently clenched between my thighs.

On a map, Sicily looks small, but it is actually quite large— the largest island in the Mediterranean—with a population of five million. Agriculture is the leading industry, and vineyards and groves of olives, almonds, oranges, and lemons abound.

But mention to anyone that you are going to visit Sicily and you'll be met with either awkward silence or one word: "Eeew!"

People who visit Italy always make excuses for not including Sicily in their itinerary, saying that it's a shame the place is so off the beaten track, or that it's too remote for a side trip. That's a lame excuse. From Naples, you can drive to it in a day.

One problem, I suspect, is Sicily's inability to be heard above the travel-industry hucksters urging tourists to visit the more "civilized" northern end of Italy. Another problem could be Sicily's flag. It is red and yellow and features a creature with three hairy legs and the head of Medusa. Doesn't exactly scream "Hey, come for a visit, and bring the kids!" does it?

Poor, lovely Sicily. At one time it was a sophisticated cultural hotbed, an exotic place of diverse backgrounds where art and academia intermingled. It was a linchpin in both Magna Graecia and the Roman Empire before becoming a full-fledged country in its own right in 1130.

But Sicily seemed to get tangled in the power plays of every tribe or nation itching to flex its territorial muscle, and that ultimately led to its undoing. By the 13th century, its economy was an unholy mess, and Sicily began a steady slide toward economic hell. When it seemed life couldn't get any worse, an earthquake ripped through the place in 1639 and killed sixty thousand people.

Sicily joined the Kingdom of Italy in 1860, but labor unrest was rife, the economy collapsed, and Sicilians left their homeland in droves. The only thing that flourished there was organized crime, and the place became known as a thug's paradise.

It still is. We drove past Catania and there, lashed to a chain-link fence, was a piece of cardboard upon which some-one had scrawled in big black letters, *"Vergogna."* Shame. It was a reference to a horrific incident that had occurred the previous month. Following a football match between Cata-nia and Palermo, forty-year-old police officer Filippo Raciti, a husband and father, was killed when a homemade rocket was hurled into his squad car.

An international outcry erupted. Public attendance at foot-ball games was immediately and indefinitely banned, and the president of the Catania team resigned. Everyone, from the cops to the Vatican, castigated the light punishment Italy's judges doled out to sports hooligans, and put much of the blame on the Mafia. Raciti himself had had firsthand expe-rience of the Sicilian justice system: A week before he was killed, he attended the court appearance of a football goon he had arrested. After the judge delivered a mere slap on the wrist to the accused, the goon walked right up to Raciti in the courtroom and laughed in his face, then strolled out the door to freedom.

That's the thing with Italy; it can be achingly beautiful and at the same time heartbreakingly ugly.

Between Catania and Enna we drove through the predictable swath of boxy, bland shapes that is sadly characteristic of suburban highway architecture—a sight that always sends me into a stupor—and then somewhere on the outskirts of Enna the scenery changed dramatically. We found ourselves meandering through pure, unadulterated, empty countryside, on a fluid ribbon of highway. The road was an architectural marvel built upon colonnaded, fluted underpinnings that must have been inspired by a Roman aqueduct. The loveliest thing about this drive was that it lacked the astonishing mass of visual distractions normally found on superhighways. There was nothing around it. No billboards, buildings, signs, or service stations whatsoever; the elegant band of asphalt with contours that mimicked a river weaved silently through a rich, lush landscape. It was one beautiful drive.

Italy's reputation as the purveyor of pleasure and passion clearly extends to its highways. When Italians construct a road, I don't believe for a minute that they merely survey the area, draw a plan from A to B, and then summon a squad of bulldozers. I imagine they ruminate on it, ponder the landscape over a steaming cappuccino, then walk it, talk to it, take in both the dominant and the subtle changes in elevation. A sketch begins to take form, infused with the rich repertoire of the Italian experience. The soft curve of this autostrada, for example, might have been the curve of a voluptuous woman glimpsed striding through a piazza, or a coastline driven in the summertime, or a path strolled hand in hand with a lover, or a ski run mastered on holiday.

And if I may be permitted to take this a few steps further:

When Italians design something, they don't design it solely
for themselves, they design it for their lovers, in-laws, friends,
neighbors, priest, and God, not necessarily in that order. I
simply could not imagine it being done any other way.

It also occurred to me—and of course by now I was an
expert, having been in Italy a total of six days and having
driven almost four hundred miles—that Italian engineers
never build straight roads. They intuitively know that the
ideal is never what is most expedient and cost-effective; the
ideal is to make a driver jump out of her car and stand in such
awe of a section of road she has just travelled that she can do
nothing else but squeeze together five fingers, kiss their tips,
and release them with a shout of "*Bravo! Bellisimo!*" Which I
did. And then I took a photo for good measure.

Sure, you can believe that the decision to build a winding
road rather than a straight road has more to do with slowing
down speeders than about design, but then you would completely misunderstand the Italian mind. And frankly, such
roads don't slow anyone down; they just make drivers (like me)
revel in the thrill of leaning into a curve like Mario Andretti,
feeling your body sway in a gentle rock until your back arches
slightly and your pelvis starts to tingle. Driving in Italy is a
rapture of passion and gasoline.

I glanced over at Mom to share with her this sparkling
observation, only to discover that she had nodded off, her
head tilted back against the headrest and her mouth slackly
agape.

Not again! How could someone travel all this way just to
fall asleep in the midst of such beauty?

My mind do-si-doed back to our earlier conversation about
love. Perhaps my mother didn't really care that she was in Italy,

or anywhere for that matter, she just wanted to be with me. I guess that's love—the unexpressed variety.

I pumped the brakes slightly to see if the sudden movement would jerk her awake.

"What on earth are you doing?" she said with obvious irritation.

"Oh, hi. You're awake," I smiled.

"I was not sleeping; I was just resting my eyes," she snapped. She surreptitiously wiped away a small pool of drool that had collected in one corner of her lips.

"How can you sleep?" I protested. "Look at this! We're in Italy. Look at this road. Have you ever seen anything so beautiful?"

"Jane, it's just a highway," she said. "For heaven's sake, I think you're the one who needs a rest."

I steered the car toward an exit heading south—a smaller, less impressive highway—and bade a reluctant farewell to the A19.

We passed a small construction crew doing road repairs; all of them were working with their hands. Two or three were wielding scythes—scythes!—to cut back the roadside brush; another was on his knees with what looked like a screwdriver, picking away the old tar from the road. There wasn't a piece of gas-fuelled machinery around, a point that pleased me greatly.

I took a quick look at the map as our car picked up speed again.

There are a number of enchanting, well-known places to visit in Sicily, but our destination this day was a not-so-well-known one: Racalmuto, which shares a bond with Hamilton, Ontario, the city where I have lived for the last twenty years. During much of the 20th century, boomtown Hamilton was the industrial and manufacturing heartland of Canada. Around 1945, the city put out an urgent call for skilled workers. When the people of Racalmuto, where poverty was rife, heard this news, a few brave Racalmutese boarded a ship and headed west to check it out. Within weeks they were writing home to confirm that—*mamma mia!*—jobs, good wages, new housing, and an economy in breathless overdrive were up for grabs.

The news triggered an incredible exodus. By the mid 1950s, much of Racalmuto's population of sixteen thousand had emptied out and relocated to Hamilton. Today, there are more people in Hamilton who hail from Racalmuto than there are people in Racalmuto (its current population is under nine thousand).

And so with great anticipation I steered the car toward Racalmuto. The verdant rolling hills and the fact that I have long harbored a dream to live in Italy gave me an idea. Maybe I could be the first Hamiltonian to relocate to Racalmuto! I kept my eye open for a suitable property.

"There's a place for you!" crowed Mom. She has a way of reading my mind.

It was a sprawling ruin with small windows, none of them with glass and all of them of different shapes and sizes. The roof had fallen in on itself. A string of arches and the remnants of an arbor indicated what might have been a garden. Two smokestacks at either end of the property made the place look like a crematorium.

"Isn't it perfect," sighed Mom. There is no ruin too hopeless or too eerie for her imagination.

And then it all changed. As we plugged farther west, the lush rolling hills gave way to a landscape of scrub and stone.

By the time we reached the exit for Racalmuto, conditions were downright pitiful.

We followed the road leading into town. Large weeds had sprouted where the road met the sidewalk. We drove past a small, desperate-looking olive grove with nary a leaf in sight, and I offered a quick prayer that its owner would have a decent yield—or at least a yield.

Racalmuto is built in a bowl surrounded by hills, so as we descended the streets I scanned the horizon for a landmark that might point us to the center of town. A church steeple came into view, and I steered the car toward it, but road construction detours forced us off in another direction. We kept looking for a sign directing us to the *centro storico,* signs we had become familiar with in every Italian village, town, or city we had visited, but we did not see one in Racalmuto.

We drove down cobbled streets where the road abutted the front doors of homes. This is a quaint feature of almost every European town, but here it just looked dangerous and pitiful.

The buildings were all painted in the same worn color of buff, or at best a deep but dirty yellow. Paint was peeling off iron balconies, and the buildings themselves showed signs of advanced neglect.

"No wonder they all left," Mom deadpanned.

I would later learn that the name Racalmuto comes from the Arab name *Rahal-mut,* which translates to *il casale dei morti* or "farmhouse of the dead." Talk about your self-fulfilling prophecy.

I'm not quite sure what I was expecting from Racalmuto, but it was something better than this. The place had an air of suspension, as if waiting for all those men who had departed for a better life in Hamilton to swagger deliriously into town with sweat lighting up their grimy faces, their fists and the pockets of their work trousers bulging with gold coins and dollar bills.

Perhaps this was the bad side of town, I thought. I tried another route and hoped for a prettier streetscape.

"I believe someone once told me that there is a Hotel Hamilton here," I said. "Let's try to find it."

We drove around and around. The streets were largely deserted except for the requisite clusters of old men in dirty white undershirts standing outside a bar gesturing to one another. .

I got out of the car and approached one such group, asking directions to the Hotel Hamilton. I was met with polite shrugs. When the men asked where I was from and I answered, "Hamilton," the word produced a glimmer of recognition, as if it had rekindled a dim but bittersweet memory. But the men were not helpful, and as is so often the case in small, insulated towns, they did not seem acquainted with the world beyond the next street corner.

On another street I approached a group of women and had better luck. One of them attempted to give me directions but said it would be easier if we just followed her in her car. She drove to the autostrada and pointed to the other side of the highway.

A large unattractive sign announced "Hotel Hamilton," with the words "Ristorante, Pizzeria, Self Service" printed underneath. Behind it, on an elevated patch of land, was quite possibly the sorriest-looking piece of modern architecture in existence.

We waved our thanks to our guide, drove across the highway, and sat in the parking lot staring at the Hotel Hamilton, a bright white square slab located behind a gas station.

"It sure isn't how I'd pictured it," I said to Mom. "For some reason I imagined something old, grand, and ornate."

"Me too," she said. Then, trying to find something positive in the situation, added, "At least it looks clean."

We sat in a sort of dumb silence for a moment, as if trying to convince ourselves that we were actually going to be spending the night there. It was the polar opposite of all the photos you see of charming *pensiones* and hotels in small-town Italy.

Eventually I heaved a sigh.

"I'll go in and see if they have a room."

I somehow knew they would.

The lobby was deserted save for a startled front-desk clerk with a spiffy beige suit and slick black hair. A large board dangling with keys to every guest room hung on a wall behind the clerk as he bent over the room register and studiously perused it, rubbing his hands together before allowing that there was a vacancy. I acknowledged the rate of sixty-five euros a night including breakfast and signed us in.

The best part about room 105 was its gleaming mahogany door and an oval-shaped brass plate that displayed the number. Behind the door was a room that had all the warmth of a student dorm. Twin beds were covered with plain green bedspreads of a utilitarian design; the blond wood credenza-cum-dresser was remarkable in its utter lack of personality; the closet rod was set at a height that would have been comfortable for a six-foot-seven-inch-tall basketball player. We left our clothes in our suitcases.

The bathroom was bright and clean and sparkled like a toothpaste advertisement.

The prospect of a warm and ample lunch gave us renewed hope, and after we had settled ourselves and had a quick wash, we made our way to the hotel restaurant. We were ready to tuck into some yummy Sicilian food.

The dining room was empty. I coughed loudly in the hope of summoning someone, but no one came. I heard clattering sounds in the kitchen and tentatively pushed open a swinging door.

"Buongiorno," I called out in a pleasant if slightly timid voice.

Eventually a man of about forty, slightly heavyset with sandy-colored hair and a matching moustache, came forward, wiping his hands on a very soiled apron and cocking his chin toward me as if to say, "What the fuck do you want?" He was either a waiter or the cook.

I politely explained that we were hungry and would like lunch.

He gestured roughly toward a table, threw down two menus, and disappeared.

"Let's just ask for a pizza," said Mom. "The sign outside said they serve it."

But when the waiter came back for our order he said emphatically, "No pizza!" and made a cutting motion in the air with his hand. It seemed unwise to press the point.

And so it continued. The rough service bordered on hostility that, in another country, might have been grounds for a war crimes tribunal.

We ended up ordering the soup. It was quite possibly the worst concoction my stomach has ever entertained: a can of chickpeas that had been dumped into a pot, boiled for five minutes, tossed with some dried (not fresh) herbs, and plopped down in front of us so harshly that the contents slopped onto the table top. No apology was given; no effort was made to clean it up. The waiter retreated to a nearby wall and glared at us with narrowed eyes while sucking angrily on a cigarette.

In retaliation, I dug into my purse and fished out my journal and a pen. I began to write in it furiously with the hope that he would think I was a food or travel writer and that he would be moved to amend either the food or the service. He did neither.

We finished off with weak tea and paid the bill of fourteen euros. Frankly, meals like that make me question the purpose of eating.

There was obviously nothing to hold our attention at the hotel, so we returned glumly to our car and drove to Agrigento, about fifteen miles away. The sun made a surprise cameo appearance. Well, maybe things are looking up, I thought.

Agrigento is by far a larger center than Racalmuto and would have yielded nicer hotels and restaurants, but the night before, in Taormina, a tour guide in the dining room had warned us about Agrigento's robust car-theft trade.

Agrigento has another, more positive claim to fame, however—the Valley of the Temples. It is home to the largest and best-preserved collection of Doric temples outside of Greece. As we sped along the autostrada we could see a magnificent example on top of a hill, and we turned off to explore.

Tourist organization is not Italy's strong suit, and Agrigento was no exception. There were no signs indicating where to buy tickets, let alone what to do if you happen to have someone with you who has great difficulty walking.

Despite numerous queries (I had memorized the handy, *"Mia madre è disabile"* from my phrase book) no one was helpful. I drove to the turnstiles that formed a barrier across the road leading to the temples, but it was an automated system and there wasn't a real person around to ask for assistance.

"Don't worry about me," said Mom as we returned to the main parking lot. "I'll stay in the car."

"That's hardly fair," I protested, looking around for someone who had a smidgen of authority for this attraction. "I don't like leaving you in the car."

"No really, I'm fine. You go on ahead. There are some shops around so I'll be alright."

"OK. I promise I won't be long."

I finally found tickets for sale at a gift shop, but when I asked about wheelchair accessibility I was met with big shrugs and small smiles. I paid for one ticket and struck out briskly toward the temples. I glanced up at the sky and considered returning to the car for my umbrella, and then chided myself for not channeling more optimistic thoughts from the universe.

"It will not rain," I chanted to myself.

I was already through the turnstiles and more than halfway to the Temple of Concord, a distance of about a quarter mile, when the sky opened. Smarter people than I casually pulled out umbrellas from purses and pockets and carried on without concern. I pretended to be oblivious to both the rain and the alarmed looks from my fellow tourists, who obviously felt that a woman my age should be better prepared.

I focused on the ruins rather than the rain streaming down my face, and on the massive gnarly trunks of several olive trees that were as ancient as the temples themselves.

The scale of the eight temples was fantastic—every stone larger than a human, every column defying an easy explanation as to how it was all put together. Four thousand years ago, the Greeks developed cranes, winches, and derricks, but that

knowledge does not diminish the marvel of how these enormous structures were built. It would take a full day or two to
wander the entire site, poke around the digs, peer into the
catacombs in hopes of finding a human skull, and visit the
museum that is reportedly chock full of locally found artifacts,
but rain and an elderly parent alone in the car prevented me
from venturing too far.

By now I was drenched, though that barely hints at my
condition: I looked like I had been dragged through the Mediterranean Sea for a week. People regarded me the way they
would a homeless person—with pity and veiled disdain. I put
on a brave face, activated my I'm-ignoring-your-glares force
field, and floated winsomely back down the dirt road toward
the car park.

When I reached the car Mom was fast asleep, her head
thrown back and her mouth wide open. I glanced around
embarrassedly in case a lynch mob had assembled to punish
me for leaving a little old lady locked in a car. I rapped gently
on the driver's-side window before unlocking the door. She
jolted awake.

"There you are!" she said, snapping to life and fussing
busily. "I've been out and about myself and bought some postcards. How was your walk?"

Then, zeroing in on my soggy appearance, "We really have
to do something about that hair."

Naturally, the sun came out as soon as we began the drive
back to our hotel. We took a detour through Racalmuto once
more to see if the place had improved since our visit a few
hours earlier. Even in the sun, even after a good soaking by the
rain, it had not. I hoped it was just the time of year, because I
really wanted Racalmuto to be beautiful.

We trolled the streets looking for a place to eat. We were famished. Hunger always seemed to strike us when Italy was shut down for siesta.

I parked the car and Mom, and I set off on foot to see what could be scrounged in the way of food. The rain-slicked streets were deserted, and there was an ominous silence to the place, as if someone might suddenly burst through a door and start firing a machine gun.

I spied a man walking toward me, but he turned out to be one of those life-size statues that are placed on park benches or on sidewalks to throw you off guard. There was no identifying plaque on this particular statue, but later on, having consulted that great oracle Google, I deduced it to be the Sicilian novelist and dramatist Leonardo Sciascia, Racalmuto's famous son.

I found a bar and purchased a bottle of Sicilian wine and two stale croissants.

"This is going to have to serve as dinner," I told Mom upon returning to the car. "I'm not going into that hotel dining room again."

Back at the hotel we sat on our beds in our pajamas, munching croissants and gulping wine.

"You finish it off," said Mom. "I'm not that keen on wine."

With that, she turned out her light, curled onto her side away from me, and prepared to fall asleep.

"But it's only seven o'clock!" I protested.

"It's dark out. That means bedtime," she said. "Good night!"

7

Messina, Catanzaro Marina

"To have seen Italy without having seen Sicily is not to have seen Italy at all, for Sicily is the clue to everything."

Goethe penned that in 1788, and I could not agree with him more. Although there was much more to see of Sicily—coastal Cefalù, Palermo, and a few interior villages were places I had a desire to explore—it was going to require a future visit to delve further into its charms. And so, to paraphrase Julius Caesar, *veni, vidi,* vamoose.

I suppose this is a downside to renting a home base when on holiday. My sense of frugality—which inexplicably seizes me at the most inopportune times—made me mindful that we were paying for hotel rooms (and lousy ones at that) as well as the rental of the *trullo* in Alberobello.

We checked out of the Hotel Hamilton in the morning, having availed ourselves of what passed for a continental breakfast (the less said about it the better), and made our way back to Messina.

We took the same route we had travelled the day before, mainly because it was the fastest route, but also because it had been so lovely that I did not mind revisiting it.

"We should stop very soon," Mom said quietly about a half hour into our journey.

This was code for "I have to go to the bathroom. Badly."

I pressed down on the accelerator pedal and kept my eyes open for an Autogrill.

Italy's highways are strung with this bright, polished fast-service chain of restaurants. They have acres of freshly prepared food, and everything exudes deliciousness. The other nice thing about Autogrills is that almost all of them have accessible washrooms.

Ten minutes later, around Enna, I spotted an Autogrill. We slipped out of traffic and followed the exit lane into the spacious parking lot, right up to the front doors and into an empty handicapped parking space.

In the rearview mirror I saw a tour bus lumber into the parking lot.

"*Andiamo!* You better hurry!" I alerted Mom.

I jumped out of the car and ran around to the passenger side to yank her out, but she was so slow moving her arthritic legs into position that by the time she was out of the car and on her feet, the busload of more sprightly seniors—from Germany—had swarmed the Autogrill with the same goal—to find the washroom.

Mom hustled off to the ladies' room, and I hung back to poke about in the Autogrill's large gift area, where a mouthwatering variety of cheeses, chocolates, meat, pastas, sauces, oils, and wines were arranged as if it was about to be photographed for a food magazine.

Occasionally I craned my neck over the food displays to check on Mom, who I could see standing patiently, a grim look on her face, in a long queue for one of four cubicles.

She seemed OK, so I sauntered over to the bar and ordered a cappuccino.

The downside of Autogrills is their organization, or rather lack thereof. There are often a lot of staff behind the counter preparing food and laying it out attractively, but the whole operation seems to fall apart when a customer attempts to actually order something. I often found it safer just to order a cappuccino.

At the coffee bar, a gaggle of senior men from the German tour bus had gathered. If you want to witness "survival of the fittest" in action, or if ever you have reason to explain the concept to someone from another planet, then an Autogrill is the place to be when a coach tour rolls in. It is a ton of fun watching tourists and natives duke it out over who was first in line. Italy and Germany were about to square off, so I took my cappuccino to a table and settled in for the action.

To be fair, the Germans were at the coffee counter first, but they were milling about in such a fleshy mob of disarray that you could imagine Hitler spinning in his grave. The Italians, their home advantage notwithstanding, are amazingly unflustered when they tangle with opponents who hail from a country where a modicum of civil order is enshrined in the constitution. The intensity of this particular meet was heightened by the fact that it was ten o'clock in the morning, a time when both cultures were in a state of advanced caffeine withdrawal.

A German who had already placed his order at the bar threw the first volley by complaining about the gauche behavior of an Italian who was at his elbow and who had audaciously stridden up to the front of the loose queue to place his order.

Unbowed, the Italian returned a dismissive shrug and exchanged quick words with the barista. A few of the Italian's countrymen moved closer to the bar to run interference. The Germans cried foul in a booming baritone, throwing the argumentative Italians momentarily off guard. Italians dislike loud voices unless they are their own.

A melee ensued, with the Italians predictably but entertainingly casting arrogant sneers at the Germans and making slow brushing movements on their sleeves, a gesture meant to dust off the trivial and provincial antics of the Germans. The Germans were ultimately edged out because of a lack of conversational Italian and, with rueful expressions on their faces, shuffled into a stout, straight line.

I drained the last of my cappuccino and proceeded to kill more time perusing the lavish assortment of Easter goodies, which included chocolate bunnies the size of young children. But what was taking Mom so long?

I wandered back to the ladies' washroom. No one was there.

"Mom?...Mom?"

A small, sheepish voice finally came from behind one of the cubicle doors: "Yes?"

"Are you OK?" I asked tentatively.

The cubicle door creaked open slowly, just a crack.

"I've had a terrible accident," she whimpered, her head bowed in shame.

"Oh dear," I commiserated.

It appeared that the more continent and mobile of the German bus travellers had rushed in, hogged all the stalls, and left Mom to wait in line a very long time. By the time her turn came for a cubicle her defenses had fallen faster than her trousers.

"What can I do to help?" I asked softly.

"Can you bring me some fresh clothes from the car?"

She was miserable and embarrassed when we resumed our journey. She barely spoke.

"It must be awful to not have control over your body," I offered.

"It is. It comes out of nowhere—the urge to go, I mean," she said. She turned her head away from me. "Without any warning. I wish there was something I could do about it. This is why I don't want to go out with anyone."

She had had a couple of suitors since my dad's death, but she had kept them at arm's length. At first I thought she was being unduly prudish, but now I understood. For someone as fastidious as my mother in matters of appearance and social decorum, incontinence was the worst possible curse.

"Don't worry," I said perkily. "We'll be back in our little *trullo* tonight. Let me know if you need to stop again."

The sun came out when we turned north at Catania, but it did not brighten Mom's spirits.

"Look!" I said, pointing enthusiastically. "Mount Etna!"

The volcano's trademark smoky, wispy plume was etched ominously across the sky like a signature, but even mighty Etna could not alleviate Mom's funk. I considered amusing her with a quip that she and Etna had something in common—they are both in a constant state of eruption—but then I thought better of it.

"Did you know that Etna is so big that its plume and lava flows can be seen from the International Space Station?" I said, trying to draw her into conversation. She responded with little more than "Hmm" and a slight smile.

And then, "Are those houses?"

"Why, yes they are," I answered, rather perplexed myself by the sight: Etna, the largest and most unpredictable volcano in Europe, has a bourgeoning housing development creeping up its side, along with farms and vineyards.

125

"What sort of a marketing slogan do you suppose you'd need to get homebuyers clamoring for a piece of real estate like that?" I wondered aloud. "'Go with the flow?' 'Bank on a boom market?'"

In fact, probably no slogan at all. Nothing better illustrates the diffident and fatalistic attitude of Sicilians than a subdivision making its way up the side of a volcano.

Etna erupted not long after we left the island, but an even bigger blast occurred several months later, in September 2007, with lava spewing thirteen hundred feet into the air before coursing thickly down its side like drool from a Saint Bernard. I have no idea how the housing development fared during the fireworks, but I did read that Sicily closed its airport for the day as a precaution, and farmers on the mountain leaned their hoes against the shed for a spell. Within twelve hours it was business as usual. No biggie.

IT WAS noon when we reached Messina. I dutifully followed the *"Traghetti"* signs to the ferry terminal, a route that led us down a wide, handsome street lined with lush green palms waving languidly and an assortment of yellow-and-white Baroque buildings.

The ferry terminal was very different from the one at which we had disembarked. For starters, there was a huge lineup of cars and people, and a festive quality pervaded the quay. People were stretched out on the front of their cars squeezing in a few minutes of sunbathing. Well-marked ticket kiosks with streamers looped along their canopies, as well as cafés and souvenir stalls, were all doing a brisk business. There wasn't a truck in sight.

126

The biggest surprise was the fare: It was double what we had paid on the way over. It was suddenly clear that our maiden voyage to Sicily had been made by cargo boat.

Onboard this very modern ferry the atmosphere was genteel. It was kitted out with a two-storey car park, comfy padded seating in expansive lounge areas, bright, clean washrooms that didn't require a sailor's key to access, some shops, and a few cafés serving a wide selection of sandwiches and pasta. All these conveniences for a mere thirty-minute passage.

We barely had time to gobble down a *panino* and a drink before it was time to join the mad dash back to the ferry's parking garage. We shuffled to the elevator and waited patiently for the lift while our fellow passengers scurried around us as if a fire alarm had been sounded.

Based on our speedy drive to Sicily down Calabria's west coast, I assumed the return trip to Alberobello would be just as quick and we would be home by nightfall.

Everything went swimmingly until we drove off the ferry at Reggio di Calabria and I made a wrong turn. In Italy, wrong turns can undo you. Before I could figure out what had happened, we were plunged into a crowded, gritty, labyrinthine suburb with an air of desperation and poverty.

Mom pressed the button to raise the automatic windows, and I engaged the security locks on our doors. It took us a good half hour to find our way out. When we eventually rejoined the autostrada it was another quarter of an hour before it dawned on me that we were heading up the east coast of Italy instead of the west.

The eastern portion of the coastal highway—despite being called an autostrada—was a plodding two-lane road that forced us on a slow march through every single village—some of them prosperous and well-tended little places such as Pilossi, Brancaleone, and Locri, with cheerfully painted balconies and landscaped front gardens; all of them without any sign of a living soul.

127

In some parts of Calabria only thirty miles separate the east and the west coasts, but the differences between the two are substantial. The west is pastoral, majestic, and more sedate; the east has a scrubbier terrain but also a flashy resort-like feel. In the west you see olive trees and firs; in the east everyone has an orange or lemon tree in the front yard. The life seems more hard-won in the west, easier in the east.

Road construction and heavy truck traffic dogged our progress the entire way. We were forced to take detours that drew us into an interior land of wild dill, stone farmhouses, farmers threshing the fields, and sheep grazing on hillsides. It sounds idyllic, and under normal circumstances I would have found the journey pleasant, but with an incontinent and discontented passenger beside me it was torture. I could sense Mom's longing for the familiar surroundings and the somewhat dull routine we had carved out for ourselves back at the *trullo*. I was anxious to get back, too, if only to relinquish the grind of driving all day. It felt like my ass had been permanently glued to the driver's seat.

After four and a half hours of stop-and-go traffic, in which we covered less than a quarter of the distance we had done in the same amount of time a few days earlier, it became obvious that home was another day away. The sun began its quick dip to oblivion, and we resigned ourselves to a hotel for the night. We stopped in Catanzaro Marina and, finding no practical accommodation, surrendered the contents of our wallets for a small suite at the Hotel Palace.

May I ask a stupid question? Why do so many first-class hotels exude low-class attitude? Does it have something to do with making the guest feel grateful to be in this rarified atmosphere, or is it an acquired snobbism on the part of the hotelier who could just as easily be working at a Travelodge?

The front desk staff of the Hotel Palace regarded my mother and me the way most people would greet Martians, something you do not expect from an establishment that bills itself as "an international hotel." The bartender refused to smile at me, despite my repeat business, which I conducted entirely in Italian, and the chambermaids averted their eyes.

The coup de grâce was our departure the following morning. After settling the bill of 218 euros (suite, small dinner, and big breakfast), I went to retrieve our car from the hotel's parking lot across the street, only to discover that it was boxed in by two other cars. The hotel summoned its parking attendant, one of those older middle-aged men who believe that a pimp roll, a baseball cap, and a stained T-shirt will fool the ladies into thinking he's thirty years younger. Well, perhaps very drunk ladies.

Sloppy Joe grumpily swaggered out to the parking lot and a few minutes later returned to the hotel lobby, made quick eye contact with me, and then skulked into a back room. No one said a word.

Several minutes passed until curiosity got the better of me. I walked outside to our car and saw that it was still somewhat blocked in—enough that I feared I would do damage to the surrounding cars if I tried to wriggle out of our spot.

I returned to the hotel's front desk to ask for assistance, but I got only shrugged shoulders and indifference. No one offered so much as to carry our luggage out the front door. This is what passes for five-star service these days?

So, picture this, if you will: A harried, middle-aged woman fumbling with three unwieldy bags (well, four if you count my mother), and an old woman on the verge of an asthma attack, leaning heavily on her cane, and with what breath she has apologizing for not being physically able to help her ragged, middle-aged daughter.

"Look at this!" I finally screamed in the parking lot. "How the fuck am I supposed to get the car out of this spot?"

"Never mind," said Mom. "Just get in the car and leave it to me. I'll guide you out. Trust me."

And didn't she do just that. Good ol' Gimpy.

As we exited the parking lot I flipped a finger at the Hotel Palace and gave Mom a high five with the other hand.

"Great work, Mom. You know, that was probably the finest example of teamwork that we have ever experienced."

"No, there are others," she smiled. "Your memory is short."

We got lost going out of Catanzaro Marina, but a gas jockey—thank God for Agip gas stations—provided excellent directions that got us across the narrowest part of Italy and onto the Reggio di Calabria–Salerno A3. As soon as we hit the autostrada—and I have never been more pleased to see a superhighway—I unclenched my sphincter and floored the accelerator pedal.

Zipping past the rugged landscape with its panoramic vistas and tunnelled mountains—I loved the tunnels in

Italy—I concluded that the west side of Italy's southern end is more picturesque than the east.

Too bad it wasn't as breezy a drive up the coast as it had been down. It seemed that Italy's construction workers had decided that this particular Thursday was a perfect day to begin the work week. Amid this flurry of construction I couldn't figure out the reason for all the half-finished villas we saw during the entire time we were in Italy. Some looked as if they hadn't seen any action in several months.

May I just mention here that Italian work crews are a very smartly dressed lot? Rarely did we see anyone wearing jeans or mud-splattered T-shirts and boots. Most wore dark slacks (not dirty ones, either) and a polo shirt topped by a navy sweater. They all looked so presentable and clean—even those driving dump trucks and front-end loaders.

Here is another roadside observation for you: Road construction in Italy does not require the crew to rip up a six-mile radius to complete a project. There is a reverence for the land that you don't encounter on North American work sites. Italians have road building down to an art—after all, they've been perfecting it for three thousand years—whereas North Americans have been building roads for maybe two hundred years and feel compelled to haul out every vestige of heavy equipment to construct a shuddering tangle of cloverleafs and turnpikes. Italy still uses its hands and tries not to disturb the land, while North America bulldozes the daylights out of everything in its path. I suppose North America is sort of like the short, chubby guy who owns the flashiest car: He has to make up for his shortcomings somehow.

The Italians have not, however, found a way to perfect traffic flow, and so, like anywhere else on the planet, dust-clogged construction zones and snarled traffic go hand in hand.

It was dark by the time our car crawled up the long drive-way to our *trullo*. I turned off the ignition, said a silent prayer of thanks to the travel gods, and checked the odometer: We had covered nearly a thousand miles in four days.

8

Alberobello, Matera

OVERNIGHT, A mysterious, itchy infection sprouted around my eyes, and by the time I awoke the next morning they were swollen and virtually sealed shut. I had also contracted Mom's cough and runny nose, and my throat had a sandpapery quality that augurs the onset of a cold.

I staggered to the bathroom mirror to examine my condition. A serious misjudgment of the distance between my face and the mirror caused me to bash my nose against it's surface, which triggered a nosebleed of Biblical proportions.

I groped around for some toilet paper to staunch the flow.

Really. Could things get any worse? I had imagined looking glamorous and worldly during my trip to Italy. I had fantasized about sashaying down a charming cobblestone Italian street of imposing Renaissance and Baroque buildings. A warm breeze would cause the fabric in my long, white,

multigored skirt to flutter gently; the sleeveless top (in matching white fabric) would show off slender, tanned, and toned
arms decorated at the wrist by a stack of thin silver bangles.
Large silver hoop earrings would catch a glint of sunlight and
sparkle against my dark hair. In those dreams my hair was a
deep chestnut brown, lush with a bouncy curl; my eyes were
dark and sultry, enhanced by a hint of kohl around the edges
and mascaraed lashes. My lips shimmered with a cranberry
gloss. My body was smooth and tanned from top to toe, its
color and texture like Baileys Irish Cream. My breasts would
sit up high and firm. Italian men would halt their conversations in midsentence as they watched me stride by. Like the
Girl from Ipanema, I would be regarded by one and all as an
exotic, mysterious creature.

   In reality, I was exotic and mysterious in the way the Creature from the Black Lagoon is exotic and mysterious. My eyes
were crusty, my hair was thin and frizzy, and my body was a
pudgy billboard for the sweets I had stuffed into my maw the
previous Christmas. If I so much as sashayed in this condition
it might very well bring Italy to its knees in laughter.

   I assembled a grumpy list of afflictions I had endured on
this trip: rainy, cold weather; mediocre food; my mother's
bouts of incontinence; colds; strategizing my mother-daughter showdown; and now a painfully itchy eye infection and a
nosebleed.

   There was no one to telephone for help, and come to think
of it, nothing with which to telephone. I had no choice but to
find a clinic or hospital.

   On the bright side, we were in an area of Italy that was so
off-season and so off the tourist radar that I could drive into
Alberobello practically blind and the odds were I wouldn't hit

anyone. We followed the universal blue "H" signs and found Alberobello's *ospedale* behind a service station. Never one to pass up an idle wheelchair, Mom grabbed the first one she encountered at the entrance to the hospital and used it as a walker as we made our way down the hall to the reception desk.

Without asking, the hospital staff pounced on Mom, incorrectly deducing that she, not me, was the one in need of medical assistance. I hastily explained the situation as best I could—Jesus, did they think I actually looked this bad all the time?—and was shown into an examination room. Three medics, a woman and two men dressed in fluorescent-orange stretchy pants and dark navy fleece jackets, appeared. They stared into my eyes, prodded the areas around the lids gently— not one of them wore latex gloves, by the way—then stood back, gravely holding their chins, to consider the situation.

I tried to be helpful: *"Mi fanno male gli occhi,"* I said, explaining that my eyes hurt. *"Allergica alla primavera,"* I added, offering some medical history that might suggest this was a seasonal allergy.

The three nodded silently and then proceeded to confer most intently with one another. There was a lot of gesturing, heated discussion, serious looks, and more thoughtful chinholding. At one point it looked as if they might convene a medical conference on my behalf. Amid their raised voices and wildly waving hands the word *"infiammazione"* (inflammation) was spoken a few times, so I knew they were heading in the right direction.

They were very nice—at least when they weren't shouting at each other and gesticulating randomly—and soon they presented me with eyedrops and sodium chloride, with orders to bathe my eyes twice daily.

"No charge," the woman said proudly. "In Canada, all is no free, eh?"

I was in no mood to argue, but for the record, my experience in Canada as well as other countries—England, Spain, and Hungary immediately come to mind—is that small amounts of medication, enough to last the duration of the holiday, are often dispensed to travellers at no cost.

The medication worked a treat almost instantly. It was cause for raucous, riotous celebration.

"Let's go for lunch," I said to Mom.

We drove to Green Park, an *agriturismo* that had been recommended in an information package at our *trullo*. But when we arrived, it was closed. I pressed the buzzer and waited for a young man to appear. The park was not just closed that day; it was closed until after Easter, he said.

There are so many disappointments for the off-season traveller.

"WHY DON'T we ever stop and tour around," Mom wondered aloud one afternoon as she padded around in her white sandals in the kitchen of the *trullo*. She had brought with her the same useless wardrobe as I had—on my advice.

"Well, let's see," I said, looking up from the map that was spread out before me. I had been reviewing a list of places I had hoped to visit but somehow knew I would not be able to on this trip. "You've been unwell since we arrived and you've had no desire to get out of bed, you can't walk, you shit at inopportune times, and you expect someone to always be nearby with a wheelchair. Except for at the hospital, have you seen a wheelchair here?"

I did not want to sound mean, but someone had to acknowledge the elephant in the corner. And yes, a wallop of resentment was gathering within me. We still had four more weeks in Italy, but I just knew I would not get to experience the *passeggiata,* the traditional evening stroll Italians of all ages engage in each night. I would not get to hike the hills or take off for a full day without worrying about my mother worrying about me. I would not be able to explore some of the farther-flung towns without leaving her alone in the car. Or tuck into those great Italian meals I had heard so much about, unless the restaurant serving it was accessible for someone with a walker. Because I had to be constantly vigilant to my mother's needs, I knew this was the most relaxed I would be on this holiday, and that wasn't saying much.

My resentment was also about my lack of sleep. Travelling with my mother was not a restful experience. Her illnesses and various health issues worried me. When she awoke, I awoke; when she made fitful utterances in her sleep, I awoke; when she shifted in her bed, I awoke. It was like being a first-time parent with a highly sensitive radar tuned to the needs of a newborn.

Granted, being incontinent on the Continent was no picnic for Mom. It was an awkward, shame-inducing inconvenience. And yes, people don't plan to get sick on holidays—that just happens.

At the same time, incontinent resentments were beginning to spill out of me. Mom had misrepresented her disabilities to me. She may say that she's "perfectly healthy," but that's not the reality. Call me a pessimist, but puffing wildly after walking ten paces or showing signs of acute distress after scaling three steps does not indicate good health.

Mom could not see, or rather she refused to admit, that our lack of excursions was entirely due to her inability to get around and her preference for staying in bed. When she gets bored, it somehow becomes my fault.

I was prepared on this trip to modify my normally hyper-speed pace to suit her, but I was not prepared to sit and stare into space for six weeks, move only when my mother wanted to move, and go to bed when she wanted to go to bed, which is what I was more or less doing.

And then there was the sticky issue of moral accommodation. Growing up, my mother had exerted strict control over everything I did, said, wore, and, without success, thought. She was not flexible about my desires or wishes. Now she wanted me to be flexible with her. She didn't ask this outright; she considered it my duty as a daughter. It just didn't seem fair. And yet I did it, like all daughters do, out of a sense of duty, and partly to prove to her that I was a good girl.

What *are* the expectations of adult children, and who sets them? Had I already unconsciously set them for my children? Are you allowed to refuse the expectations, or are they considered obligations that come with being part of a family? During rushed, infrequent visits with friends, I had listened to them talk about juggling jobs, emotions, children, grand-children, and elderly parents. They adore spending time with their grandchildren, but spending time with their parents is another story. Grandchildren are giggly and cute, and they generally do what they're told. Elderly parents are often grouchy and demanding. They dribble from various parts of their body. But who can fault them for their crabbiness? They're experiencing loss on a daily basis, the type of loss that awaits us younger ones who are next up at bat: loss of strength, dexterity, memory, eyesight, hearing, independence, mobil-ity, control of their bodies. What's more, everyone is trying to rip them off. The worst part is that their partners and dearest friends are dropping like flies.

When it came to my mother I knew this intellectually, but still I felt a sense of irritation around her.

"OK, here's an idea," I offered Mom, as a gesture of good-will. "Let's go out for dinner tonight. Even though I look like a Cyclops and I'm feeling about as attractive as one, we'll go out. And let's try to be Italian and eat later than five thirty."

Around 6:00 PM, we drove into Alberobello. We trolled the tacky souvenir shops to kill time, passing groups of old men who were clustered on the café patios enjoying an early evening coffee.

Italian men seem to have more time for socializing than their counterparts anywhere else in the world. They were always outside in small groups, pondering or arguing one issue or another. When they aren't honing their debating skills, they stare unapologetically at anyone who passes by. The appearance of Mom's walker as she steered it toward them caused a stir. As if catching a whiff of their interest, she veered the walker off the sidewalk and onto the road, walking behind the parked cars to avoid a full and close inspection.

There was also a practical reason for her detour. Italian men refuse to step aside for anyone. We encountered this situation a few times throughout Italy—never once did a man get out of the way to let my mother through. It was left for me to clear the path, and not always nicely.

"C'mon you lazy bastards; move over." A few of them grudgingly shuffled a couple of centimeters to one side while casting heavy-lidded, indignant looks; others stood gape-mouthed at the metallic red contraption Mom was pushing.

Farther along the promenade, a huddle of Japanese tourists turned away from a display of tea towels and postcards to observe this fantastic device. They began a furious discussion that included pointing.

"Just you wait," Mom said to me. "Next year, all the Japanese will have one of these."

A promising restaurant presented itself up a side street, and I scampered ahead to scope it out. Once there, I noticed its entrance had steps that Mom would have difficulty negotiating, plus the restaurant did not open until 8:00 PM.

"I don't know how any of these people stay in business with these hours," Mom said when I returned with my report. "It's ridiculous."

There was only so much walking we could do before Mom began to tire. I fetched the car, and we drove around the tight, snaking streets of Alberobello with the car's heater on full blast.

We eventually found a restaurant in a converted *trullo*. We took our seats in a charming but empty dining room and asked for a bottle of wine.

This particular day had special meaning for us. A year earlier Mom had been rushed to the hospital with heart problems. I raised a glass to her recovery and health.

"Well, it wasn't really a heart attack," she said coyly. "It was an angina attack."

"Did you say a vagina attack?" I asked with mock horror.

She wheezed with laughter.

"Oh you," she playfully scolded me. "No, it was congestive heart failure."

"Well, look at you anyway," I said. "Did you ever imagine a year ago that we'd be in an Italian restaurant..."

"...and eating shitty food?" she said conspiratorially.

More patrons had materialized, and their presence gave the place a bit more ambiance.

We dined on a dish of orecchiette pasta (locally made, the owner assured us) with boiled tomatoes, parmesan, a scant amount of basil, and enough olive oil to lube a car. It was quite possibly the second worst meal I had eaten. Ever. The soup in Racalmuto held first place.

The TV, a ubiquitous presence in restaurants these days, hung from the corner of the ceiling and was broadcasting a program that had captured the attention of our fellow diners.

"What's everyone watching?" Mom turned rigidly in her seat to face the TV. It was a football game. "Oh, those overpaid idiots."

The owner arrived with our coffee and glumly set the cups on the table.

"*Il conto, per favore,*" I smiled, asking for the bill.

"Well, this is the worst coffee I've tasted," Mom commented, after taking a delicate sip and puckering her lips in distaste. "Why can't these people ever get it right?"

We gathered our things and were about to leave the restaurant when a worried look crossed her face.

"I need to use the washroom," she said.

She moved toward the restroom while I hurriedly paid the bill. I dashed off to get the car and sprinted back into the restaurant just as Mom was emerging from the washroom. She looked a little pallid.

"You didn't make a mess in there, did you?" I asked.

"Nope," she said.

"I got the car for you anyway...you know, just in case we had to make a quick getaway."

"Really, Jane, I'm not that bad," she chuckled.

"I think they have bylaws here about bathroom usage," I said, holding open the car door for her.

Another round of wheezing laughter.

IT WAS cold the next morning, so Mom stayed in bed. She remained there for three days.

I could tell when she was out of bed by the rhythmic clicking of her cane on the terra-cotta tiles.

Her breathing had taken on a Darth Vader–like draw, and to amuse myself—I know, this sounds so cruel—I would hum the *Star Wars* music that signals Vader's approach.

Nothing made me more tense, however, than hearing her go into the kitchen to make tea. She is not accustomed to gas cooktops, and I would hold my breath whenever she turned on the gas. I would hear the click-click-click of her attempts to spark a flame with the barbeque lighter, and then a sudden loud *whoosh!* as the flame made contact with the gas. An anxious silence would follow.

My breathing resumed when her puttering did: the sounds of her rifling through bags of potato chips, bread, pasta—everything seemed to come in cellophane bags that were irritatingly loud—or she would fidget with the packages, occasionally emitting an exasperated "oh, dammit" as she struggled to pry something open. The rustling and the crinkling would shatter the quiet. Then Mom would shuffle back to her bedroom and close the door, and silence would reign once again.

Her coughing made it difficult for me to sleep, and with the combination of the relentless rain and the cold—the temperature could not have been more than a few degrees—I, too, found myself retreating to my bed and wondering whether spending six weeks in Italy with her had been an insane idea. I wasn't certain she would physically make it to the halfway mark of our trip. I wasn't certain my patience would hold out that long either.

The rain continued to pelt our hilltop *trullo,* and I mulled over the idea of whether I should broach round one of The

Talk that I was desperate to have with Mom. But it didn't seem right to suggest it, given how ill and tired she was.

The more time we spent isolated in the *trullo,* the more boredom and frustration poked and prodded me. Maybe it was folly to think we could mend our fences here, or anywhere. While the storm raged outside my window, another one was brewing inside me, one that included thoughts of hurling the red walker to kingdom come.

WHEN I wasn't holed up in bed memorizing sexy sentences from the Italian phrase book, doing a Sudoku, or stewing about the negative energy in my relationship with Mom, I was hunched over a road map of southern Italy.

One morning, I had smoothed it out on the dining room table and was sounding out some of the place names—Ostuni, Galatina, Copertino, Squinzano, Grotta San Biagio—feeling the vowels exercise my mouth, rolling the gr in Grotta, enunciating the sharp t's, stretching the u in Ostuni until it pursed my lips.

Time was running out on our stay in Alberobello, and there were at least half a dozen places I still wanted to visit. The story of Saint Joseph, the flying friar of Copertino, was so fantastic that I just had to see for myself the town and the church where Joseph had launched his fame. Then there was Padre Pio, the Capuchin priest who bore the stigmata. The 40th anniversary of his death was the following year (his body would be exhumed for the celebration), and I had a hankering to spend a day in San Giovanni Rotondo, where Pio had lived, to get a sense of the buzz. With crushing disappointment I resigned myself to the reality that I would not make it to any of those places in the two days we had left in this region.

I glanced at the *trullo*'s front door, which was open to the stone patio. Sunshine lapped tauntingly at the doorway. A dog barked in the distance, the birds twittered, and a light breeze caused a rustle among the olive-tree leaves.

I left the map and walked outside to assess the conditions more closely. I squinted at the sky: it was sunny now, but the temperamental Italian climate is not to be trusted.

I walked around the outside of the *trullo* and saw Chris, the property manager, skimming leaves out of the swimming pool. I wandered over to join him. That's when I learned about the "stupid tax."

"Yeah, you want to watch out for that," he said as he turned the skimmer's net to scoop up a bug. "It's the Italian revenge against tourists who come here and don't bother learning the language or the monetary system. You go into a store and you see these Americans standing with their hands cupped, loaded with coins, and asking some store clerk to take the amount owing for a cup of coffee or their lunch. The Italians always help themselves to more than what the bill has come to. And who can blame them? They figure it's the price for putting up with ignorance."

It seemed unwise to tell him that that was precisely how my mother operates in a foreign country.

Mom was sitting at the other end of the patio reading a book. Oversized, owl-like glasses were perched on her nose; her hair was in curlers.

"Let's go somewhere today," I said.

My eyes were improving, and though my cough was worsening, and Mom's cough was still bad, staying cooped up in our Italian Alcatraz was making me antsy.

"I'd better not," she said. "I've taken a laxative."

"Why would someone with incontinence take a laxative?" I asked.

"Because sometimes I can't get my system working and I have to help it along," she said with an air of petulance.

"How long do you think that will take?" I asked.

"Give me a couple of hours," she said.

144

"Wait for laxative to take effect" had not been on my list of things to do in Italy.

I stood for a moment, thinking of ways to pass the next few hours.

The air had warmed up, though it could not be called hot. It was still too cool to swim. Twice that morning I had stretched out on the chaise longue with a book, but each time, as soon as my bum hit the chaise, the sun scurried behind a cloud and the temperature dropped.

I decided to take a stroll around the hilly terrain that encircled the *trullo*, mainly to escape a squawking magpie that had taken to hectoring me on his territorial prerogative vis-à-vis the patio. I climbed to the highest point on the property and surveyed the undulating Apulian terrain. All was silent and in a state of reverential repose. The hurly-burly of life felt eons away.

I picked my way slowly back toward the *trullo*, stopping to admire the variety of trees along the way—olive, fig, walnut, apple. Against a weathered wall, a tall stand of bamboo had begun to sprout shoots. That little excursion killed twenty minutes.

With Mom needing to stay put, I gave her a peck on the cheek and got into the car.

The trepidation I had experienced two weeks earlier was long gone. I felt an easy familiarity with my surroundings now and began to entertain thoughts of moving here permanently.

I always do that—it is how I take the measure of a place I'm visiting. I have a nomadic spirit that is always on the lookout for a new place to settle.

On the outskirts of Alberobello I spied a DOK grocery store. The information package that had been left for us at the *trullo* mentioned this place, but each time we went searching for it we couldn't find it, no matter how intently we followed the directions or studied the landscape. Today, for some reason, it appeared loud and clear.

Inside the store I grabbed a metal buggy and started rattling up and down the aisles admiring the products.

The more I wheeled around the aisles, the more confident and less intimidated I became. By the time I hit the checkout counter, I felt practically native. I heaped my cartload of groceries onto the conveyer belt, casually commented on the sunny day that lay outside, paid the bill, and wished everyone *ciao*. Hmm, I thought to myself, maybe I *could* live here.

In the parking lot, while I was swinging the grocery bags into the car, an imposing edifice up the road caught my attention: two courses of six thick columns flanked by two small, squat square-shaped towers. On a rise just behind the entrance was a white building in the Greek style, sporting four Ionic columns. Intrigued, I drove toward it, found a place to park by the side of the road, and got out to explore. I walked purposefully through the entrance and evaded two security guards, who were busy exerting their authority on an older couple, who I guessed were tourists.

That's how I ended up in *il cimitero monumentale,* Alberobello's cemetery.

The entrance, hailed as the most beautiful of its kind in Europe, was designed in the Egyptian style in 1890 by Antonio Curri, an architect from Alberobello. I climbed steadily up a set of stone stairs and found myself amid a colony of midsize mausoleums arranged in a way that resembled a small neighborhood street. I followed a second flight of steps to the top level and arrived at a large expanse of land. A tidy crushed-gravel pathway, lined with cypress, tall and stately like soldiers, stretched serenely toward the horizon. On either side of this treed border lay a glossy green park studded with statuary and raised stone graves. Curri had designed all this according to his vision of Heaven, and it was every inch that.

The place was teeming with people. Never have I seen such bustling activity in a cemetery. Ninety-nine percent of them were women, devotedly scrubbing away the grime that had accumulated on the headstones of loved ones. Others were pushing huge ladders against a wall of burial niches to wipe the dust from the nameplates or replace flowers in the vases attached to them. And there were many more sweeping dirt out of the mausoleums or from around the monuments, or tending the burial plots that were landscaped like mini-gardens around the crypts. A flurry of spring cleaning had gripped everyone.

The mood was very un-cemetery-like. The cemetery was a happy place, a world away from the blaring traffic and commerce on the street below. The women—many of them young and attractive—chatted amiably with one another while their young children skipped along the paths and played hide-and-seek among the crypts. If you were a guy looking for female company, this would be a good place to come on a Saturday morning. It was a very different atmosphere from what you would find in a North American cemetery, and I suspect this has something to do with the Italian attitude toward death.

I was driving back along the winding country roads when another sight caught my attention: a derelict *trullo*. It was another landmark I had passed several times, but I had never mustered the courage to stop and take a closer look. Now that I was fired up with confidence—after all, I'd been to a grocery store and a cemetery in a foreign country all by myself in the last hour—my boldness was boundless.

I parked the car on the side of the road and walked through tall grass to the front entrance of the ruin. The interior walls were stained with age, and the place was littered with oil drums and an old, rusting vegetable display case that probably came from a grocer's.

Still, the building's stone bones were good. I appraised its location thoughtfully, paced back and forth in front of it a few times. What about the cost and the work? How would I get plumbing and electricity into it? What about the insurmountable headaches of renovating a property in a foreign country? How would I furnish it? I fantasized about my family and friends coming to visit me—the lazy *al fresco* luncheons that would turn into wine-soaked conversations and laughter that would last into the evening.

I noticed a farmer working in a far-off field and figured the property must be his. Dare I approach him?

I came to my senses and got back into the car.

"I found a neat *trullo* down the road that needs renovating," I told Mom when I returned to our *trullo* and was unpacking the groceries.

"How exciting! Maybe we should take a closer look at it," she said, gleefully rubbing her hands together. These are the moments when I know she's my mother and I realize that I come by this renovation madness honestly.

Then, noting the grocery bags on the counter, she said, "Why did you buy all these groceries? We're leaving in a day or two."

"I finally found that grocery store we were always looking for," I said. "The DOK? I guess I was so excited that I bought more than we needed. Sorry."

"You didn't happen to see any clothing stores, did you?" she asked. "I need clothes. My wardrobe looks like a three-year-old packed it. I left all my nice outfits at home."

"Why didn't you bring them?"

"I was saving them for a special occasion," she said, trying to sound prudent. But who was she kidding? What's not special about a trip to Italy?

"Truthfully," I said as I put a carton of milk in the fridge, "for someone who suffers from incontinence I don't know where you got the idea that white slacks would be practical. Speaking of which, are you able to go out now?"

"Not quite, but soon."

So I returned to the patio and the chaise longue with my book of Sudoku puzzles.

Not ten minutes later I heard Mom calling my name. I turned my head and saw her looking around frantically near the back door of the *trullo.*

"Jane? Where are you?"

She shuffled jerkily from one corner of the patio to the other calling my name.

"Over here!" I called out. "Here! HERE!" I waved my arms, but she still couldn't hear or see me. God, I wish she would get a hearing aid.

She disappeared around a corner of the *trullo,* still searching and calling my name.

I got out of the chaise and ran after her. No matter how close I got to her and yelled, "Here I am!" she could not hear me.

When I finally caught up to her I was about to tap her on the back, then thought better of it. I doubled back around the other side of the house so that she would see me approaching rather than be frightened half to death by my coming up behind her.

"Where were you?" she asked worriedly. "I thought you were lost, or that you'd fallen into a hole and I'd be stuck here alone forever!"

"I was just sitting over there, in the chair beside that shrub," I said calmly, pointing to my spot in the sun.

"I guess you blend in with the bush," she smiled, collecting herself. "What are you going to do about that hair?"

"Let's go out sightseeing," I said brightly. "Has your laxative taken effect?"

"I think I'll be fine," she said.

OUR DESTINATION was Matera, an hour or so southwest of Alberobello.

Matera is one of the oldest towns in the world, and the area has yielded evidence of settlements dating back to the Paleolithic Age—more than ten thousand years ago—when hunters found shelter in the caves hollowed out by the receding Ice Age.

Even a cave dweller yearns for upward mobility at some point, and so, with flint axes in hand, they began to carve homes and places of worship out of the natural caverns and clefts of the massive limestone rock face that dramatically dominates Matera's landscape.

When we got out of the car to look at Matera across the gaping Gravina canyon, we forgot for a moment that we were in Italy. The sight was more suited to the Middle East: tier upon tier of bleached-stone homes and caves. Mel Gibson thought so too, which is why he chose it as a stand-in for Jerusalem in *The Passion of the Christ.*

"This is incredible," enthused Mom. "I've never seen anything like it."

Turning to me, she added, "You must feel very at home here."

She was referring to my teenage desire to be a troglodyte. I stretched an arm across her shoulder and gave her a little squeeze of thanks for having remembered. It had been so long ago.

One evening—I was about eighteen at the time and just finishing high school—the dinner table conversation casually (though in hindsight it perhaps wasn't so casual) drifted to a question about what I planned to do with my life. I matter-of-factly told my parents that I had decided to live in a cave in Switzerland, grow my own vegetables, and play guitar. It did not matter to me that I had never been to Switzerland, had never grown a vegetable, and did not play or own a guitar. It was the early 1970s and I had a hippie's soul.

I gathered from the quick, shocked glances my parents gave each other across the dinner table that they weren't exactly on board for this, but they did not dismiss my idea, which I thought was rather decent of them, and the subject was gently changed.

Two weeks later, I came down for breakfast to find a return plane ticket and a note from my parents. The note informed me that they had taken matters into their own hands and submitted an application under my name to Carleton University, in Ottawa. I was instructed to fly to Ottawa that day, properly register, find a place to live, and be back by dinnertime with a full account of my expedition.

I did what I was told. You might imagine that I would be angry about this, but I wasn't. Sometimes I need a kick in the ass. They could have kicked me toward university or kicked me toward Europe. The point is, I needed a kick in some direction to get me started. At the time I had no idea what to do with or make of my life.

"I think your father and I made the right decision for you," said Mom. "You were...well...what do you think of the idea now? Would you have been happy living in a cave?"

"Only if it had been a cave with a modern bathroom and a kitchen," I joked. Here was a colony of caves the likes of which I never thought existed and, as often happens when a piece of my past resurfaces, I tried to envision what my life might have been like had I heeded my heart rather than parental intervention. I might not have had the stability or the means to become a parent, and that would have been a shame. I love being a mom. Then again, I'm a pretty resourceful soul, and I would have made my situation work. I would have eventually found a job. I can't say that Switzerland would have been my first choice as a place to live, but maybe someone might have told me about the Italian caves, and I would have relocated here. I would have learned Italian. Maybe met a rich, sexy Italian. So many maybes.

We drove across the canyon into Matera itself to see the place up close.

If any place deserves to be walked it is Matera. Apparently, the Italian authorities concur: It is illegal to bring a car into the *centro storico* of some towns, and security cameras are constantly on alert, whirring into position to pick up the license plate of transgressors. (Six months after our trip, a traffic ticket from Matera arrived in my mailbox. I considered fighting the fine just for the chance to return to Matera, but the rental car company had already conveniently deducted the amount from my credit card.)

"You get out and look around. I'll be fine," said Mom after

151

we had driven along the Via Madonna delle Virtù at the canyon's edge.

"It's OK," I lied. "It's not fair to leave you in the car."

But she insisted, and so I pulled the car over to the side of the road, jumped out, and ran up a narrow flight of worn stone steps, two at a time, nearly knocking heads with a gargoyle. The stairs delivered me to the courtyard terrace of a charming hotel. A few white iron patio tables and chairs were set out. Green plants in terra-cotta urns contrasted vividly with the sun-bleached stone walls.

From the terrace I looked down on a maze of cobblestone streets and lanes. Roads ran across the rooftops of some of the cave homes; tier upon tier of tufa stone dwellings, some with elaborately carved door frames, were packed tightly together. The small windows and doorways were starkly silhouetted in the glare of the afternoon sun. I made a mental note to return here one day soon.

I dashed back down the steps to the car. Surprisingly, Mom had not fallen asleep.

We drove through as much of the town as we could, passing caves that had been transformed into stunning modern boutiques, restaurants, and wine bars. A call center had taken over one entire cave complex, housing its computer system in one part of the cave and the call center of five hundred people in another. From Stone Age to high tech—this is the sort of mix of ancient architecture and modern life that I find riveting.

Not that long ago Matera was Italy's shame. As recently as the 1970s people still lived in caves—and I don't mean the renovated models. Health and hygiene were appalling; the child mortality rate hovered around fifty percent. When malaria began claiming the lives of many of the residents, the Italian government was stirred to action. Modern-day troglodytes were evicted and relocated to suburban apartments.

Daylight was waning as we began the return journey to Alberobello, driving though the countryside rather than taking the main roads. We passed gigantic stone gates marking where a large villa, monastery, or convent had once stood and drove through small towns where filigreed iron balconies created canopies over shop entrances and where children played football and rode their bikes in piazzas dominated by churches.

"It's too bad we only get one kick at the can of life," Mom sighed sadly as she gazed out of the car window.

"Why's that?"

"Now I know what's available, and it's too late," she replied.

"What would you have done differently?"

"I would not have changed my man or my children, but maybe I would have bought a grand old gate in Italy and built something beautiful behind it. I might have chosen to live somewhere different."

We turned off the ss172 onto the road that led to our *trullo,* and I pointed out the abandoned *trullo* I had snooped around earlier that day.

"It's adorable!" gasped Mom. "You need to find a real estate agent."

9

Castel del Monte, Potenza

HAD WE stayed in Alberobello a few more days, I might
very well have called a real estate agent. I had become
quite attached to the area—to the hobbitlike *trulli,* the low drystone walls embracing broad fields, the quiet, simple rural life,
and the ancient olive trees with their gnarly trunks and sprawling limbs. It seemed an easy sort of place, an authentic place;
the kind of place that might show patience to a newcomer.

The next morning, with rain shelling our car like gunfire,
we bade a final farewell to our *trullo* and set our sights north-
ward to Castel del Monte, between Bari and Melfi. I wasn't
entirely certain where we would be spending the night, but
based on my map, Melfi looked as good a destination as any.

Our first stop was a gas station.

I had developed a fondness for Agip gas stations. I'm not
sure why—perhaps it was their medieval-style logo of a fire-

breathing wolf with six legs, or maybe that their corporate colors of red and yellow reminded me of the gas stations I frequent at home.

"*Il pieno, per favore,*" I said to the gas jockey.

A chuckle came from the passenger seat.

"What's so funny?" I asked Mom indignantly. I mean, had she bothered to learn a word of Italian?

"What on earth did you say to that man?" she giggled, trying unsuccessfully to restrain her mirth.

"I said, '*Il pieno, per favore.*' It means 'Fill it up, please,' and before you start criticizing my pronunciation may I remind you that..."

Mom clutched my arm and, her eyes brimming with tears of laughter, gasped hysterically: "I'm...sorry...but to me...it sounds...like you're saying...'I play...piano...for a whore'!"

Well, we had a good laugh about that one. I almost joined her in the incontinent department.

Thereafter, on a couple of occasions when I was feeling cheeky, I would quickly mutter my mother's English version to the gas jockeys, and without so much as a raised eyebrow they dutifully filled up the tank. Mom and I would crack up like schoolgirls.

We followed the highway north to Bari. I had considered taking a brief tour of the city, but the amount of traffic turned me off the idea immediately, and I decided we would simply press on.

"Look! IKEA!" said Mom with the same sort of excitement Columbus probably displayed when he first set eyes on North America.

"You aren't serious about stopping at IKEA," I said.

"Why not?" she pouted. "My friend Kitty's daughter is a buyer for IKEA; I could take a photo of the store for her. Besides, I like IKEA."

I felt it best to ignore her.

The rain had finally subsided and the sun was doing its best to apply some much-needed heat to the air. We turned off the E55 and followed the signs to Bitonto, which was en route to Castel del Monte, one of the homes of Frederick II. Everywhere I went in southern Italy I encountered references to old Freddie, so I felt obliged to pay his ghost a visit.

Entering Bitonto, I shared a historical nugget with Mom:

"The funeral cortege of Frederick II passed through this very town—and right through that piazza—in December 1250, on its way to Taranto, where a ship was waiting to take his body to Palermo for burial. And just think, we're heading to one of Frederick's castles right now."

"Look!" Mom said excitedly. "STOP! A clothing store!"

I swerved the car into the first available parking spot. The passenger-side door was open before I had the car properly stopped and the hand brake engaged.

She didn't give two hoots about Frederick; she wanted to shop.

I could hardly blame her: both of us were in desperate need of warm clothing. I had tried to make do with the clothes in my suitcase—a wardrobe fit for a heat wave—but no amount of layering could sufficiently warm me up.

We descended on the boutique like a SWAT unit and emerged fifteen minutes later with sweaters.

The fabled Via Appia conveyed us out of Bitonto into the flat, big-sky countryside. Distant snow-capped mountains abutted lush green fields and gentle valleys arrayed around their bases.

There was so much to take in, and to some eyes the ordinary looked extraordinary.

"Look at all those crosses," sighed Mom, pointing to a series of structures along the roadside. "Isn't that a marvellous sight?"

"Those are electricity poles, Mom."

IT WAS around noon when we drove up to Castel del Monte, the perplexing octagonal fortress that was built, and some say designed, by Frederick II in 1240 to secure his control over the Apulian territory. It is one of more than two hundred buildings he erected during his thirty-eight-year reign. The construction guild of the day must have been giddy with gratitude to him. The creamy-pink-hued limestone facade and crownlike shape give it an almost playful innocence when you first lay eyes on it, but as you draw closer you get a distinct sense of the creeps.

The castle has baffled historians and archaeologists. It is not grand enough to be a pleasure palace, not menacing enough to be a fortress, too pretty to be a prison, too geometric to be a hunting lodge. Castel del Monte proved perplexing for us, too. Frederick had obviously not built it with Mom in mind. There were no signs anywhere to indicate access for the disabled.

We parked the car in the parking lot—a long distance from the castle—unfolded Mom's trusty friend the red walker, and made a slow, torturous journey along a rough dirt-and-pebble road and then up uneven steps leading to the castle.

It nearly killed her. She walked for several minutes with labored breathing and a pinched look of agony on her face. She was so out of breath and in such pain that I feared she would collapse.

"Stay here and let me find out if there's a better way to do this," I finally said.

I sprinted ahead and up a dozen steep steps to the castle door.

"Mia madre è disabile," I explained impatiently to the young man at the ticket wicket. It might take a village to raise a child, but it takes a loud, edgy voice to advocate for a disabled senior. I hoped he would be able to allow me to drive my mother right up to the castle, where a ramp or something would make climbing the stairs easier for her. He conferred with a colleague and then told me to ask my question to someone at the restaurant down the road from the castle, across from the parking lot. As for entering the castle, he said, Mom would still have to climb the dozen steps to the front door.

I ran back to Mom to relay the information. Her face was glistening with perspiration.

"I'm afraid we have to walk all the way back to the car," I winced, wishing with all my heart that I could have given her different news.

The look on her face did not match her words: "I'll be fine."

Off we set, slowly and painfully, back to the car. Once I got her settled and stowed the walker back in the trunk I went into the restaurant and asked that the chain rope barrier be unlocked so that we could drive up to the castle.

"Momento," I was told.

Why is my *"Andiamo!"* so often met with *"Momento"*?

After a wait, during which time I was able to tap out the score to the *William Tell* overture on the steering wheel, we proceeded over crushed stone to the castle. I parked the car as close as I could to the entrance steps.

"How are you feeling?" I asked Mom. "Those steps look steep."

"I'll be fine," she said determinedly, and struggled out of the car. "There's a railing, so that should help quite a bit."

She slowly worked her way up the steps, using the railing to pull herself up one stone riser at a time. My mind drifted back twenty-some years to when I had patiently ascended many stairs with my toddlers, teaching them to move one leg up a step before bringing the second leg up to join it. Then the next step, and the next. Where had those years gone? No one told me then that I would be repeating the lesson with my mother.

Once Mom reached the top, I bent down slightly and gave her a look of victory along with quiet applause, in much the same way I had done for my children. The term "second childhood" was beginning to make sense to me.

The next hurdle for Mom was lifting her legs—which have difficulty bending because of a mass of arthritis strangling her knee joints—over the foot-high threshold of the castle door. She steadied herself on a door frame nearly a millennium old and, taking a deep breath, managed this too.

At the ticket wicket I faced the same young man I had earlier. This time I asked for a wheelchair. He looked just as dumbfounded as he had about my first request. Again, he conferred with his colleague.

"No wheelchair," he said officiously.

"What is it with you people and your fucking lack of services for the disabled?"

Well, that's what I wanted to say. Instead, I turned to Mom and rolled my eyes.

"I'll manage," she said, forcing a smile. "Come on, let's take a look around this joint."

Now, I know things like osteoarthritis and asthma and guiding one's mom and her infernal red walker around the kingdom were not uppermost in Frederick II's mind when he embarked on his Italian building spree, but eight hundred years later the issues are still ignored. I found this especially surprising at tourist attractions where every possible means is often used to entice visitors. And it's not just the disabled that this concerns, it's people like, well, like me, who accompany a disabled person. I had lost count of the number of times I had run back and forth and hither and yon to make sure my mother saw the things I wanted to see. My knees aren't getting any younger, and once they're shot, then my mother's care declines exponentially. Doesn't it make sense to design and plan things for the enjoyment and use of all ages? Wouldn't accessibility benefit us all—from the elderly in wheelchairs all the way down to tots in strollers?

I parked my rant while I wandered the rooms of Freddie's somber castle. There were few windows in the place and even those were curiously undersized; bow slits permitted light on the eight towers.

The towers each contained spiral staircases, lookouts, and even bathrooms—one of the few surviving examples of medieval plumbing. I hoped Mom would not have to test Frederick's invention.

It was sure different from its pink-and-playful exterior. Inside, Castel del Monte is dark, depressing, and suffocating. As you move through the rooms your eye is drawn to one of three portals leading into an octagonal-shaped interior courtyard that once displayed an octagonal fountain or bath. Frederick appears to have been rather fond of those crazy eights.

The eight rooms on each of the two levels were all inter-connected, making it impossible to leave the castle without first passing through every room. I could not imagine being thrilled to receive an invitation from Frederick to spend a weekend here. It seemed like a place more suited for punishment.

After Frederick's death, the castle was used primarily as a communications link in a network of fortresses, and much later, in the 1600s, it sheltered the area's noble families from the plague.

And then, inexplicably, the castle fell into disuse and disrepair. By the 1800s it was openly used by shepherds, criminals on the lam, political refugees, anyone, really, who wandered by. Vandals stripped it of its marble, mosaics, fur-nishings, and architectural integrity. Entire fireplace mantels and hoods are missing, and based on the massive size of the fireplace openings, taking them could not have been an easy task. But the overarching question you find yourself asking is, What level of greed or ignorance triggers the sense of entitle-ment required to strip a place—even an apparently abandoned one—bare? I suppose this is a question of trifle concern when you are in a country like Italy with a huge supply of heritage buildings and fabulous architecture.

The Italian government belatedly stepped in and pur-chased Castel del Monte in 1876. It took them another fifty years to figure out a restoration plan, and the project contin-ues to this day.

We North Americans assume that historical preserva-tion and restoration are somehow ingrained in the European psyche, but that is not always the case. Places like Castel del Monte were and still are left to the mercies of scavengers and squatters. These days it seems that nothing gets saved from the wrecking ball without UNESCO storming in and planting its World Heritage Site designation, which it did for Castel del Monte in 1996. And God bless UNESCO for doing so. Architecture is a visible record of a country's history, and its preservation is a visible indicator of a government's commit-ment to that history.

But there is no point in saving a building if you don't nail up a sign educating visitors about its significance. Italy fails miserably in this regard. Seldom is there an identifying label, sign, or explanatory plaque attached to anything of historic interest. You see tourists walking around in a state of utter panic and wonder, searching for something, anything, that will twig them to the raison d'être of the object to which they have been directed.

Yes, there's always a guidebook to purchase in a gift shop for five euros, but you get tired of carting them around, and by the end of your trip you've added twenty pounds of guide-books to your luggage—books you rarely crack open again.

In a little guidebook available in Castel del Monte's gift shop—yes, I broke down and purchased one—the reader is assured by the Office for Architectural and Environmental Assets of Apulia that the Ministry for Cultural Assets and Activities has "adopted a policy aimed at improving both the quality and quantity of the expectations of the tourist inflow."

You know what would really help? A filing card tacked up beside an attraction upon which are scribbled a few facts. That would go a long way in meeting "the expectations of the tourist inflow."

I came across a staircase—unmarked, naturally—and fol-lowed it upstairs in my pursuit of information.

I wandered from empty room to empty room and ended up in the *sala del trono*—the throne room. (This I gleaned from the guidebook.) Four worn stone steps led up to a cozy window seat, where I plopped myself down and let my eyes roam the countryside that stretched clear to the Adriatic Sea. A thick collar of firs and pines encircled the castle; this served as both a natural barrier and prime hunting land for Frederick.

Of all of Italy's historical characters, Frederick is one of my favorites. I marvelled at his diverse accomplishments, the most unusual being his book on falconry: *De Arte Venandi cum Avibus (The Art of Hunting with Birds)*, the first scientific examination of ornithology pertaining to such birds.

I found it remarkable that a man who ruled a vast empire— he was king of the Romans and king of Italy, Germany, Burgundy, Sicily, and for a time Cyprus and Jerusalem—who was always sparring with the Church, who managed to hang onto his far-flung empire despite a constant stream of marauders trying to wrest it away from him, who built a slew of fortresses and castles, still had time to tend to his birds and to write an academic treatise about it, to boot. Frederick wasn't the type of guy who slept in.

A staircase in the tower adjoining the room in which I stood led to the rooftop terrace where Frederick practiced his falconry. I was told quite emphatically by one of the castle staff that *no one* was permitted on the roof, but that didn't stop me from jiggling the door latch in case someone had left it open.

Sadly, it was locked, so I turned my attention to the interior of the room, and to its slender, soaring ribbed vaults, its complex brickwork pattern, and its clusters of columns—some elongated and fluted, others embellished with a profusion of acanthus leaves. You could see where vandals had stripped away the pink marble that would have framed a delicate, sweeping arch or doorway. Even by today's standards the precision of work visible on the remaining decorative features was rather breathtaking.

I imagined this empty room decorated and furnished: Was the bed placed over there? Did a servant hang or store garments in that niche? Was a large, plush, ruby-colored carpet, a gift from a Persian sultan perhaps, rolled out on these floors?

It is a game I constantly play with myself. First, I imagine a room decorated during the peak of its ancient glory. Then I mentally clear everything out and furnish it with my own stuff (or stuff I wish I owned). By the time I leave I feel a sense of ownership. It's sort of like a dog that urinates to mark its territory.

A brief gust of wind rattled the window. A shudder rippled through me, and I felt it best to leave.

I returned to the first floor, where I found Mom speaking excitedly to two people behind the ticket wicket who had absolutely no grasp of English.

"I've lost my daughter!" I heard her say. "You have to find her for me."

"Is everything OK, Mom?" I asked, walking briskly up to her.

"Oh there you are!" she exclaimed rather agitatedly. "Where were you? I was going to have them send out a search party for you. I thought something bad had happened to you."

"I just went upstairs," I said, looking at my watch and noting that I had been gone barely fifteen minutes. "Are you OK?"

"I'm fine! I was just worried."

Why was this woman always thinking she would lose me? I took her hand and guided her outside and down the steps to our car. She had always been an independent, self-sufficient person, but I was beginning to notice in her the neediness and fearfulness that comes with age.

As we drove away I glanced back at the castle. Its pretty pink coloring was vivid against clouds like steel wool that were gathering ominously behind it.

We stopped at the restaurant at the entrance to the castle's driveway and were greeted inside by the warmth and cinder smell from an open fire.

I ordered us each a glass of red Castel del Monte wine and perused the menu.

The waiter tried to push the orecchiette, the small lamb's-ear-shaped pasta for which every place we had visited so far claimed the best recipe and preparation. I had no intention of offering up my taste buds as a guinea pig again. Instead, I chose the antipasto—prosciutto, *bocconcini* cheese, provolone, artichokes, grilled eggplant, and zucchini. It was a tasty repast.

"Thank God you ordered this," said Mom, tucking into her lunch. "I couldn't have faced another plate of pasta."

Sufficiently fed and watered, we returned to the car and jacked up the heater.

I pulled out my trusty road map and with a finger traced a westward route that might lead us to a bed for the night.

"Where to next?" asked Mom brightly. She is always perky after a meal.

"Melfi, I think. It's not too far. We'll spend the night there."

"Do we have reservations?"

"Nope. We talked about that this morning, Mom. We're winging it today. Remember?"

"What's in Melfi?" she asked.

"Haven't a clue, but I hope it has a hotel," I said, starting up the car.

What I really wanted was a rest. The constant driving was unravelling me. I wanted to find a place where I could flop onto a sofa and receive hourly injections of gin and tonic. I didn't want to have to think or plan, make a decision or answer a question.

166

"Look at that snow cloud up there," Mom remarked, peering through the windshield.

"Nonsense," I scoffed. "It's the first day of Spring. Besides, this part of Italy doesn't get snow."

Within the hour ankle-deep drifts were lining the road. I looked down at the open-toed sandals on our feet and let out a long groan. What happened to global warming?

We somehow missed the exit for Melfi and found ourselves reading signs for Potenza.

A tough wind began buffeting the car. Snow swirled in front of us, wisps danced on the hood of the car and shot madly into the sky. I pressed the accelerator pedal harder in order to make Potenza before nightfall.

It was 6:00 PM when we checked into the Grande Albergo Potenza. Standing sheepishly at the front desk in our light clothes and sandals, we looked like refugees beside the bemused businesspeople in sensible dark wool coats, hats, and gloves.

In our hotel room we raised the blinds to an evening sky and faced a snow-covered mountain range and twinkling lights in the distance. Below us, cars sloshed through the street bearing inches of snow on their roofs. It looked as if we had been transported to a Swiss ski resort. It was enough to make me double-check the road map to make sure we hadn't made a wrong turn somewhere and ended up in the Alps.

The next morning a light dusting of snow was added to the previous day's accumulation. I dragged our bags through slush to the car. By now I had learned to ignore the stares and gasps from people when they saw sandals on my feet. I pretended to belong to a religious order that had taken a vow of immunity against fashion and weather.

We joined the morning rush hour out of Potenza and slipped back onto the E847 heading west toward the Amalfi Coast and Sorrento.

Surely it would be warm and sunny there.

10

Amalfi Coast, Sorrento, Capri

THE LAST thing I expected on the Amalfi Coast was snow, but that's precisely what we got.

We had just come through some of the densest fog—*la nebbia* as the Italians refer to it—I have ever seen. It was like driving through cotton batting. We could not see signs or lane lines or other cars. The fact that our car was on a tilt was the only clue I had that we were on an incline. It was thoroughly scary. Then, inexplicably, the sun broke through, and we were reading road signs for Salerno and the Amalfi Coast.

"Andiamo!" I blurted at the interminably pokey and lumbering garbage truck in front of us in the right-hand lane. Honestly, when you are in a hurry to get somewhere, a garbage truck can always be counted on to pull in front of you.

I boldly pulled out into the middle lane to pass. As I did, the exit sign for the Amalfi Coast appeared. I could not get back into the exit lane in time, and we sailed past it.

In Italy impatience is punished by a dearth of exits for many, many miles. Off-ramps and on-ramps are not always paired up in Italy, as they are in North America, where a travel error can be corrected fairly painlessly. In Italy, there might be an off-ramp to a city, but its corresponding on-ramp might be ten miles away, if one exists at all.

Twenty minutes and a litany of profanity later, we reached an exit, turned off, and doubled back through a maze of traffic-clogged narrow streets in Salerno.

It had been my New Year's resolution to give up swearing. I had regarded my meltdown that first night in Italy as a one-off—and seriously, I defy anyone to get into a car in a foreign country at night after twelve hours of flying and not swear. I thought I would be able to atone for my transgression some-how, but I was hopeless. It was probably a good thing that my mother was hard of hearing.

Still, I don't like swearing. I'm really trying to break the habit. I swear.

"Next time I take a holiday," I promised God, "I'll spend it at an ashram or a convent. I promise to make this up to you."

In the midst of a chaotic, traffic-choked, horn-blaring section of Salerno I somehow managed to spot a very small sign that read Costa d'Amalfi with an arrow pointing to the right. I slid the car over to the right lane and followed the sign. Within seconds, the crowds and cars disappeared, and we were motoring along a spectacular road. That's the thing with Italy: a scene, like a mood, can change without warning.

The Amalfi Coast is a thrill ride. Yes, the autostrada in Sicily was exhilarating, but this was an entirely different kettle of fish. This was iconic: Huge rock faces on one side; a sheer drop to the Mediterranean on the other. When rain, then snow began splattering our windshield I refused to surrender to any sensation less than sheer excitement. It is also a breathtakingly narrow road, a point quickly reinforced when your car encounters a gigantic tour bus that comes screaming around a tight, rocky corner from the opposite direction like a *Tyrannosaurus rex* chasing its dinner.

We would not, however, be enjoying sun-drenched seaside cafés or darting into the tiny shops that crowd the main road through small, sexy places like Praiano and Positano, the sort of places where you should be strolling along in stylish sandals, white slacks, and large, white-rimmed sunglasses, your hair held back by a Hermès scarf. Not for us. Not this time. Not in the friggin' snow.

"Let's stop for lunch," said Mom. But because *mia madre è allergica a pesce ed a tutti i frutti di mare* our options were rather limited. It didn't help that in the slushy downpour, driving had turned into a nail-biting exercise of dodging tour buses, cars backing out of garages chiselled into the rock where you didn't think a garage could exist, or delivery trucks blaring their horns at you to move along when you became mesmerized by garages chiselled into the rock face.

THE SUN was beaming and mopping up the remnants of a sloppy morning when we arrived at our hotel in Sorrento, the small, charming, family-run Hotel Villa Margherita.

At the check-in desk I asked about meals but was told that the hotel's restaurant, shown on the Web site with an enticing lemon-grove patio and hanging lanterns, was closed until April. Ditto for its rooftop terrace with a clear view of Mount Vesuvius. I had stopped counting the number of off-season letdowns.

However, precisely because it was the off-season and

there were only one or two other guests registered, the owner
offered us separate rooms at a reduced rate.

Without consulting one another or making eye contact,
Mom and I lunged at the offer.

"That sounds..."

"Fine, yes..."

"We'll take it."

The owner—Maria—arched a delicate eyebrow, and a
glimmer of a smile appeared on her lips as she made the neces-
sary adjustment on our registration form.

"Really, I think it's best for us, and..." Mom said quickly
to me.

"Absolutely," I nodded vigorously. "No need to..."

"We both like our privacy..."

"And you've been so ill, you'd be more comfortable..."

"Besides, we're here for four days..."

"You're absolutely right."

The thirty euros extra this would cost us each over the
course of our stay would preserve our sanity and our relationship. The price even included breakfast.

The rooms were comfortable and clean; mine had the
bonus of a small balcony, though the weather was too chilly
(and as it later transpired, rainy) to use it. The bathrooms were
cramped affairs with the smallest shower stalls imaginable.

"If they'd just get rid of that useless bidet there would be
room for a proper shower," Mom remarked. "What is the
point of them anyway? I've been using them to store my curlers and makeup."

We wandered back to the lobby to inquire about places to
eat. Maria suggested we dine at nearby La Campana, a place
within easy walking distance, though not so easy for Mom.

We arrived at the restaurant at 6:00 PM. We were the first people there. An unctuous waiter greeted us and led us to a table.

I tried to figure out the theme of the place—there was a South Seas vibe going on amid the grass-hut interior, or maybe it was supposed to be a maritime look, with its fishing nets and paddles as décor art.

The food was mediocre but hearty, definitely geared to the tourist trade.

When the bill arrived I discovered we had been grossly overcharged on a few items, and two other menu items had been added on.

I called the waiter over and pointed this out. He expressed mock surprise, bowed, and went to confer with someone in the kitchen. When he returned he admitted with more bowing and apology that, yes, the bill had "a few errors."

It was not the first time this had happened on the trip, and I barely masked my anger. I was well aware of the "stupid tax" that Chris, the property manager in Alberobello, had told me about, but I was finding that in many places, even if you spoke a bit of Italian and knew your way around the euro currency, you were targeted for simply being a foreigner.

We settled the bill, and I staggered out defiantly, though perhaps a bit wobbly, with the half-empty bottle of wine ordered at dinner stowed in my purse.

"How was your dinner?" asked Maria brightly when we returned to the hotel.

I mentioned the incident involving our bill.

Her face flushed with rage. She immediately picked up the phone, dialed the restaurant, and gave someone at the other end an impressively blistering tongue-lash, the gist of which, as far as I could tell, was, "If I'm going to recommend your establishment to my guests then you better cut the crap. This is what gives Italy a bad name."

"*Allora,* I am sorry," Maria said gravely, hanging up the phone and composing herself. She smoothed her trousers as if she had been physically involved in the dustup. "The restaurant is sorry, too. They invite you to return and your meal will be free."

We thanked her and declined the offer.

The lack of guests at the Hotel Villa Margherita allowed us to get to know Maria and her family a little bit during our stay.

Her Italian parents had immigrated to Montreal, where she and her brother were raised. For reasons that were not shared, the family minus the father returned to Sorrento and bought the hotel. At just twenty-four, Maria was a mature and astute businesswoman.

Often, when my mother and I returned to the hotel after a sightseeing excursion, Maria's extended family would be hanging out in the lobby. Some of them would be watching TV; the grandmother would be playing with an excitable toddler strapped in a stroller; a sister-in-law would be lounging on a wicker sofa, flipping through a magazine; Maria's brother would be in the hotel's restaurant working on repairs; and Maria herself would be canoodling with her boyfriend in a corner. In this little Sorrento hotel, life played out in all its glorious passion. This is what I love about Italy—the live-out-loud life.

"What do you think of Maria and that fellow of hers?" asked Mom as we made our way to our respective rooms one evening. There was a disapproving tone to her voice, so I already knew her opinion.

"I think it's wonderful that they're allowed to kiss and show affection in front of everyone."

I said this without mentioning that our own family had taken a dim view of public displays of affection, even between married spouses. "It shows there are no secrets. It's good for the family dynamic—you see your daughter kissing a guy and you know that guy might be your son-in-law one day. So you forge a rapport with him and start drawing him into the family unit. Quid pro quo gets established. Eventually, he's truly like your son and he knows he can't get away with abusing your daughter. If he's not committed to the family then he won't be committed to your daughter. I see lots of psychological and sociological benefits to being permissive with your adult child's sexual expression. I mean, within reason."

"That's a lot of malarkey," snorted Mom. "Kissing in public is undignified."

THE SUN was shining the next morning.

"Quick!" I said to Mom. "Let's go out and see the sights."

We decided to go to Capri.

We drove through Sorrento's bustling roads and down through an impressively deep chasm toward the port. We parked the car, and Mom, her walker, and I shuffled onto an awaiting hydrofoil.

Mom decided that this would be a good time to start singing "The Isle of Capri," and she looked around, hoping those within earshot would join her in song.

"You're too uptight, Jane," she said, noticing my rolled eyes, and continued singing alarmingly off key, as is her wont. I made the usual embarrassed smiles to our unimpressed and glaring fellow passengers, most of whom were young, haughty, and glamorous.

The hydrofoil was the floating epicenter of Black Sunglasses and Bored Looks. This was where "cool" came to chill. Sunglasses are as prevalent as cell phones in Italy—no one is seen without either. And while my stance on cell phones remained unbowed, I noted that Italians' cell phone conversations were shorter and quieter than those of North Americans. I didn't have to listen to someone's loud and excruciatingly detailed recounting of their annual medical examination or reports of bowel regularity or how much pasta cost at the local grocery store compared with a competitor's price.

Nothing screams "not cool" like a walker. While my mother was lost in her little wartime singsong, passengers either stared at her like she was a crazy woman or stole furtive looks of disgust at the walker You would have thought that a bloodstained gurney had been rolled onboard.

A young woman sitting kitty-corner to me was almost reeling at the fact that she had to sit with two relics and a walker. She stared at me contemptuously, as if holding me solely responsible for the aging process. I locked eyeballs with her defiantly and felt a cruel smirk emerging on my face. "One day, young lady, your long, glossy chestnut hair will be streaked with gray, your pert boobs will settle somewhere around your navel, and you'll wake up one morning to find wrinkles on your face (you and some of your more charitable friends will call them 'laugh lines,' but it won't help) and a weird puckering on your once flat, smooth tummy. And maybe, just maybe, you'll become incontinent. I do hope so—it might add texture to your personality."

The red walker was rocking unsteadily against the movement of the hydrofoil as I tried unsuccessfully to hold onto it. An infuriating design oversight of this particular walker was its lack of a strong locking mechanism. Like a testy and rambunctious two-year-old, the walker escaped my clutches and rolled against the wall, where three Italian crew members were discussing the mechanics of the gangplank and did their best to ignore the commotion. They did not offer to tether the walker to a railing and, in fact, did not even acknowledge the walker, not even when it eventually banged into the knees of a snoozing passenger. Definitely not cool.

In the meantime, the hydrofoil glided quietly across turquoise water beneath a high ring of fluffy clouds that created a dome effect. It was like sailing through a marine cathedral. Mount Vesuvius lurked in the background.

When the hydrofoil docked at Capri we let all the busy cool people push and elbow their way off the boat first, and proceeded at our own pace to the island's main drag.

"I want to see the Blue Grotto," I said to Mom. "Will you be OK until I return?"

She smiled and nodded, and toddled off to contentedly troll the numerous souvenir shops and fast-food eateries of which Capri has an unhealthy abundance. I scurried to a nearby ticket booth to purchase passage on the next boat to the Blue Grotto and grabbed the last seat on one that was about to pull away from the dock.

If you have not come to Capri to shop its overpriced shops you have likely come to experience the Blue Grotto, one of those curiosities of nature. Pictures of it show a dark cave with stunningly bright blue water that looks as if it has been lit from the bottom of the sea, which in a way it has. The light comes from an opening farther underwater through which sunlight passes, producing an eerie but brilliant otherworldly glow.

The sun came out as our motorboat, crammed with about a dozen passengers, skipped over the choppy waves of the Tyrrhenian Sea, past rocky cliffs topped with the pastel-colored homes of the superrich.

It was a short trip, perhaps fifteen minutes. At the mouth of the grotto we joined a small flotilla of similar boats that had gathered in a loose (how Italian!) queue. We waited to be transferred into skiffs that would take two of us at a time into the mysterious and infamous cave. It looked like it was going to be a bit of a wait.

As we sat bobbing in the water, I observed the tricky business of actually getting inside the grotto. The top of the cave entrance is low to the water line, and visitors are conveyed through the small opening in wooden skiffs in which they must lie absolutely still and prone. They are guided by boatmen who carefully maneuver the skiff with the help of guylines or chains permanently attached to the cave entrance. However, all this skill is rather moot if a sudden sea swell occurs midentry: the skiff and its occupants could be smashed to smithereens.

I glanced nervously at the sea and became an instant expert in monitoring wave activity. Hmm. This could be dicey. The water had become choppier. I wondered how Mom, who was contentedly cruising the souvenir stalls, would cope if I was suddenly cast into the sea.

Just then a muffled groan came from the waiting passengers. The grotto's gatekeeper had given the signal—crossing his thick hairy arms then stretching them quickly apart—"*finito.*" All further visits that day were cancelled because of too-high swells.

We sullenly made the trip back to Capri's harbor. No refunds. No rain checks. Just a "try again tomorrow." I was supremely disappointed.

Mom had settled herself in a café at the far end of the souvenir promenade and had just ordered tea when I joined her. I placed an order myself.

"What a shame that you couldn't get in," she said. "What will you do?"

I shrugged. "Guess I'll have to come back to Capri another time."

When I had finished my tea I announced that I was going to walk to the center of town to check it out. "There's an arrow over there pointing to the *centro storico*."

"OK. I'll look around a bit more here and make my way back to the ferry," she said. "I'll meet you there."

I set off to explore, happy for a chunk of time to myself. I followed the arrows and the steps. Up and up I continued. The sun beat down on me as I climbed along a blindingly white, walled passageway. On either side of the white stucco walls were gardens and small homes with a view of the turquoise sea. Occasionally a burst of red bougainvillea cascaded over the wall and broke the bleached monotony. It was pretty, but the novelty quickly wore off. The walk became a long, demanding trek of interminable steps.

Thirty hard minutes later, dripping with perspiration, my face flushed from sunburn and exhaustion, I arrived at the top.

Turning a corner I entered the town's main piazza. Scads of cloth-covered café tables and bamboo club chairs were occupied by the Black Sunglasses Gang, their smooth, tanned, beautifully sculpted faces turned toward the sun as they sipped their afternoon Campari.

On the edge of a wall was an arrow and the word *"funicolare."* As I was soon to discover, a *funicolare* conveys people from Capri's harbor to the hilltop town, and I had completely missed the sign. I wish I could be like the people who know there is a *funicolare* and who don't arrive in the midst of an elegant setting with sweat-stained clothing and wild hair.

Unlike me, Capri is tidy. It is an evidently well-heeled place, the type of place that looks as if it has never dealt with home-lessness, traffic congestion, pollution, or needle-exchange centers. The people lounging on the café chairs or saunter-ing along the shop-lined lanes seemed blissfully unaware and unconcerned about anything but their own gratification. A sense of moral superiority washed over me as I surveyed this state of slothful decadence. 179

"They should be doing something useful with their time," I said to myself. Was that my mother speaking? Or was that the voice of someone who wished to be draped over one of those café chairs, too?

The novelty of posh boutiques and hotels and gelato shops faded quickly, which tends to happen when I don't have money, so I looked around for something less expensive to grab my attention.

I spotted an ambulance. It was the narrowest vehicle I'd ever seen, toylike in its design, and I followed it through the winding, skinny streets. It stopped near a hotel, and when the back of it was opened I saw that it was no wider than a stretcher. Other service vehicles in Capri were similarly adorable—how else would they get through a warren of streets barely wider than an arm span? To North American eyes, design in Italy often seems rendered in miniature.

Being prone to frequent bouts of stubbornness, especially when my ignorance and stupidity have been uncovered, I defi-antly took the steps rather than the funicular back down to the ferry. Partway down, I came upon a group of teenage American boys who were part of a school trip. (Two questions here: Since when did North American schools start organizing class trips to Capri? And is it possible for me to redo high school?) I overheard the boys' worried conversation about whether they would be late for the return ferry to the mainland.

When they spotted me, there were hushed, rushed decisions to appoint one of them to ask me the time. One young fellow began madly flipping through an English-Italian phrase book.

"Pardon, *signor,* I mean, *signorina,*" he stammered as a few of his mates huddled around him and stifled a giggle.

"*Sì?*" I answered with a smile, deciding not to correct his use of *signorina.*

"*Che*..." then whispering to his friends asked, "Is it pronounced chee or kay?"

"It's pronounced kay, I think," one of them replied.

"OK, *che ora*..."

"No, no!" demanded another friend. "Ask her where the ferry is?"

"Um, *dove*..."

"It's pronounced dough-vay, you idiot."

"Then *you* ask her!"

"Would it be easier just to ask me in English?" I interjected helpfully.

I wish I had a photograph to show you of their shocked faces. It was priceless.

"It's OK, I just look Italian," I smiled.

"We're supposed to be at the ferry by three thirty," one said.

"It's quarter to three now," I said, checking my watch. "I'm heading there, too, so you should make it in time as long as you don't dawdle. Where are you guys from?"

"The States. Vermont."

"North American schools do trips to Capri now?" I asked.

The boys looked at me with that "Uh, DUH!" expression.

And that, ladies and gentlemen, is how you go from *signorina* to fossil in ten seconds.

THE NEXT morning I fetched the car, and Mom and I drove to the shops off Sorrento's Piazza Tasso with the happy aim of shedding some euros. We had done no shopping since arriving in Italy, unless you count the handful of fridge magnets I had purchased along the way.

Mom was looking for a rain jacket. She has twelve at home, but it had not occurred to her to pack one for our trip.

I pulled a stylish coppery-brown jacket off the rack and asked her to try it on. It fit perfectly and looked very elegant on her.

"Well, I don't know," she said, looking at her reflection in the mirror.

"What?" I asked. "It's perfect! It makes you look stylish and sleek."

"I don't think it's me."

"But you always talk about wanting to update your wardrobe. Why are you drawn to the same frumpy clothes?"

"I beg your pardon? My clothes are classic. I've had some of them for forty years."

"My point exactly," I argued. "Why are you so resistant to change? You ask for my opinion and help and then you don't listen. Never mind. Suit yourself."

In the end she bought it, but I must check her closet at home and see if she has kept it.

We ventured into a few other shops, but the smallest amount of exertion was now too much for Mom's legs.

She wanted to go back to the hotel and rest. I was just getting into the shopping spirit! I walked her back to the car and bit back the urge to give vent to all the boredom and irritation that was roiling inside me.

I was tired of constantly changing our plans to suit Mom's disabilities and being limited to where we could go or what we could do. I felt terrible for even thinking such thoughts. It wasn't entirely her fault after all, but a part of me wanted to berate her. "Maybe if you had looked after yourself rather than spending so much energy on old homes you might have been able to get around easier in your later years."

Everything I did or wanted to do was subject to *her* limitations and wishes. What about *my* limitations and wishes? This was my trip, too. I felt like parking her at the Hotel Villa Margherita for a few days so I could run free and see the side of Italy I wanted to see—the coastal cafés, the small hidden restaurants that served the food people raved about, the clusters of real people who live away from the tourist areas, maybe a distillery where they make Sorrento's signature liqueur, *limoncello.* This wasn't a holiday; it was like visiting Italy under a probation warrant.

Occasionally she let me off the leash, but I could tell from the look in her eyes that she was doing so reluctantly. She knew I would stumble across something fascinating, and it would make her miserable that she had missed it.

To keep me close at hand she would try to get me to nap when she napped. Nap? I'm in Italy! I didn't come here to nap! "And excuse me," I wanted to say, "I'm not one hundred and twenty years old, in case you hadn't noticed. I do not nap."

But Mom would insist, and when I objected she would point to my rising irritability as justification.

"You know you always get bitchy when you don't get enough sleep," she would admonish.

No, actually, I get bitchy when I have to drag a fucking walker and an incontinent gimp from one end of Italy to the other, I felt like saying.

Of course, I did not utter these sentiments. I didn't dare. So much of what passes between mothers and daughters is unsaid. Those tight smiles between women have nothing to do with Botox.

Instead, I dutifully delivered her back to the comfort of the hotel. As soon as Mom was settled in her room, I closed her door softly, then turned around and set off on foot back to the Piazza Tasso.

Sorrento is a bit of a historical oddity. It has managed to keep a low profile throughout its long history, which dates to pre-Roman times. This must have required some skill, because it is located directly across the bay from big, boisterous, hairy-chested Naples.

Sorrento is a genteel, picturesque seaside town, unmistakably elegant without the pomposity that often afflicts towns that know they are beautiful. It is relatively small, about twenty thousand people, and now one of the most popular tourist destinations in Italy. It is easy to see why: It has a manageable scale, it is tidy, and it has a laid-back vibe. Unlike almost every other Italian town or city, Sorrento is built on flat terrain, a boon to those with walkers and motorized wheelchairs who want an Italian town without the inclines. The downside, of course, is that Sorrento is a boon to those with walkers and motorized wheelchairs who want an Italian town without the inclines.

I followed the scent of lemons down a rain-soaked laneway and found two young men loading up the back of their small pickup with the bounty from a backyard grove. Fresh, tart, young—no, not the men, the lemons—they produced a heady, magnificent aroma, something I cut, pasted, and saved in the part of my brain that is reserved for olfactory memories. I longed to possess the language to tell these men that the smell of the lemons was heavenly.

There was a buzz in the air when I reached Piazza Tasso. Preparations were underway for a major event that afternoon in front of the Fauno Bar: the unveiling of the new Maserati.

Flags sporting Maserati's corporate ink-blue color and stylized trident logo fluttered excitedly on tall, lean standards; massive terra-cotta urns filled with lush greenery were hoisted into curvy ironwork plant stands on casters and rolled into place.

And then the main attraction arrived—a sleek, inky-blue racing car. It was reverently unloaded from a flatbed truck, eliciting gasps from all the men in the crowd, who salivated at its smooth angles, curvaceous and slightly raised back end, voluptuous front end, luscious butterlike upholstery, and aloof style. Put a pair of dark sunglasses on this baby and it would be indistinguishable from much of Italy's female population.

"Che bella macchina!" The swooning chorus was delivered with the sort of moan normally associated with the sexually frustrated. I wondered whether the lusty glances and sighs projected at the car were secretly meant for the cool, slender beauties in their tight, ink-blue skirts, jackets, and matching stockings and shoes who worked the crowd. There was not a blonde among them.

"Quanto costa questo?" I asked a young Maserati rep.

"Ah, this is a racing car, so it is not for sale," he said. "It would cost about two hundred and fifty thousand euros. The cars for everyone else"—more sedate sedans began arriving in the piazza as we spoke—"are not so much."

"I see," I replied, rocking on my heels and nodding knowingly, as if I were accustomed to discussing high-end cars.

The truth is, I know zip about cars. I can't imagine discussing cars for more than ten seconds. But I had read somewhere and somehow retained the information that the 2008 Maserati GranTurismo, considered a masterpiece by those who equate car showrooms with art galleries, clocks in at around 100,000 euros. Only about 4,000 would be manufactured.

I lingered longer than I would have usually at a car event. The fact that I had spent so much time on the road in the last few weeks might have piqued my interest in things automotive. When I discovered that the GranTurismo's trunk space could not accommodate a walker I lost interest and wandered away.

My eyes landed on an immense bower of wisteria that was draped over a high black iron gateway across the street. It was the entrance to the gardens of the Albergo Vittoria, a hotel that is not ashamed to display a plaque beside the gate announcing that Enrico Caruso died here in 1921.

I decided that a walk through the gardens would be a pleasant way to pass the time, but just as I entered the gates a security guard intercepted me explaining that a wedding was taking place and that unless I was a guest I couldn't get in. There was no way I looked like a guest, so I retreated.

I stood on the sidewalk for a moment wondering what to do next. I wasn't ready to go back to the hotel.

A couple of well-dressed men strolled by, arm in arm. One of them—a dark-haired man with thick black glasses and a red foulard around his neck—was chatting and gesturing dramatically to his partner.

I took off after them along the Corso Italia. They paused in front of a Baroque-looking building and then walked toward the entrance. I followed them in and soon found myself in a large, bright reception room that had been turned into a gallery of local art.

I wandered around pretending I had money, and privately selected a few paintings. All of a sudden, one of the men I had followed in appeared at my side.

"Parla italiano?" he asked.

"No," I replied. *"Inglese.* I'm Canadian."

"Ah, how lovely," he said, switching to English. "You seem very interested in these paintings. Now tell me, which ones catch your eye? I want to buy something but I always need help choosing."

He was an eccentric fellow, from Dubai, he said, and he mentioned that he collected paintings from every place he visited.

"I'll come back after you've had some time to look at everything, but I really want your advice," he said kindly, perhaps noticing the look of wide-eyed fear on my face.

I strolled around the room and soon fell into easy conversation with a few other people as we compared notes about a painting's subject or the view that had prompted inspiration for an artist.

I surprised myself at how easily I could banter about cars one minute and art the next. In a foreign country I feel more intelligent and articulate than I do at home; I can rise to the point of relative brilliance when no expectations are placed on me. I think that's one of the reasons I like to travel. It is only when I'm in another country that I can see, hear, and appreciate myself most clearly, when my true self emerges.

About twenty minutes passed, and the man from Dubai approached me again.

"Well?" he asked eagerly.

I pointed out a few canvases, but even the one I was most taken with—a field of big blood-red poppies and soothing spikes of lavender—did not impress him.

"No, I want you to see this," he said emphatically. He linked his arm through mine and dragged me to a cluster of small portraits.

"It's important to buy art that has people in it," he counselled gently. "That scene of the poppies is nice but it could be anywhere. Faces, however, they are so evocative of the area, so distinctive. Don't you see? Which of these do you like best?"

I chose one of a young girl with large dark eyes like melted chocolate, and one of a middle-aged woman whose posture indicated confidence but whose eyes betrayed her vulnerability.

"Yes, excellent choices," said the man approvingly. Pointing to another study he said: "This woman here, she looks too perfect, doesn't she? Women who are too beautiful lack mystique and depth."

He thanked me for my help and gave me a warm hug, then turned around to find someone to process his purchase.

Well, that was a productive use of my time, I told myself, and exhaled with satisfaction. I left the gallery and returned to the street.

The rain had resumed, and I pushed open my umbrella and moved confidently toward the narrow streets that emanated like tentacles off the Piazza Tasso and disappeared into a medina-like labyrinth. I selected one that looked promising and set off to see what adventure it held.

An Internet café presented itself, so I ducked in and tapped out a quick message to Zoë, updating her about our whereabouts and relating my failed visit to the Blue Grotto.

She happened to be online—again. She was at school working on a project in the library, she explained hurriedly, and was just coincidentally checking her e-mail.

I didn't care about the excuse. I was thrilled to be connected, however briefly and tenuously, to my daughter.

"Sucks about the Grotto," she wrote, "but don't worry 'cuz you and I are going to go to Italy together one day, and we'll visit the Grotto then."

I loved her optimism.

When I left the Internet café the sound of metal security shutters being pulled down for *siesta* by their shopowners was reverberating through the town. It was a sound I never liked to hear: The streets were always being rolled up just as I was getting into a groove to explore.

A *gelateria* was still open for business, so I ducked in, even though it was definitely not gelato weather. It was obviously an establishment of some repute because its walls were covered with framed newspaper clippings and autographs from famous Italians. A huge chocolate statue of a naked woman dominated the middle of the shop.

I moved to the counter and, from about twenty or so flavors of gelato, I chose pistachio. A small dish of it was handed to me. The moment I tasted it I knew I had made the wrong choice. This almost never happens to me.

I sulked to the side wall and picked away at it anyway. What was going on with my taste buds? I am a veritable addict when it comes to ice cream, and pistachio, well, how could something so promising taste so bland?

"'Ow's your gelato?" a cheerful man next to me said. In his hand was a cone of what looked like chocolate gelato.

He was visiting from Brisbane, he said, by way of introduction.

"You probably made a better choice," I said. "This isn't terribly yummy."

"Neither is mine," he confessed. "What's the big deal about gelato anyway? Give me real ice cream any day. But, you see, the wife and I missed lunch today, and at this point I'll eat anything."

And then, conspiratorially, he asked, "'Ave you by chance, um, eaten anywhere interesting?'"

"Sadly, I haven't," I answered. "What do you make of the food in Italy?"

"It's shit," he said. "All we heard about before we came to Italy was how incredible the food was. I guess you need to travel with a food writer to experience that side."

We traded stories about our respective travels through Italy.

"I visited a brothel yesterday," he said, leaning over and lowering his voice.

"Is that a fact?" I answered, not quite knowing how to respond. I took a quick glance at his wife, who was talking to someone else.

"Oh, it was all above board," Brisbane laughed. "We were at Pompeii. Did you know there were more than twenty-five brothels uncovered at Pompeii?"

I confessed I did not, but I did tell him that we were headed for Pompeii the very next day.

11

Pompeii, Mount Vesuvius

A THUNDEROUS BOOM that nearly shattered my eardrums shook me awake the next morning. It was followed by apocalyptic lightning, a torrential downpour, thrashing wind, the works: A perfect day to visit Pompeii and Mount Vesuvius.

Mom had signed us up for an organized tour. She finds coach excursions thrilling; she loves the precision and organization and, of course, someone else making the decisions. She figured that a bus tour would be a treat for me because it would mean I would not have to drive. Bus tours, however, come with their own stresses.

After breakfast, we drove our car from the hotel to the appointed rendezvous point, a distance of two blocks. I retrieved the red walker from the trunk, popped open the umbrella, and with my free hand guided Mom across the street.

And there we waited. And waited. Sheets of rain abused us from every angle for the better part of an hour. It was also humid, and after a while I could not tell which parts of me were wet and which were sweaty. I was pretty certain my makeup was running down my face.

"Something's not right," Mom said eventually.

"No shit, Sherlock," I said amid a crash of thunder. By now small rivers had formed on the road, and the branches of the trees that were providing a modicum of shelter for us were swaying dangerously.

"Maybe we should go back to the hotel and ask Maria to find out what happened," she said. "But I don't think I can walk back to the car."

I opened her folding cane so she would have something to lean on while I pushed her walker back to the car (this is not a good look for me, by the way) through the rain, loaded the walker into the trunk, and then drove the car across the street, got out, and helped Mom in.

We circled the block back to the hotel, and had just got out of the car and were dodging large puddles on our way to the hotel's entrance when Maria came bursting out the front door.

"Where have you been? The bus is waiting for you!" she cried.

"We just came from there, and there was no bus," I replied as rain sluiced off my face and clothing.

"They have arrived, and now they are wondering where you are!"

We turned around and shuffled back to the car, the rain pelting us mercilessly.

Mom struggled into the car, and I folded up the walker once again and stowed it in the trunk.

We drove back to the prearranged corner, where the hulking coach was idling, cloaked in an exhaust fog of impatience. I put the car in park, got out, helped Mom out of the car, steadied her as she negotiated the steps of the bus, then returned to the car, got back in, and drove to a nearby parking spot on the street.

Gathering my purse, I got out of the car, locked the door, and quickly opened the umbrella, which promptly blew inside out as a gust of wind did its best to throw me off balance. I steeled myself against the wind to retrieve the red walker for the umpteenth time from the trunk of the car, unfolded it, and pushed it half a block to the waiting bus while simultaneously trying to control it with one hand and battling the wind over control of my umbrella with the other.

And then I snapped. Right in the middle of the intersection. In front of a church.

"Fucking rain! Fucking trip!" I screamed like a lunatic into the Sunday-morning streets.

I was ready to collapse and let the rain and the wind sweep me into a sewer.

The foul weather had exhausted me, but so had the responsibility of caring for my mother. I was wiped from being in charge of every single detail of this trip and having to undertake every request, errand, and duty every single day and every single hour of that day. Any time I had to myself was used to recharge my patience and energy. I did not even have the luxury of wearing myself out; someone else was taking care of that! How do people care for loved ones around the clock without going completely mad?

By the time I reached the bus my fury was as apparent as my drenched appearance. My hair was matted to my skull, and my mascara must have looked like skid marks on my cheeks. I'm sure I looked like a madwoman.

The bus driver was waiting by the luggage hold to take the walker from me, but instead of handing it to him I swung the walker and threw it as hard as I could into the hold. I wanted to smash it to bits. I was angry at it, angry that my mother's life had come to the point of having to depend on it, angry that it now exerted control over me.

"We held the bus for you," the young tour guide said sweetly as I heaved myself up the steps of the bus, water squishing from the sides of my shoes.

"No you didn't," I snapped back. "We waited an hour in this weather for *you*. Could you not have had the decency to phone the hotel to say you were going to be late?"

I glanced down the aisle. A busload of dark, murderous eyes stared back at me, eyes that said they had no patience for a cranky passenger holding up their tour.

"Oh well, we're here now," Mom said nervously in a sing-song voice, patting my arm as I sloshed into the seat beside her. "You can sit back and relax for a change."

Well, what can I say? When you travel with a person who has a disability, one of you has to be the bitch, and it most certainly isn't the person with the disability.

One of the things I was discovering on this trip was my mother's chipper attitude. For the most part she was unfailingly happy and easygoing. A gentle, almost beatific smile was always on her face—even when she was in pain. Except for the first day or two and the odd seat belt infraction since, which I put down to forgetfulness rather than recalcitrance, she had been compliant to a fault.

This was not the mother I remembered from my childhood.

I remembered a distracted, intense, on-the-go woman who had no time to join me in the sandbox and no interest in dressing up Barbie dolls. My mother-daughter "quality time" was spent accompanying her to the grocery store or to an interview she had to do for a story she was working on. She did not approve of idleness; our family was in a constant state of motion. Now, in Italy, she was different. She was urging *me* to relax and slow down. Who was this woman and where had she been during my childhood?

During our travels through Italy everyone loved Mom. They found her refreshing—even inspiring, according to a few people. They marvelled at the way she persevered despite her physical limitations and how engaged she seemed.

I, however, was the riled, harried daughter, the woman with the pinched face, the snapping voice, the set-in-stone itinerary to follow, the one *in charge*. At which point during our lives had we swapped roles?

Several months earlier I had been out with a friend for a drink when I realized to my alarm that my posture was exactly like my mother's: leaning across the café table with my elbows resting on it, slowly rubbing the palms of my hand and then aligning my fingertips to form a dome. My head-nods and some of my verbal responses to my friend's conversation were my mom's to a T. I looked at my hands and fingers and realized they were the same shape as my mother's, right down to the nail shape.

I immediately shifted my body in the chair to settle into un-Mom-like poses—hanging an arm over the back of the chair and swinging one leg over the other, or twisting to one side of the chair, arm bent on the chair back to support my tilted head in my hand. I have no idea what my friend must have thought about these sudden, frantic contortions.

Now, with Mom beside me on the coach heading to Pompeii, I glanced down at the backs of my hands and noticed with quiet alarm the ropy veins that were lurking beneath my thinning, somewhat crepey skin. Oh Jesus. I turned my head slightly to look at Mom and thought of the White Stripes' song "I'm Slowly Turning Into You", a ditty that reminds us that the traits we despise or ridicule in others are often the traits we possess ourselves.

195

THE CLOSER our tour bus got to Naples, the denser and more maddening the traffic became. The autostrada was a mess, as small trucks refused to yield enough space for a large bus to change lanes, and cars darted in and out erratically without signalling (an infraction that should be punishable by death, in my opinion). How the bus driver managed it without becoming unhinged was a mystery to me. Traffic around Naples, I had been warned, is the worst in the country, perhaps on the planet, and the unanimous advice—from friends, guidebooks, television programs, and newspaper reports— had been to avoid Naples like the plague.

The traffic wasn't the only drawback.

"Don't go to Naples," an Italian friend had told me. "If you do, be careful. Neapolitans are always out to screw you."

With a ringing endorsement like that, I had without a smidgen of regret nixed Naples from our travel plans.

"It's too bad we're not going to Naples," pouted Mom, looking beyond the gridlocked traffic and suicidal driving habits in front of us.

"It's a dangerous place," I told her.

"Nonsense," she scoffed.

Uh oh. I knew what was coming. She was going to try and wheedle a trip to Naples out of me.

Before she could open her mouth I managed to divert her attention with a loud "Whoa! Did you see that?" as the bus driver deftly nosed his shiplike vehicle into a four-foot opening in the bumper-to-bumper logjam, bypassing the mayhem and hitting the accelerator.

I suppose you have to expect traffic like this in a place where 6 million people live in the most unstable volcanic area on the planet (second place goes to Sicily's Mount Etna) and where the evacuation plan states quite plainly that it can only reasonably save 600,000 of them. In other words, if the Gulf of Naples is the epicenter of volcanic disaster, it is also the epicenter of denial.

Back in Roman times, folks who lived in the vicinity of Vesuvius had no idea their mountain was a luxuriant forested bomb. All they saw was a staggeringly impressive landmark: Before its infamous eruption, Vesuvius measured about 6,500 feet; today it is just over 4,000 feet, having literally blown its head off more than fifty times since the Big One in AD 79.

In AD 62 an earthquake had rumbled through these parts, an early warning signal for what was to come, but back then people didn't know about earthquakes. They went about their daily life unaware of the magma huffing and puffing beneath the surface, until August 24, AD 79, when the pressure came to a terrifying climax just as everyone was polishing off their pastrami sandwiches and preparing to bed down for siesta.

The eruption first manifested itself as a silent, gigantic ash column four miles high, resembling a nuclear mushroom cloud. Then, with a massive deafening boom—representing the power of three atomic bombs—it tore away a mile-long stretch of one side of the mountain and unleashed a ferocious combination of fireworks, bubbling mud, poison gas, lava,

white-hot stones, and ash. Many of the townspeople bolted
for the caves along the shoreline and the lower levels of their
homes to wait out the storm.

Over the next twelve hours pumice and ash rained down
on the city of Pompeii and the nearby seaside resort of Herculaneum. When it stopped, both places had disappeared
from the face of the earth, and the coastline around Naples
had been totally reconfigured. Lava covered everything and
had consumed almost all of the towns' 25,000 people. So
profound was the horror of this event that no attempt was ever
made to rebuild either town; they were left as graveyards.

In the late 18th century, archaeologists accidentally discovered Herculaneum and Pompeii under about eighty feet
of ash and stone—roughly the height of a four-storey building. Today the two sites compose the most fascinating tourist
attractions anywhere, not so much because of the ruins, which
are rather incredible, but because of the way tour guides talk
about "the eruption of '79" like it was 1979.

Our bus rolled into the parking lot and deposited us
smack-dab in the midst of a raft of souvenir stalls that jammed
the entrance to the ruins of Pompeii.

"Do you think you can manage this?" I asked Mom skepti-
cally as we regarded the long walk from the parking lot to the
ruins proper.

"I'll see how far I can get with my walker," she said calmly.
"If it gets difficult I'll just turn around and come back here.
You go on ahead."

We were each given a headset and a small receiver that could
pick up our tour guide's patter as we surged through antiquity.

"I don't want to listen to anyone," said Mom, handing the
headset back to me. "I just want to look."

She made it as far as the entrance to the first attraction, the small, thousand-seat Odeon. She scanned the theater's ruins, gave me a been-there-done-that look, pointed her walker in the direction of the coach parking lot and the souvenir kiosks, and toddled off.

As our tour group moved to the colonnaded remains of Pompeii's gymnasium, our guide suddenly raised her arm for silence and gave me a puzzled look.

"Where is your mother?" her booming voice crackled through the receivers and headsets.

"Don't worry about her," I replied buoyantly, in an effort to make nice after my earlier tirade. "She travels at her own pace."

All heads in the group swiveled toward me and emitted the sort of glare reserved for child abusers and death-camp commandants. I used the next few moments to become engrossed in the contents of my purse until the group moved off to consider my punishment.

We shuffled through bathhouses; we saw bake ovens and frescoes, chariot-rutted roads, and roadside *tabernae* and *thermopolia* (the Roman equivalent of fast-food joints). There were gracious homes with atria and tidy courtyards with wells, fountains, and chapels. Mosaics and intricate tile work framed gardens, doorways, and pools. A plethora of sculptures, bronzes, and friezes testified to the importance and proliferation of art and architecture in Pompeii. It really was a remarkable place.

The city was also prolific when it came to sex. The Aussie I had met the day before in the Sorrento *gelateria* had been right: Pompeii had quite the booming brothel trade. The brothel we toured, the Lupanare (sex wolves, anyone?) had ten rooms on two floors, each kitted out with a single stone bed. That couldn't have been comfortable. The front hall was decorated with a series of colorful frescoes that, upon closer inspection, revealed explicit advertisements for the various services this particular establishment offered. Would you prefer your sex doggie-style? Standing? Crouching? Missionary? Perhaps a little fellatio with your threesome?

While the others in our tour group obediently filed upstairs to check out the other rooms, I hung back and studied the frescoes, tallying my personal expertise and wondering whether prostitution would have been a suitable career path for me.

After two hours our group circled back to the parking lot. I spied Mom trolling the souvenir stalls. She did not look happy.

"This is a very dirty place," she scowled at me with disapproval. "They have posters and statues of a man with a very long, um..."

"Penis?" I asked, picking up a small statue of Priapus from one of the souvenir tables. All around us were posters, key fobs, pens, calendars, statues of every size of Priapus and his impressive organ.

"Oh, it's disgusting," she said, shaking her head and scrunching up her nose.

"You could give these to the ladies in your bridge club," I teased. "They'd appreciate this kind of souvenir, don't you think?"

"Really! What an awful thing to suggest," she snorted. "Put it down."

My eye fell on a series of fridge magnets replicating the erotic brothel scenes I had admired earlier. I collect interesting fridge magnets during my travels, and these would have been perfect. But Mom was hovering. If she caught me buying them there would be no end to her nagging about how such a purchase was indicative of my moral decline.

"Actually," I began, still holding the statue of Priapus and adopting a scholarly look, "There's an interesting story here. This guy was the Greek god of fertility for..."

"Oh really, Jane."

Mom spun around her walker, flicked her head, and marched away.

After lunch—and it would have been a good pizza had the rain not intercepted it during the waiter's journey to our *al fresco* table—the tour bus took off for Vesuvius. Clouds the color of gunmetal moved stealthily across the sky.

Turning into an upscale residential area, our bus followed a paved, tree-lined road upward and ever upward. My ears popped several times during the ascent, while Mom remained resolutely still, eyes closed, as the hulking bus rounded hair-pin turns. Mom is not a fan of heights. I tried to interest her in the dense pine forests that lined the road opposite the sheer cliff or in the profusion of broom that appeared to be mere weeks away from blooming into its distinctive yellow flowers. She refused to open her eyes.

Gradually the bucolic green gave way to a barren moon-scape of gray, black, and brown, where thick, dark ropes of lava from the last eruption, in 1944, had cooled into shapes that resembled massive pythons rippling beneath the surface of the earth. Craggy, misshapen rocks lay exhausted on a landscape that had been battered and beaten to within an inch of its life.

"If you want to see the crater you will have to hike to it— it will take about a half hour—and it will cost you an extra six euros," announced the guide as the bus pulled into an almost empty parking lot.

I leaped out of my seat. A long walk was precisely what I needed.

"You're going?" gasped Mom, grabbing my arm. "Don't fall in!"

I was the first off the bus and strode excitedly toward the entrance gate. At the turnstile I looked behind me to see how many of my fellow busmates were also taking the challenge.

Not one. I could not believe it. I was about to stomp back to chastise the lot of them when two figures morosely descended from the bus. I think their spouses had shamed them into it.

I paid my entrance fee and set off through thick fog on a barren path of reddish-brown dirt that, as I could faintly make out, switched back and forth to the summit.

It was a spooky walk. Occasionally the ominous silence was broken by the skittering of small pumice rock. I picked up a few pieces and stuffed them into my coat pocket as souvenirs.

I passed groups of young teenagers on a school trip, wearing the bored, blasé expression of a generation that requires constant stimulation. It is a sad day when you cannot get kids excited about walking up the side of a volcano. This particular group was milling around a rest stop braying for Cokes. Please, God, I muttered, let the volcano burp right now. God wisely ignored my supplication.

Before I knew it I had reached the top and the gaping crater. Bulbous, gnarly rocks had risen haphazardly around the perimeter. Through wispy threads of fog I spied a few patches of snow on the floor of the crater—a good sign, I reasoned.

I imagined the site in full explosion—angry blasts of lava, rocks being hurtled in every direction, the roar of the eruption. It reminded me of past arguments with my mother. And now here it was, dried out, benign, exhausted.

It is not readily apparent when you visit the crater, especially in inclement weather, but Vesuvius is heavily monitored by the Osservatorio Vesuviano in Naples. Seismic measuring stations, GPS and satellite imaging, ground-measurement radar, and chemical analysis of the gases arising from the fumaroles and vents are all used to track magma activity. This information would at least give people a head start in case Vesuvius wakes up.

Scientists figure Vesuvius is having a fifty-year rest, which means it is somewhat overdue to blow. Time to dust off the evacuation plan, although that is little consolation. The plan states that it would take a week to ten days to evacuate the entire population in and around Naples. Well, that sealed my decision: There was no way we were going into Naples.

"A week seems like a long time when you consider how much Vesuvius destroyed in just half a day back in '79," I said to our young tour guide once we were back on board the bus.

"They are trying to get people to move out of the *zona rossa,* the red zone—the area around the mountain," she said. "They have offered them money to leave."

"And do they take it?" I asked as our coach descended from the desolate summit and reentered the leafy, placid life of the world at sea level.

"Not many do. People are stubborn here," she said with an apologetic smile and that Neapolitan shrug that conveys, "What can you do about it?"

The participants of the Second International Conference on Early Warning in 2003 decided to get busy on improvements to the evacuation plan. "The final objective is that in about twenty to thirty years the lead time will be reduced to two to three days," it reads.

That night, safely back in Sorrento, Mom and I dined on the top floor of the Hotel Mediterraneo, directly across the Gulf of Naples from Vesuvius. The mountain's peak was now veiled in a cloud. A prettier scene could not be imagined as the pink-orange of sunset intermingled with the fading blue sky. A dinner cruise ship glided peacefully in the Gulf as the twinkling lights of Naples began to light up the coastline.

Amid such beauty is it any wonder the Italian soul is lulled into complacency? Volcanoes, schmolcanoes.

12

Viterbo

IF I'D told her once, I'd told her a hundred times. "After Sorrento we are going to Viterbo. We are spending three weeks there, and Colin is visiting us for three days."

We were at the halfway mark of our trip, and I reckoned that a brief interlude with Colin would smooth the increasingly ragged interactions with Mom. Yet Mom persisted in maintaining a mental block about Viterbo. How many times did I have to repeat myself?

Of all places, I figured Viterbo would be a surefire hit with her. The charming 13th-century town house I had found for us was right smack-dab in Viterbo's San Pellegrino district—the medieval quarter, according to the Internet description. Its owner, who lived in the U.K., had supplied me with lots of information about both the town and the house. She had elderly parents, too, she had said, and was sensitive to my mother's needs.

As for Viterbo itself, the place positively oozed religious history. It is located about seventy miles northwest of Rome and once vied with the capital as the official papal residence. It was where popes and cardinals went when the political intrigues in Rome got too hot. The word "conclave" was coined in Viterbo; Thomas Aquinas preached from Viterbo's pulpit; and Frederick Barbarossa, the Holy Roman Emperor from 1122 to 1190, walked its streets. When Franco Zeffirelli was looking for a medieval location for his 1968 film *Romeo and Juliet,* he chose Viterbo over fair Verona.

With the added promise of antique stores right outside our front door, I knew this would be the perfect place for Mom. For me it would be a chance to give up driving for a while and immerse myself in small-town Italy, to put down temporary roots that might—who knew?—one day turn into permanent ones. I could hardly wait to get there, even if my travelling companion seemed certifiably amnesiac about the idea.

The sun was shining as we made our way up the A1 auto-strada. Traffic was light, the drive was relaxing, and we had not made any wrong turns. Mom was unusually quiet, the result of not getting her way.

"Why are we going to Viterbo?" she asked for the umpteenth time.

For Christ's sake!

"Why do you keep asking me that question?"

"Because you didn't consult me on this."

"That's crap," I retorted. "You told me you were leaving all the plans up to me. I told you about Viterbo. I showed you pictures of the place we're renting. Why are you suddenly surprised by all this? And how come you're questioning our plans now? This was booked months ago."

She didn't answer. She set her jaw and stared out the window.

When we entered Viterbo I followed the signs to the *centro storico* until we arrived on Via San Pellegrino. The cobblestone street narrowed until it looked as if it could no longer handle vehicular traffic. I pulled to the side of a small, deserted piazza, deciding that the prudent thing was to set out on foot to locate our accommodation.

"You stay put," I instructed Mom with as much good humor as I could muster given that she was being totally recalcitrant. "According to the directions, it's not far from here."

On a dark sliver of a partially covered street a few short blocks from where I parked the car, I found Signora Marconi's home; Signora Marconi was the keeper of the key to the house when its owner was not in residence. I knocked on the door. A tall man answered. It quickly became apparent that neither Signor nor Signora Marconi understood English.

I pulled out my phrase book. As usually occurs in these instances, I could immediately call to mind phrases such as *"Voglio fare l'amore con te"* (I want to make love to you) but not, "Hi, I'm the person who rented the town house over on such-and-such street. May I please have the key?"

Eventually I was able to make the couple understand why a weary Canadian was standing at their door. Signora Marconi grabbed her black sweater and the house key and led me back up the street to Via San Pellegrino, across to the next block, then down another wedge of cobblestone.

An ominous feeling began to gather in my stomach the farther we progressed down the tomblike lane. The cobblestones were rough like cobblestones are, only a bit worse. I wondered whether Mom's walker was equipped with shock absorbers.

The distance down the street was not far for an able-bodied person, but for an old gal with dodgy mobility it would be like an obstacle course. Oh dear, I thought.

"*Essa,*" said Signora Marconi, pointing out the town house. Its obvious charm was muscled out by the horror of a dozen or so steep steps to the front door. Oh shit.

"Now, calm down," I told myself. "Let's reserve judgment until we see inside."

But within seconds of stepping over the threshold I knew. This would definitely not work out for Mom. At all.

The town house had two bedrooms: one on the lower level and one on the upper level. Mom would have to sleep on the pullout sofa in the kitchen—on the main level—if she was to avoid steps inside. I could already hear her loud, defiant protestations. At least there were laundry facilities and a bathroom on the main level.

I pretended to listen while Signora Marconi explained in Italian how to work the heating system while I tried to come up with a way to sell this arrangement to Mom. It wasn't like we had an alternative.

In the kitchen a black iron spiral staircase led to a loft bedroom. Ah yes, the loft bedroom. From the moment I had viewed images of it on the Internet I had dreamed of this loft with its exposed ancient stone walls and angled roof lines. I had already claimed it as my nest for three weeks and imagined Colin and me spending some serious cuddling time there.

I made my way up the steps eager to get a real-life glimpse of the loft. I craned my neck, and BANG! The crown of my head made contact with the sharp edge of one of the iron risers.

A sledgehammer of pain ripped into me, setting off weeks of pent-up stress. I burst into wild sobs. Signora Marconi stood awkwardly, her hands folded in front of her, not know-ing where precisely to look at this moment, or whether to comfort me or wait out my tears. I tried to compose myself, but each time I did, another wave of convulsive sobs over-whelmed me.

Through the blurry film of tears I spied a small welcome basket thoughtfully prepared for our arrival by the town house owner: maps, crackers, a letter with my name on it, and a bottle of red wine. I managed to tamp down the urge to grab the bottle, smash its neck, and empty its contents into my giz-zard. Instead, I picked up the map of Viterbo and the letter, and turned to leave.

Signora Marconi and I walked hurriedly back to her home. We each tried to make small talk but neither of us could put our sentiments into words that were understandable to the other. Besides, I was holding back the emotional floodgates, and every time I opened my mouth it seemed another round was rising in my throat. I tried desperately to figure out what to do next.

At Signora Marconi's home her teenage daughter, who spoke the barest amount of English, explained on behalf of her mother that parking was not allowed anywhere near Viterbo's medieval quarter. Mom and I would have to park outside the district and cart our luggage in on foot. This situation was get-ting worse by the moment. I told them as carefully and clearly as I was able that the town house would not work out.

"*Non solo uno notte,*" I said. Not even one night. I told Signora Marconi's daughter that I would call the owner that evening and explain the situation.

I returned to the car and found Mom in the same position I had left her—sitting ramrod straight, purse clutched on her lap, a grim, stony look on her face. I got into the car and made sure the windows were tightly rolled up. Then I let loose another round of uncontrollable, convulsive sobs.

They were sobs of disappointment, but also of exhaustion—a larger explosion of pent-up frustration, weariness, self-pity, and sleep deprivation than I had unleashed in Sorrento. I was tired. Tired of driving all over goddamn Italy and maneuvering our car through smaller and smaller towns with increasingly narrower, tighter roads, dodging pedestrians; tired of being responsible for directions, accommodations, and restaurants and for conducting all our business in Italian, making sure the itinerary flowed, and troubleshooting when it did not. I was tired of the crappy weather, the crappy food—I would have killed for a big salad with something more than iceberg lettuce.

Mom had offered to take off a bit of the pressure by doing some of the driving and letting me catnap instead. And that might have been an option had I wanted to end up in Slovakia or, worse, a ditch. Right now, all I could think about was that a big chunk of our plans, including our accommodation, were suddenly down the drain.

"You poor dear," said my mother, patting my arm stiffly. "I knew it wouldn't work out."

Well, thanks. That just made me feel a ton better.

"What are we going to do now?" I wailed. "We were supposed to stay here for three weeks and now we have nothing else booked."

"We're going to find a hotel," Mom said matter-of-factly. "Start the car and just drive. We'll find one."

After a couple of inquiries and many rejections, we landed at the four-star Hotel Nibbio, just outside Viterbo's fortress walls. It did have a room for us, but it lost a star when no one helped us with our luggage. Parking was in a rear laneway, but despite there being a convenient door to the hotel from the laneway, patrons were not allowed to use it—even to convey luggage. It made no sense at all. The hotel also had no wine bar and no restaurant. Deduct two more stars.

My first call was to the owner of the Viterbo town house. I explained to her why it could not work out for us. She kindly agreed to a refund.

The next call was to Colin, who was due to visit us later that week. The plan had changed, I told him weepily, and at the moment I did not have an alternate one.

I made a third call to an acquaintance I had run into in Toronto a few months earlier who was now living in Italy. Sofia had invited me to come and stay with her and her husband. Rarely do I take up people's kind offers of hospitality, especially those I barely know, but that was about to change.

"You must come and stay with us," Sofia enthused on the phone when I told her of our predicament. "When can you come?"

"How about tomorrow?" I asked boldly.

"Tomorrow won't be convenient, I'm afraid," she said apologetically. "Our car's in being repaired. The day after?"

Done.

I called down to the hotel's front desk and told them we would be staying an extra night. It would give me a chance to come up with a Plan B—and perhaps a Plan C.

Mom and I ordered pizza and wine from a nearby restaurant and brought it to our room.

One of the things Mom and I had discussed when we first planned this trip was to use our time together to air past grievances and come to an understanding and acceptance of our stormy past. I had asked her to come up with three things about me that had gnawed at her over the years. I said I would do likewise about her.

"Well," Mom had harrumphed defensively. "You won't have much of a list when it comes to me because I was a perfect mother."

Now as we sat in silence pulling apart the pizza I figured, well, there's no time like the present to get a start on this discussion.

"Remember that list of three things I asked you to come up with?" I finally asked. "Feel like talking about it now?"

Without batting an eye or questioning what I was talking about, Mom snapped open her purse, pulled out a small piece of white paper—it looked as if it had been folded and refolded many times—and plunged right in.

"First of all, you were indifferent to me and to your father when you were growing up," she began, without so much as a preface to her remarks. "You never listened to our advice. You were always telling us to shut up. You were so single-minded."

I opened my mouth to respond, but she was already on item number two.

"Second, you changed once you came home from university. It was Thanksgiving weekend, your first year in Ottawa. You were never the same to us.

"Third, your choice of husbands. You never listened to us. And the result? Well, you made some very poor choices."

I glanced at the bottle of wine. I was the only one drinking, but it looked as if this discussion could outlast its contents.

"Even when you were little you never bonded with us," she continued, gathering steam and changing the rules of

engagement by broaching item number four. "Your independence was hurtful. Whenever we went on holidays to a cottage
you would find another family on the beach and stick with
them. You completely ignored us."

I did?

"What did you do about it?" I asked. Obviously I could not
recall those instances.

"What *could* we do?" she said, shaking her head. "We
tried to laugh it off, chalk it up to the fact that this was just
your personality. But it caused us a lot of pain. You really hurt
your father."

Oh. OK. She's playing the dad card now. To undo me
completely when she makes a point my mother needs only to
mention my father.

Tears filled my eyes, and the nerve endings in my nose
began to tingle as if it was being pricked by tiny needles.

I missed him all over again. Like my mother Dad had been
strict and formal, but unlike my mother he could tell when my
teenage soul was hurting, and he would sit down on the edge
of my bed to soothe my wailing. He handled my outbursts by
lowering his voice and saying in a steady tone, "Now, Jane..."
My mother's approach was to match my outburst in both
volume and accusations. Whereas my dad was open to reason,
my mother considered reason a tactic used by children to
undermine parental power.

How I wished my dad were here now, not just to referee
this conversation but to be in Italy with us.

The wine was taking effect. It wasn't good wine, it was
bitter and heavy tasting. I reminded myself not to be bitter and
heavy in this conversation.

"Well, let's talk about that fourth point," I said, trying to handle this in a mature and upbeat manner. "I was three years old at the time, wasn't I? I can't explain how or why I behaved the way I did then."

It was a perfect opportunity to suggest to Mom that more hugging and less reprimanding on her part might have helped, but that would have been a criticism of her parenting skills. I did not want to turn the discussion into a tennis match, with each of us firing killer serves at the other. I was prepared to accept my share of the blame and acknowledge my imperfections, and I wanted her to do likewise. But she is a tough, unforgiving warrior and when she prepares for battle she aims to win.

I soldiered on.

"As for your second point, about my apparent change in behavior when I returned home from university that particular Thanksgiving," I said. "I do remember that weekend very clearly, but how is it possible for us to recall this one episode from two totally different perspectives?

"It was the first time I felt as if you and Dad were treating me like an adult. I was thrilled by that. I had great philosophical discussions with Dad that weekend. I can't remember about what exactly—maybe it was religion or an upcoming federal election—but I do remember the three of us sitting in the family room and all of us talking so sensibly and openly. I saw it as a watershed in our relationship. When I returned to Ottawa I told my friends what a great time I had had."

I took a deep breath.

"To address your third point, concerning my choice of husbands, well, I have no defense there," I said. "At the time they seemed like the right choice. They were both good and decent men. Relationships blossom for a reason, and they self-destruct for another reason. I wasn't perfect either. Every one of us has a different path to walk."

"Well, you're on a very crooked path," Mom replied tersely.

I had no energy left to argue. Wine and weariness were overtaking me.

"I'm sorry," I slurred in surrender. "Sorry for everything. I have no explanation for any of it. I'm just sorry. And it's true that I was—that I am—single-minded. I don't quite know how that happened."

"I guess it's time for bed, then," said Mom primly.

We embraced awkwardly, kissed each other good night, and turned out the lights.

In the darkness the conversation looped through my mind. It wasn't so much the content that exhausted me, it was the fact that we had to have this conversation. As in so many such conversations in the past, I ended up apologizing for being myself, which is rather ironic given that my mother contributed half the genetic material that was used to create me. I have some of her fighting spirit, but I also have my dad's sense of when to throw in the towel.

Why couldn't I just get past the fact that ours was a dysfunctional relationship and leave it at that? It's not like we were the only ones. Why have these conversations in the first place? What was the point of dredging up the past other than to make me feel belittled? I always ended up apologizing as if the whole mess were entirely my fault. Why didn't I have the guts to fire back and say what was really on my mind, tell her that she had been a demanding mother who rarely found a positive thing to say about me?

I had learned to tiptoe around so many things, to ignore the poison arrows just to keep peace. All we knew now was

214

how to tiptoe, not to walk with the confidence that comes with unconditional love. Our self-restraint had only built up pressure and stress over the years. Like Etna and Vesuvius we heaved and boiled under the surface of a benign facade.

Before the wine knocked me out for the evening I thought of something else. Mom had not asked about my three grievances. I wondered if she ever would.

THE NEXT morning I decided to give Viterbo a second chance. Mom wanted the morning to herself to shower and do her hair, so I set off alone to explore.

The air was sunny and cool as I crossed the Piazza della Rocca, the old city's main square. Most Italian towns began at the tops of hills and developed outward and downward. In contrast, Viterbo's took root on a small plain between two substantial hills and developed outward and upward.

I randomly selected one of the narrow streets that emanated like streamers from the square and gradually descended through the various strata of Viterbo's history: 18th century, Renaissance, medieval. I found Via San Pellegrino and retraced my steps to the town house we had intended to rent. At the foot of the stone steps leading up to the front door I tried to will it to work for us, but it was not to be. Mom's physical condition—and perhaps her emotional one—precluded any thought of adapting to the situation. That much was clear to me. At this point in her life she needed modern hotels with lifts and accessible bathrooms. Try getting that in Italy.

I walked back to Via San Pellegrino and wandered along the cobblestone street to the small Piazza San Pellegrino. There I sat down on a church step and surveyed my surroundings. Everything was built from volcanic, gray *peperino* stone—the large smooth cobbles of the street, the walls, the fountains, the churches. Black wrought iron and the occasional wood-plank door provided the only relief to a drab, morose palette.

There was an abundance of Romanesque arches, covered balconies, nooks and crannies, and simple but elegant architectural detailing. I loved that. But there was also an unsettling stillness to the place. When a sound arose, it cut the air like a shock wave and ricocheted off the high walls. The beating wings of pigeons sounded like a flock of pterodactyls; the brief whine of a circular saw sounded like someone screaming. I heard a man whistling for his dog, a sound that in the English countryside would have sounded friendly but here was abrupt, piercing. Water trickling from a nearby fountain sounded like blood dripping.

I decided to have a look in some nearby shops, none of which had signs indicating the manner of business being conducted inside. I ventured into an antique shop and found its owner deep in conversation, sotto voce, with a client or friend. Everyone seemed to speak in hushed tones here. My presence was acknowledged with a wary *"giorno"* and a too-long stare, and then the whispering resumed.

In another shop I found a collection of beautiful, small blue-and-green majolica plates for five euros each. Mom collects majolica, and for a moment I considered buying them—as a peace offering or as a distraction, I'm not sure which. Then I reconsidered the purchase, mainly because the owner seemed agitated by my presence, as if having a customer in his shop were highly irregular.

I ducked into a third antique shop. There I was tempted by a bed tester of ornate gilded wood, from which hung about twelve inches of gloriously faded fabric. But again the owner eyed me so contemptuously that I left empty-handed and with the strong impression that Viterbo's shopowners could use a lesson in customer service.

I proceeded along Via San Pellegrino to see if a cheerier welcome could be found. At another piazza a gang of geezers, whispering among themselves like spies, regarded me with such dark and sour-looking expressions—they actually stopped talking and stared directly at me—that I did not feel comfortable venturing farther. What a grumpy town! It was a shame, really, because I completely missed two buildings I had hoped to see—the Cathedral of San Lorenzo and the Papal Palace, of which I had read so much. Instead, I retraced my steps rather quickly out of the Dark Ages.

I found myself in Piazza Dante Alighieri but saw no sign or memorial to the poet, just a plaque explaining that the church there was the last valuable piece of Romanesque architecture. I did come across another wee church, however, with a notation indicating that it was the Chiesa di San Marco and that it had been consecrated in 1198 by Pope Innocent III.

I wanted desperately to fall in love with Viterbo, because I adore medieval art and architecture, but this place wasn't throwing me a bone. I walked around some more and came to the conclusion that Viterbo was fine for a few days but not for three weeks. A week of this, and I would be resorting to self-flagellation as entertainment.

Up the steps from Via Cavour a very pretty building of *peperino* stone caught my eye. Its main entrance on the upper level was accessed by a side staircase supported by a sweeping arch on one side without any visible underpinning on the other. It was quite the engineering puzzle. A plaque explained that this was Casa Poscia, built in the 14th century, and that it possessed the best preserved example in all of Viterbo of a *profferlo,* an outside staircase with a small arcade beneath it. It was a decorative feature that offered privacy and protection to the main house, which was accessed from the upper level only, while providing commercial space at street level for the homeowner.

Casa Poscia itself had an endearing history. It was known as *la casa della Bella Galiana* and had been the home of the most beautiful girl in Viterbo. Hundreds of years ago young swains would loiter in front of this lovely structure with the hope of catching a glimpse of the fair maiden.

And how apropos that today beneath Casa Poscia's arch, in the space where the father of the most beautiful girl in Viterbo once conducted his business, is a lingerie shop. The meshing of the modern and the medieval was alternately fascinating and amusingly jarring. Shops with such names as Pink, Lunatic, Barghini, and Bum Bum occupied space in buildings that six or seven hundred years ago might have sold quills, spices from the Orient, or a cup of mead to a tired traveller.

I continued making my way back to the hotel past shops displaying goods fit for modern Medicis—sumptuously trimmed brocade bedding, tightly tailored dark navy power suits, and important-looking leather handbags and briefcases.

When I strode into the hotel Mom was sitting in the lobby reading a paperback and looking very elegant and coiffed.

"I dyed and set my hair," she said proudly. "How do I look?"

"Lovely. Why don't we go for a drive and do some sightseeing?" I suggested.

The destination I had in mind was the Terme dei Papi, located on the outskirts of Viterbo. In days of yore it was the go-to spa for popes and other ecclesiastical figures when things got stressful in Rome.

A huge sign at the entrance of Terme dei Papi's sprawling American-style parking lot announced a client list that included Dante and Michelangelo.

"I do like the parking lot," enthused Mom. "Now this feels like home."

The waters in Terme dei Papi are drawn from the Bullicame hot springs, as they were in the third century by the Etruscans, and its mineralized mud, enriched with sulfur, magnesium, and sodium bicarbonate, is used in the spa's treatments. These days a shuttle bus arrives daily from Rome with a load of stressed souls looking for rejuvenation in the 100,000-square-foot thermal pool. Not surprisingly, the pool was closed the day of our visit.

Disappointingly, little evidence remains of Terme dei Papi's ancient past. The place is large and sterile looking, cleansed of its medieval architecture and replaced with the usual charmless, mall-like design. A handful of relics—marble bathtubs, sinks, the occasional Swede and German—are found around the complex as reminders of the pedigree.

I noticed a surprising number of men checking in at the reception desk, their tanned skin and trim physiques indicating that the Italian concept of the *bella figura* is as much a male phenomenon as a female one.

In the sparkling, antiseptic lobby, Mom and I sat down on a modern, white faux-leather sofa. I grabbed a brochure and ran down the list of services and treatments. They were not like any I had encountered at North American spas. In addition to the usual mud baths and massages you could have a Pap test (twenty-six euros), colonoscopy (fifty-two euros), vaginal irrigation (thirteen euros), or ear flushing (twenty euros). They didn't do manicures, waxing, hair, or makeup, which was exactly what I was in the mood for. Vaginal irrigation was definitely out of the question.

220

"Let's see if we can book something," I suddenly said to Mom. "We've been driving for three weeks. We're due for some pampering. How about a mud wrap? My treat."

Before she could quibble I had launched myself toward the reception desk and booked us in for an eighty-minute treatment.

We were directed to the elevators and taken to an upper floor, then to a smaller, deathly silent reception area where we waited for our respective attendants.

"I've never done this," whispered Mom nervously. "Do you have to take off all your clothes?"

"I should hope so," I said. "A mud bath isn't much use when you're clothed."

An attractive young woman, her hair pulled tightly into a smooth pony tail—she looked like an extra in that old Robert Palmer video *Addicted to Love*—approached me. She had all the warmth of a three-day-old cadaver.

She cocked her head as a sign for me to follow her.

I smiled "see ya," to Mom and followed my attendant down the hall.

She opened the door to a spacious, utterly bland room that was tiled—walls and floors—in dull beige-pink and lit by fluorescent lights. It was kitted out with pipes, hoses, and floor drains. There was a small window at the far end and a counter and small desk area near the door. A sink and a shower stall were on one side of the room; a stainless steel table dominated the center. A humble wooden bucket, the only evidence of warmth, cowered nearby. Was I going to have a spa treatment or an autopsy?

My grim attendant ordered me to strip down and handed me a paper thong at arm's length. She directed me with brusque gestures onto the cold, hard surface of the table. I did a quick scan of the room for sharp objects. Then she filled the small wooden bucket with goop from a pump and began thickly slathering the viscous substance on me from neck to toe on both sides of my body.

I tried to summon my inner goddess, but it was difficult to do amid the attendant's constant groans. I couldn't tell whether it was the rotten-egg smell of the mud that offended her or the fact that she was mudding down flabby middle-aged bodies for a living. No part of my anatomy was deemed out of bounds, and I wondered how Mom, who shies away from stripping in a doctor's office, was handling it all.

I was glad I hadn't purchased the small plates in the Viterbo antique shop for Mom. She has enough stuff. This trip, I decided, would be about physical pampering, not about filling suitcases with more junk to sit on a shelf.

When Mom and I met up in the reception room an hour and a half later, all evidence of her ministrations from earlier that day had been undone. With hair askew and face flushed, she looked as if she had just spent an hour hoeing a field.

"What a lot of work!" she said, collapsing onto the sofa. "Taking off clothes, putting on that little paper bikini, being rolled over and wrapped up, the showering, and then getting dressed again. I'm worn out!"

That night we lay in our beds in the dark silence, waiting

for sleep to overcome our newly cleansed bodies. I was mouthing a prayer of thanks to God for keeping us safe on our journey (to me, this is like spiritual insurance coverage) and for providing us with a positive memory of Viterbo.

Out of the void came Mom's voice: "Jane, you're a pain sometimes, but life with you is never dull, that's for sure."

222   I took that as Momspeak for "thanks."

13

Foligno, Montefalco,
Santa Maria degli Angeli

WE LEFT Viterbo early the next morning and headed northeast to Foligno to accept the hospitality of someone I barely knew.

I don't like imposing on others, especially when it means upsetting their routine and scarfing food from their refrigerator. It is one thing when this behavior is visited on relatives, who on occasion deserve to be disturbed; it is entirely another thing when the victims are people you like and who you want to like you back.

"So, these are good friends of yours?" Mom asked as we sped along the highway.

"Yes," I lied.

"How long have you known them?" she inquired. "Where did you meet them? How come you have never told me about them? Why don't I know your friends?"

I started to answer, but her head was turned toward the window and I could not be certain that she was listening to me. At times she asks questions for the sake of asking them, without really caring about the answer.

I met Sofia about twenty years ago when I began frequenting Ms. Emma Designs, the small chain of clothing boutiques she owns. She is also the designer, and on the rare occasions when I found myself with money to spend on real clothes, I would visit her shop.

I was drawn to Sofia's laugh-out-loud nature and the fact that she is the antithesis of a fashion designer. No big dark glasses, outlandish clothing, or imperial attitude. She had struck me as the type who was more comfortable stomping through the countryside in rubber boots than sucking up to fashionistas. I had dropped in to her Toronto shop a few months before this trip, knowing that she had relocated somewhere in Italy and might be able to offer advice about places to see. She had suggested at the time that my mother and I come to stay with her in Italy, but the idea seemed remote. I never guessed I would have to use the phone number she gave me to call her.

Beyond that, I really knew nothing about Sofia. I prayed the visit would be favorable and that Mom would behave.

On the outskirts of Foligno we tentatively edged our car up a gravel driveway toward a broad stone farmhouse. I recognized Sofia immediately. She was wearing rubber boots.

"Welcome! *Buongiorno!*" she cried as she and her husband, Tony, came toward us with open arms. They took us in their embrace as if we were the oldest of friends.

"Are you tired from your journey?" she asked. "Do you need a rest? No? Then I hope you're hungry, because I've made lunch," said Sofia, grabbing our luggage. "Nothing fancy, just a little spaghetti."

Mom and I gave each other pained looks: Both of us were already sick of pasta.

However, as often happens when you have tired of a dish, someone will serve it up in a different way and your appetite for it returns. And so it was with Sofia's spaghetti, tossed with herbs, black olives, olive oil, and a few chopped tomatoes. We tucked into it with gusto, and after a mouthful Mom and I looked at each other long enough to acknowledge that it was the best meal we had had in Italy. After I returned to Canada, I tried to replicate this recipe many, many times, but it just never tasted as good as Sofia's.

"How did the two of you wind up in Foligno?" I asked as a basket of warm bread was passed around the table.

"Tony had a heart attack several years ago," Sofia explained. "Our doctor told us that Canadian winters aren't the best for people who have trouble breathing in cold weather. Tony is Italian by birth, so he wanted to come back to Italy. It's perfect for me, too—did you know that Italy has the best fabrics anywhere? And, of course, we both love the lifestyle here. It's not as mental as it is in Canada."

"I was a baby when my family moved to British Columbia," said Tony as he began uncorking a bottle of red wine. "The Okanagan Valley. Are you familiar with that region? My father started a vineyard there. Canada had always been my home, but when I began thinking of retirement something tugged at my soul and led me back to Italy."

He smiled.

"Wait until you taste this," he enthused, pouring into my glass something that I can only describe as liquid garnets.

"This is wine from this area. Around here you don't go to a store for wine, you go directly to the winery. These are small wineries with an equally small production."

I apologized for lacking a discerning palate when it comes to wine. I don't know why; I have certainly drunk enough of it in my time.

"Don't worry," he smiled. "It's like anything; you have to take your time learning about something to really appreciate it. It's like Foligno and all of Umbria, for that matter. It doesn't seem like much until you delve into it and learn its stories.

"That view, for instance," he said, pointing out the window to the hill opposite, where a cluster of ordinary homes had been built halfway up the hill. "If you had looked out this window early in 1997, you would have seen a medieval village. But later that year an earthquake hit this region, and it destroyed that village. It was called Capranica.

"Capranica was never anything more than an agrarian community—that hill is Mount Subasio, an area known for its rich and fertile soil. Dante mentioned it in his *Divine Comedy*. Its narrow streets, the red stone and mortar construction, its massive walls—there was a certain medieval charm to the place, which the few families that opted to stay there fought in vain to preserve."

"An earthquake? Here? What happened?" I asked, reflexively gripping the sides of my chair.

Tony circled the dining room table filling our wine glasses.

"What happened to Capranica was emblematic of what happened to many other small towns in Italy. When national governments and the European parliament decide to finance your projects, you have very little chance of calling the shots. But the residents of Capranica resisted the idea of rebuilding their town in a geologically safer area, and in the end they won. That's no mean achievement when one considers the incredible power of money these days."

"We had just bought this place, and we were in the midst of renovating it," added Sofia, her voice tinged with remnants of a German accent. "We had some damage to our home, but not much, thank God. Our contractor said that what saved the place was its strong foundation. This," she said, waving her hand around at the upper level where we were sitting, "the part that everyone sees—that can be changed and fixed because it's basically cosmetic, right? But what holds it all up, that's the critical part of a home."

227

The conversation over lunch was rapid and free ranging, and I was thoroughly enjoying it. I frequently looked over at Mom to keep her included in the discussion. Once or twice she entered the conversation with a non sequitur, the obvious clue that she could not hear a damn thing we were saying. She refuses to get a hearing aid on the grounds that it makes her look old.

Sofia and Tony were eager to hear where we had travelled in Italy. I regaled them with stories about our excursion to Sicily and shared my observations about the social division between north and south.

"There's definitely a class system in Italy based on dialects," confirmed Tony. "As recently as twenty years ago you could not get a job on RAI"—Italy's national broadcaster—"unless you had a Florentine-Roman accent. Today, you run across the odd Neapolitan who attempts to speak like a Florentine, but those distinctions are rapidly disappearing."

"The real difference between northern Italy and southern Italy," said Sofia, "has less to do with accents and economics and more to do with dynamics. The north is a matriarchal society; the south is a patriarchal one. Did you notice that?"

"Well, I saw a lot of men hanging around with each other in cafés," I replied. "Are Italian men involved at all in running a household?"

"Women have the psychological upper hand here," added Tony. "But not the legal one. The groups of men you see in cafés and the like are there because their women want them out of the way.

"Conversely, you likely saw women and children together a lot. Italian mother love is intimate, primal; it is all encompassing. It is Madonna worship on a human scale."

"Actually, for all the talk about the mother cult in Italy," Sofia cut in, "the image of the tough matriarch presiding over the Sunday meal is a fantasy now. Mama is losing her importance in the Italian family. Italy has something called the *badanti* system, in which a woman, usually from the Philippines, is hired by a family to look after Mama."

In other words, love and caregiving, like so many things in the modern world, is now subcontracted. I cast a look at Mom, who was silently mopping up her spaghetti with a slice of Sofia's bread. Would I eventually hire a stranger to look after her?

"I'm sorry," interjected Sofia, "but I have to go to work this afternoon. Did I tell you I have a shop here in Foligno now? Tony would be happy to take you sightseeing if you're up to it."

We accepted the offer heartily; after all, Tony seemed to know a lot about Italy.

I buckled Mom into the front seat of his silver Nissan and climbed into the back.

"What sort of work did you do in Canada?" I asked Tony as he started up the car.

"I was a professor of Italian Studies at the University of Toronto," he smiled.

Well. I'd hit the jackpot!

OVER THE next two days we scoured an area of Umbria that takes up less than two inches on a road map of Italy and contains more than two thousand years' worth of history.

Tony proved to be a font of knowledge and kindness. He was also skilled at navigating his way around the villages' narrow cobblestone lanes, apparently unconcerned about doing damage to his car.

"There must be a brisk trade in side-view mirror replacements in Italy," I remarked as an ancient stone wall grazed one on the passenger side. "How many of them to do you go through in a year?"

"About half a dozen," he replied with a laugh.

He applied more pressure to the gas pedal as the car nosed its way up the steep, shadowy, skinny road. Mom muttered a prayer and tilted her head against the headrest until the road levelled out at Montefalco's Piazza della Repubblica.

An azure awning over a shop window, a gleaming copper urn filled with flowers the color of sunshine, a fire-engine-red letterbox on the side of a building—all provided intense bursts of color against the bleached stone of the buildings.

"This is very much a regular working town," said Tony as he steered the car through a portal and exited the town's walls. The words "Fuck Police" had been spray painted on a metal gate. "The Slow Cities movement has spurred a tremendous migration throughout Italy back to small-town life," Tony continued.

Established several years ago in Italy to stop the unrelenting erosion of *la dolce vita* not just in Italy but throughout

Europe, the Slow Cities movement aims to improve sustainability and the quality of life of its citizens by stopping the creeping North Americanization of its cultures, and the attendant horrors of fast food, eating at your office desk, sedentary lifestyles, and rampant consumerism. It is a gentler appreciation of life, exactly the type of life the tourist brochures portray and that lulls Westerners into an idealized vision of European life—the same vision I had fixed in my mind all these years.

We sped by cascading acres of tranquil vineyards, their crops neatly lined up and cultivated to perfection. To a neat freak like me the sight of tidy rows of almost anything makes me swell with contentment.

"Why is there a rosebush planted in front of each of the rows of vines?" I asked. It seemed a curious practice; then again, maybe the Italians just like to beautify all of their surroundings.

"The rosebushes provide a litmus test for aphid infestation in the vineyards," Tony replied. "When a bush gets infested, grape growers know it's time to spray their crop."

Was there anything this man didn't know?

In Foligno, about a dozen miles from Montefalco, Tony and I settled Mom on a park bench so that he and I could take a quick walking tour of the city.

"Sorry about my Mom," I said to Tony as we set off. "She's hard of hearing, as you may have noticed, and it's really hard for her to get around. We're finding that Italy isn't really cut out for people with disabilities."

"I don't know why it's taking Italy so long in making itself accessible," he acknowledged. "The population here is aging, too—did you know that Italy has the lowest birth rate in the world? Most Italians are now over the age of fifty, but the country is just getting around to putting in ramps to help the disabled."

"If the population is so old, how come we haven't seen another person with a walker? We feel like freaks," I said as we nimbly negotiated various sidewalk obstacles and detours as a result of construction work. "People stare at my mom as if they've never seen a person with such a contraption."

"I don't know; it's not that physical disabilities are unheard of in Italy," mused Tony.

Yet, even in nontouristy Foligno, a bustling city of fifty thousand people with a largely older population, there were no signs of anyone with a physical disability—not in the streets, in the shops, or in the square. Sure, one or two people used a cane, but nothing more than that. By contrast, you cannot walk down a sidewalk in a North American town or city without encountering someone with a walker, tripping over a cluster of them parked outside a café, or being accosted by one of those motorized scooters that are quickly bringing pedestrian road rage to a new level.

Our walk took us to the expansive Piazza della Repubblica—every settlement of consequence in Italy has a Piazza della Repubblica—where groups of teens freed from school were hanging out with friends, young professionals were chatting idly with one another at café tables, young moms were pushing babes in their strollers, and older couples with the tired look of hard living etched on their faces sat side by side, seemingly oblivious to one other.

Tony pushed open a massive oak door into the Church of San Francesco. I had specifically asked him to bring me here—it is the resting place of Angela of Foligno, patron saint of fallen women and sexual temptation.

INCONTINENT ON THE CONTINENT

Hers is a story of hot sex, sudden conversion, and hard-won redemption, all things for which I have an unhealthy fascination. Born in 1248 to a wealthy family, she was married off in her midteens, at which point she proceeded to live, according to Catholic legend, "wildly, adulterously, and sacrilegiously."

There is no mention of the type of man Angela married, which might have provided a clue as to what sparked her hot, wild stray ways. He was understandably appalled at her loose behavior, but when she turned from a good-time girl into a God-time girl, he wasn't thrilled either. I suppose there is no solace in being cuckolded by God.

Angela became a mystic, bore the stigmata of Christ, and devised a thirty-step plan to spiritual salvation. Her grave inside the Church of San Francesco became the locus for a number of miracles.

There is a sense of both shock and sympathy when you read Angela's account of her sudden reversal of behavior. Here's a taste:

> And then I began to reject fine foods, fancy clothing and headdresses. But there was still shame and sorrow, because I did not yet feel any love. And I was still with my husband—and so there was bitterness when I was spoken to or treated unjustly; nevertheless, I endured as patiently as I could. And then in accordance with God's will, my mother died; she had been a great hindrance to me. Later, my husband and all my children died within a short time. And because I had already begun the way of the cross and had asked God that they should die, I felt a deep consolation following their deaths. I knew that God

had accomplished these things for me, and that my heart would always be in God's heart and God's heart would always be in mine.

Granted, praying for the deaths of your mother, your husband, and your children so that you can serve God doesn't strike me as the most positive first step to sainthood. Still, I felt sad for Angela, sad that her spiritedness—however misguided—had been tamped down, and sad that her path to redemption was littered with so much family strife and so many bodies. As I gazed upon her small shrunken body that has, for the last seven hundred or so years, been displayed under glass, I thought about family dynamics yet again and wondered whether the sacrifices Angela had made as a daughter, wife, and mother had brought her the contentment she so ardently sought.

Tony and I left Angela and returned to the energy of Foligno's streets.

Like many parts of Italy, Foligno was going through a building boom. Scaffolding covered almost every surface, and boardwalks lined the streets where infrastructure improvements were being made.

"It's all government money," said Tony above the banging of hammers and the buzz of circular saws. "They're converting palazzos into apartments and interior courtyards into parking space."

They were gorgeous, elegant buildings, and my mind leapt once again to thoughts of whether Foligno would be a good place for me to live.

We returned to the small park where we had left Mom. She was not there; she was in Tony's car. Asleep.

"Hey, wake up," I said with some embarrassment. "We're in Italy, for God's sake. Look at all this history!"

OUR DRIVE-BY history lesson continued the following day in Spello, Santa Maria degli Angeli, Assisi, Spoleto, and the unfortunately named Bastardo.

234

"The town actually took a vote to change its name," said Tony, "but decided against it."

We arrived at the Basilica of Santa Maria degli Angeli, on the outskirts of Assisi, where Saint Francis spent a good portion of his life.

Tony wanted us to see the Porziuncola ("little piece") that sits smack-dab in the center of the Basilica's nave.

"When Francis approached Pope Innocent in 1209," began Tony as we walked toward the Basilica, "he told the Pope—quite boldly and without the slightest sense of ego—that he wanted to be the church within the Church; in other words, Francis wanted to attend to the core values of the Church that he felt were being eroded. It was a rather presumptuous statement, especially to a Pope, but Francis got away with it because of his charm."

The Porziuncola is an adorable piece of architecture—it seats about twelve people—and it is the sort of stone structure you might stumble across in the woods. In fact, that's precisely what surrounded it back in AD 350 when it was built. And here's the remarkable thing about this wee church: It was not moved into the Basilica as most people assume; the soaring Basilica was constructed entirely around it.

We shuffled through the Basilica and arrived, as all visitors inevitably do, at the souvenir shop.

You have to hand it to the Catholics. Give them a saint and

they can spin a marketing sensation that defies imagination. This shop alone had plenty of Saint Francis swag: books, CDs, DVDs, postcards, calendars, wooden icons, terra-cotta icons, and rosary beads by the bundle, some with matching earrings. There were key fobs, candies, fridge magnets, crucifixes, statuettes, posters, jewelry, religious medals, candles, bookmarks, religious cards, Christmas ornaments. It was endless.

I was flipping through a clothes rack crammed with cassocks, albs, chasubles, and other religious vestments when Mom sidled over.

"Are you thinking of those for the boys?" she asked in earnest.

"Religious garments? For my sons? Seriously?" I went through them again to see if any were printed with the slogan, "My Mom visited Italy and all she got me was this lousy chasuble."

THE NEXT day we bade a hug-filled good-bye to Sofia and Tony, who in the space of two days went from being relative strangers to our new best friends. Their hospitality had offered me and my nerves a breather from driving and decision making.

"That was lovely," said Mom as we drove down our hosts' driveway. "What nice friends you have."

I smiled in a distracted way. I was preoccupied with a troubling dream I had had the night before.

In the dream, Mom was being coerced into a long-term care facility where the walls were painted that putrid shade of green that is favored by the hospital world. I was screaming at people to leave her alone, but some authority figure felt Mom needed better care than I was giving her. No matter what I said, they would not release Mom or let me talk to her alone. Instead, the people in charge formed a barrier across the long hall and walked slowly toward me, forcing me out the door.

And then my mind moved from the dream to Mom's real-world complaints. Her back was sore, she said, and her legs felt unusually heavy. Her scattering of pills continued. She seemed forgetful—not exactly disoriented but a tad out to lunch. She didn't seem interested in the sorts of things that normally grabbed her—I could actually drive past antique shops and she would not shout "STOP!"

It rattled me, this difference between how I had perceived my mother from sporadic visits and how she was when I was with her every day, all day. Had I been too busy to notice a decline in her health, or had I unconsciously avoided dealing with the reality?

As we motored along the ancient Via Flaminia toward Civita Castellana, I suddenly wanted to go home. Sure, I was tired of the driving, organizing, caregiving, and living out of a suitcase, tired of seeing Italy through a windshield. But I also wanted life with my mother to return to normal, back to when we saw each other once every few weeks, when I was so distracted by my own life that I could absolve myself of the responsibility of caring for her every day. I craved it as much as I felt ashamed for even thinking of it.

236

14

Civita Castellana, Siena, San Gimignano

A CONTRAIL WAS unzipping a clear blue, sunny sky, and that got me thinking about Colin. He was meeting us at our next stop—Civita Castellana. I wanted to get there quickly, get a hotel room, and spend a chunk of time doing some serious primping. I could feel myself deteriorating into an old hag, and I worried that I was beginning to smell like an old-folks' home.

On top of that, it had been days since Mom had made a wisecrack about my hair. Either it looked acceptable to her, which would be cause for immediate alarm, or it was in such a wretched state that she was privately hoping its appearance would cause Colin to run screaming back to England. Then she could have me all to herself.

Conspiracy theories aside—though I made a mental note to pick up some hair conditioner—I was looking forward to being off leash for a while. Colin would be a second pair of hands and a conversation buffer between my mother and me. His soft English accent makes my mother feel that she is in the presence of British royalty, and I hoped that his company would divert her attention away from me and my flaws.

I could hardly wait for his arrival. When Mom went down for a nap, Colin and I would be able to go off together and amble down twisting, romantic cobblestone lanes. We could hold hands, my hand slipping into his strong one, rather than into the hand of someone who was gripping me like a banister. I could walk at a brisk, jaunty pace, and I could do so without dragging along an annoying red walker. I would not have to brush fallen bits of lunch from someone's shirt or keep asking that someone if they needed to use the bathroom. I would be able to have a conversation without using the words "medication" and "adult diapers."

Colin was flying to Rome—he was probably boarding his plane in London at that very moment—and then catching a train to Civita Castellana, where we would rendezvous at 5:50 PM. Just in time for a candlelit dinner in some dark *osteria*. I pressed down on the accelerator pedal.

Mom and I arrived in Civita Castellana in late morning. We circled the small town center four times to find a hotel, then ventured to the outskirts across a long bridge to conduct the same search before returning to the town center and repeating the exercise. Finally I spied a tourist office. Even before I got out of the car I knew that I was just asking for disappointment.

The tourist desk was closed, said the young man with a *"Turismo"* logo on his shirt. Undeterred, I asked him to recommend a hotel.

"No," he answered. "The *turismo* office, she is closed."

"OK, but if the tourist office was open," I posed, "and someone asked you to recommend a hotel, what would you say?"

He stared at me with a stunned look, then turned to consult with his supervisor, an unhappy, irritated woman in a very tight blouse who shooed him away and eyed me with contempt.

"*Mi dispiace,*" I said softly. "*Mia madre è nella macchina, è disabile, e vorrei un hotel.*"

OK, it wasn't perfect, and I was well aware I was using my mother's disability for gain. At some point in any journey you succumb to guerilla tactics to score a smidgen of cooperation.

"Hotel Palace," the woman snapped, swatting the air in a gesture indicating that what I was looking for was outside and around a corner.

I returned to the car and set off on another round of circling the town for the elusive hotel, or any hotel for that matter. We asked people on the street. One fellow stroked his jaw as if conjuring up a distant memory, a woman shrugged her shoulders, a man in a suit looked at me as if I had just asked for heroin, and then one old chap gestured that it was just ahead. In Italy, life is conducted through gestures. If you were a blind person you would just never find anything in Italy.

"Well, how can it be?" I thought as I followed the old guy's gestures. "We've passed this way at least a dozen times. There is nothing here!"

I drove extra slowly, making sure that absolutely every establishment we passed was not a hotel. And then a small sign presented itself, with a faded arrow pointing through a small arch flanked by rounded wooden gates. It was no longer the Hotel Palace but the Relais Falisco. Well, so much for the help from Civita Castellana's tourist office.

The driveway led into a courtyard with crunchy gravel and a central fountain that was burbling excitedly. A small patio area with chairs and tables and bright white umbrellas was inviting. The hotel looked posh and held the promise of well-heated rooms, thick coverlets on the bed, and an endless supply of hot water in the bathrooms.

We booked two rooms, one for Colin and one for Mom and me.

After a quick lunch and a long, hot bath and lots of girly pampering, I set off for the train station in Civita Castellana. I had washed my hair and styled it with the hotel's blow-dryer to a smooth, glossy sheen, flipping the ends slightly. When I was not two blocks from the hotel the weather did a dramatic one-eighty, and rain began to fall. Within seconds my smooth, tidy hair sprang into a ball of frizz. I don't know why I even bothered to try in the first place.

As I made my way through town I noticed people staring at me. Passersby gave me a head-to-toe appraisal, shopowners came out from behind their counters and stood in their doorways to have a gawk, and widows flung open the shutters of their tall second-storey windows and leaned out over their sills, clutching their knitting. A few men eyed me lasciviously. It was as if someone had instigated a phone chain alerting the population to the new kid in town. Ahead of me I could see people already craning their necks in my direction as if I were an eagerly anticipated float in a parade. At one point I paused in front of a store window as if checking out the merchandise, but in reality it was to assure myself that an enormous tumor had not erupted on my face. I could not understand the unwelcome attention. It was very unsettling.

This was one of the things I learned about Italians. They stare. They stare piercingly and without shame. They stare without a care for the obvious discomfort it might cause the object of their stare, oblivious to the fact that their staring might give offense or be construed as rude by those from another culture. Italians stare, and they do so in a deeply penetrating way.

We humans rely on eye contact with our colleagues on this planet for many reasons—for affirmation, for love, for help, for camaraderie, to let our displeasure be known, to show sympathy and solidarity. Not in Italy. When an Italian stares, especially an Italian man, he's doing so for the same reason a dog licks his balls—because he can. Furthermore, he wants you to know he can. Italian stares are all about territory and power.

On the odd occasion when I was brave enough to meet their stare, they did not avert their gaze or offer a sheepish smile to acknowledge that they had been caught in the act. They stared harder and raised their chins defiantly. I suspect that staring also has something to do with the fact that people in places such as Civita Castellana do not get out a lot. They stay so rooted to their little corner of the world that the appearance of a stranger is cause for excitement—or for outright jubilation, depending on how much money you drop in their town.

I reached the small train station on the other side of a bridge that spanned an abyss. It was a weathered station, simple in a quaint sort of way. I took a seat on a bench on the platform and waited. At varying intervals, trains three or four carriages long skittered along the tracks to the station with a clickety-clackety sound and then shuddered into the station alongside the platform, rolling to a long, screeching halt. Great gusts of steam billowed out from beneath the carriages.

I imagined Colin and me running toward each other through these very clouds of steam, locking into a tight, desperate clutch and warm, nuzzling kisses.

Before long I had embroidered the scenario into the sort of
fantasy best suited for late-night TV viewing: Tender embraces
with saliva-filled kisses and much bodily groping. We would
then dash back to the hotel, hand in hand, splashing through
puddles on dimly lit streets. We would fumble with the key to
the hotel room, giggling nervously, and once inside the room
we would launch into a session of urgent, writhing lovemaking.

Well? What else are you supposed to think about at a train
station? I continued to sit on the platform bench and wait and
wait some more.

The train station attendants eyed me with bemused curiosity. Occasionally I would get up from my bench and wander
over to ask them when the next train from Rome was arriving.
They would look thoughtfully at their watches, consult the
train schedule, and murmur an expected time of arrival.

Still I waited. A handful of weather systems passed
through during that time; afternoon slipped into evening. Still
no train, no Colin.

After three hours I figured something was wrong. I
approached a new group of attendants—the original group
having finished their day's shift—and again asked when the
next train from Rome was expected.

It was from this new group that I learned there were, in
fact, two train stations in Civita Castellana. Well, please thank
the day shift for wasting my bloody time!

I stomped back to the hotel, soaked, angry, and frustrated.
I approached the front desk clerk and gave him my lament. He
produced a piece of paper and driving directions to the other
train station.

I hopped in the car and sped off. Halfway there it occurred
to me that despite the soggy paper of scrawled directions in

my hand, I had no clue where I was going. It was pitch black, it was raining, and the invention of streetlights had not yet made its way to this neck of the planet. I retraced my route to the hotel and hired a cab.

The cab driver, who mercifully spoke English, said he had, coincidentally, just received a call from someone at the train station about an Englishman who appeared to be stranded there. We took off like a shot. I closed my eyes as the driver took reckless hairpin turns on unlit, rain-slicked roads. As a distraction, I revisited my earlier reunion fantasy. This new version ended with both of us in full body casts, limbs held aloft in traction devices.

When the taxi driver and I arrived at the train station, it was all but deserted. A barista, who was mopping up the countertop at his empty establishment and was about to turn the *"Chiusa"* sign on his shop door, said the Englishman had hitched a ride with some young locals back into town. I amended my fantasy to include a visit to a morgue and a courtroom date.

The driver and I ran through rain puddles back to the cab. We careened out of the train station and sped back to the center of Civita Castellana. Our hunch was that Colin had also discovered that there were two train stations and had headed for the other one.

We pulled up to the train station I had waited at earlier. Beside a park bench was Colin, wearing a look that said: "OK. What the hell should I do now?"

"Colin!" I squealed. If this had been a film starring Bogey and Bacall, this scene would have had audiences reaching for their Kleenex.

Except that it was nothing like that. Colin slid into the cab, smiled politely at the driver, and gave me a peck on the cheek. A peck on the cheek?

When we got into his hotel room, I tried to make like a vamp and cuddle up to him, but he would have none of it.

"I'm tired," he smiled wanly. "It's been a long day."

Maybe tomorrow will be better, I thought as I returned dejectedly to my room—the one I was sharing with my mother.

OUR CAR pulled into the last parking spot in Siena just after noon the next day, all of us anxious to experience what we had been told about Siena's Renaissance beauty.

Colin pulled Mom's walker out of the car and set it up for her, and off we went.

"Why don't you kids go off and have a look round," Mom said as we made our way down the main thoroughfare through the crush of other tourists. "I'll be fine on my own."

Normally I would have protested, or at least put up a good pretense of, "No, really, it's OK. We'll stay and walk at a snail's pace with you."

This time, I didn't ask twice. I was upset by Colin's utter lack of affection toward me—he would not so much as hold my hand—so I grabbed him by the sleeve and said to Mom, "OK, see you in an hour."

Maybe, I thought, he was nervous about appearing affectionate to me in front of my mother. He's British, after all, so it could be that. He also had not been feeling well for the last few months—maybe it was that. Ours is a long-distance relationship, and it is difficult to understand your partner's entire personality based on one-week visits every three or four months. And because our time together is always too brief, the tendency when our relationship hits a pothole is to quickly patch things up and move on rather than address the issue. It is far from ideal, but it is what it is.

We picked up a map at a tourist information center and tried to get our bearings. To its credit, Siena was the only Italian city we visited that had tourist information, knowledgeable, multilingual staff at the counter, and free maps for the asking. We huddled over the map, turning it every which way in an attempt to make sense of the labyrinth of passageways. Even Colin, a former competitive orienteer, was stumped.

It did not help that the streets were stuffed to capacity with people or that the shops—snobby Versace boutiques, MaxMara stores, and a gazillion *gelaterie*—were the types of establishments that can be found at any suburban mall. I was falling helplessly out of love with Siena before I had really made her acquaintance.

We ventured through claustrophobic lanes and several more exterior stairways until we stumbled into the vast and open Il Campo.

"I'd really like Mom to see this," I said. "She'd love this."

"Shall we stop for a glass of wine first?" Colin implored.

You would think I would have said yes, but I didn't. I was suddenly overcome with concern about Mom and began to rush through the day-tripper-clogged streets to find her. Colin did his best to keep up.

She was not easy to find. We checked in all the cafés and hotel lobbies. "Have you seen a small white-haired lady with a walker?"

"She was just here," said a doorman at one hotel. "I think she turned that way."

Off we went. Up ahead a small clot of police officers and tourists were huddled around something. I immediately recognized the wheels of the red walker. I had a sinking feeling in my stomach.

I pushed through the crowd and past several towering police officers. In the middle of a tight circle was my small mother, sweeping her hair away from her eyes and holding court with her story about how she had lost her daughter and wasn't quite sure where or how to find her.

"Mom?"

"Oh, there you are!" she exclaimed, turning her head. "Here's my daughter!"

The crowd stared at me with immense resentment.

"You should look after your mother," one of the police officers scolded me.

That stung. The rest of the crowd nodded their heads in agreement and began murmuring to one another. I fully expected a long torch to be lit as everyone mobilized behind the first person to shout, "Burn the negligent bitch!"

"But she wanted to be left on her own to amble about," I pleaded to the police officer and anyone else within earshot.

"Look. After. Your. Mother," the cop boomed sternly.

Mom did not come to my defense but simply toddled away with her red walker.

"Now, where did you park?" she called out to me. "I've had a delightful time, but I'm a bit tired now. Wasn't that funny? All those nice policemen?"

I could barely contain my anger when I caught up to her.

"Why did you go to the police?" I asked.

"Well, I didn't know where you were," she said, her big brown eyes giving me a look of utter innocence. "You were gone so long."

"We agreed to meet up in an hour, and in fact we were back

in less than an hour. Did you hear that policeman say that I should take better care of you? How do you think I feel?"

"Well, it's done now. Aren't those scarves in that shop window pretty? Did you and Colin see anything interesting?"

I could not talk. I was too upset. Had Colin not been there I would have sat down and wept. Colin, meanwhile, did the British thing of keeping the conversation cheery and chatty while I nursed my bruised ego. We found the car, hoisted the walker into the trunk, got Mom buckled into the front seat, and off we went.

I stared grimly out the windshield. It wasn't enough that my boyfriend was freezing me out; my mom was allowing police officers to accuse me of negligence. No doubt the episode colored my attitude toward Siena. For years I had listened to people raving about the place, that it was the perfect Italian city, that it was romantic beyond words. But Siena failed to cast its spell on me, and I felt a bit cheated.

Ditto for the Tuscan countryside. We sailed silently alongside pale gold fields and dark green cypress standing at attention. I can see why North America loves Tuscany. It looks a lot like North America, or rather a North American version of Italy: a little too idyllic and pretentious. A pang of longing shot through me for the drystone enclosures and the adorable little *trulli* of the South. I missed the tougher, more authentic way of life.

"Where are we off to now?" chirped Mom.

After a long pause I replied tersely, "San Gimignano."

I had heard great things about San Gimi, the same great things I had heard about Siena. On our approach to San Gimi, the setting sun cast a burnished glow over the golden brick stone and red-tiled roofs. We found our way into yet another cobbled labyrinth but could not find our way out. We circled the *centro storico* endlessly and finally took a random road that angled steeply downward into what turned out to be a dead end. A dead end so tight it was almost impossible to turn the car around.

"What the...?" I fumed.

I threw the car into reverse and after a series of to-and-fro shunting managed to turn it around. I stared up and up at the steep incline in front of us. I could not imagine that anything short of a crane would get us back to the top.

"How are you going to get out of this one now?" snapped Mom. "I am not walking up the hill. You'll have to carry me."

I tried to gun the accelerator pedal and plow up the hill, but we only made it halfway before the engine cut out and the car rolled back down.

A small crowd of locals gathered to watch.

"These towns are ridiculous," Mom snorted. "What a stupid country."

We had all become exceedingly testy. The distance travelled, the unexpected warm and humid weather, the lack of a proper meal, and our individual resentments against each other began to come to a boil.

"Let me drive," said Colin with uncharacteristic irritation.

He got out of the backseat, slammed the door, and slipped behind the steering wheel. He got us up the hill, but by the time we reached the top, an acrid odor had filled the car.

"You've burned the clutch," I snarled. "That's brilliant. Thanks a lot!"

I exhaled loudly for effect, and when we had exited the medieval walls of San Gimignano I ordered him to turn in at the first hotel.

He did, literally.

"Why here?" I demanded.

"You told me to pull into the first hotel, and so I did," he shot back.

"Well, couldn't you be a little more discriminating?"

"Fine! *You* tell me when and where..." he said, putting the car angrily into gear.

"STOP IT RIGHT NOW!" bellowed Mom. "I am getting out here, and we are staying here! Do you understand?"

I looked at Colin.

"I'll park the car and bring the bags," he said stiffly.

The Hotel Villa Belvedere was an old villa of faded pink that had been converted into a family-run B&B. It had a commanding view of the Tuscan countryside from its perch, and I noticed a pool—closed, naturally—off to one side of the garden.

The owner, a handsome young father, pulled himself away from the afternoon football game on TV and took his place behind the marble front desk.

He responded to my query for two rooms politely and affirmatively. And yes, he added, one of the rooms was on the main floor, Mom's preferred location.

Before exiting the front door to relay the information to Mom and Colin, I turned and asked, "Do you have a bar?"

"Yes," he said, nodding toward a room to the left. "And we serve dinner and breakfast."

We brought our luggage to our respective rooms. A few minutes later Colin, Mom, and I rendezvoused on the front patio to slake our thirst.

"I'm having a Scotch after that drive," said Mom in a don't-try-to-talk-me-out-of-it tone of voice. She had two in quick succession and retired to her room for a nap.

Colin and I sat in silence watching a large red-gold sun melt into a distant wheat field. Colin is such a contrast to me. I wished I had his patience, his ability to willingly adjust his pace to accommodate others. I sat there wishing that I were a nicer, gentler person.

Suddenly Colin reached for my hand. His touch caused me to jump.

"Why didn't you hold my hand in Siena?" I asked. The words were still leaving my mouth when I realized it was the wrong thing to ask. I hurriedly added as lightly and softly as I could, "Just curious."

He pulled his hand away as quickly as he had offered it, his jaw tightened, and he stared ahead into the distance for a minute. Then he stood up.

"Is there anything else I've done wrong today?" he demanded. He stomped off to his room.

I proceeded to drink in slight excess of my normal limit before staggering back inside to my room and falling on the bed into an inebriated slumber.

Two hours later we all met up again in the dining room, cheerful, rested, and showered, with nary a mention of the earlier fracas.

"How about an after-dinner walk?" Colin said to me.

I looked at Mom.

"Of course, go on," she said. "I'm ready for bed anyway."

"Are you sure?" I asked. "We'd hate to come back and find that you had called the police."

"I'm sure," she said.

"We might be longer than an hour," I probed.

"Whenever you get back," she smiled.

Hand in hand and back on speaking terms—such is

the mystery of the British that they can be angry at you one minute and then act like nothing was ever amiss the next, without ever raising the subject—Colin and I walked across the road toward San Gimignano's fortressed walls and took the first turn in. It was now dark, and the cobbled piazzas had emptied of tourists. Dark corners, shadowy figures, and dead silence gave it a spooky but enchanting atmosphere.

We passed a few hotels, whose inviting glow drew us in. They were romantic places, most dating from the 11th century, awash in medieval and Renaissance atmosphere with vaulted ceilings, arched entranceways, vine-covered facades, exposed stone-and-beam rooftop restaurants. How had we missed this earlier in the car when we were dodging tourists and trying in vain to find some place that said "hotel"? It really is true what they say about seeing things differently when you're on foot than when you're in a car.

"This," I said to Colin with a sweep of my arm, "is what I hoped to see in Italy."

"Well, let's pick up some brochures and plan another trip," he smiled.

We stopped in for a glass of wine in a low-ceilinged trattoria, had a gelato farther down the road, and doubled back for a cappuccino. We were trying to cram every experience you could possibly want in Italy—well, every legal one—into one hour.

Then, with a blanket of stars overhead, we bid a reluctant *ciao* to San Gimi.

15

Pisa, Florence

OVERNIGHT, OUR rental car miraculously recovered from the trauma of the previous day. It was going to need more than a tune-up at the end of this journey—it was going to need therapy. Come to think of it, so was I.

In the sort of cheery humor that comes from a good night's sleep and a satisfying breakfast, we set off for Pisa.

Pisa was only about an hour or so away from San Gimignano, so we took a secondary road through golden swaths of Tuscan countryside.

No sooner had we arrived in Pisa than Mom insisted we look for a hotel.

"But it's only eleven o'clock," I protested.

"I don't care how early it is, I am not going through what we went through yesterday," she said, folding her arms in front of her and staring resolutely ahead. I was well acquainted with that body language.

We followed signs to the "Grand Hotel 4★" and pulled up to the front doors minutes later. The star system had obviously not been updated in this decade, or the previous two, for that matter, but I'm sure that in its glory days—likely 1968—the hotel's four-star rating had been well deserved. I approached the front desk and inquired about rooms.

"We're in luck," I said brightly to Mom when I returned to the car. "And the price is fairly reasonable: 160 euros for the two of us, including breakfast. Colin, a single is a hundred."

"That's fine," he said, reaching for his wallet.

"Well, maybe we should check that place out across the street," said Mom, not moving from the passenger seat.

I followed her eyes to a small *pensione.* I dutifully walked over and checked it out—eighty euros a person but no breakfast.

"What about that one?" Mom pointed to another *pensione* farther down the street.

I let out a huge sigh and sprinted up the street to check that one, too.

"Same price, and there are no lifts in either one," I said when I returned to the car.

"Do they have main-floor rooms?" she asked.

"I didn't ask."

Mom sat mulling this over a minute, working her lip. Colin and I waited for her verdict.

"OK, that's long enough," I snapped after fifteen seconds. "We're staying here."

Honestly, indecision stretches my tolerance. When you want a hotel and a perfectly adequate one presents itself, what's to decide?

What the Grand Hotel lacked in esthetics it more than

made up for in location. When I threw open the shutters in our room and thrust my head out, a little thrill rose up.

"Look!" I shouted excitedly to Mom and Colin.

Both poked their heads through the window and saw a clear view of the Leaning Tower of Pisa.

"You can't beat that for a view, eh?" I smiled at Mom. It was the most excitement I had felt in quite some time.

254

"I suppose," she said indifferently and wandered off to unpack her bag.

The tower kept us—well, Colin and me at least—enthralled all day. Even better, all the main sights of Pisa—the tower, the Duomo, and the baptistery—were all located in one grand park. All we had to do was roll Mom and her red walker down two short blocks and there it was. Connecting them all was a string of souvenir stalls. Mom loves this sort of playground.

Colin and I climbed the tower and took photographs until our cameras ran out of disk space.

What struck me and has remained with me ever since is how this little tourist mecca made so many people happy. Without exception wave after wave of visitors disgorged into the piazza with the same jaded, travel-weary look, but when they saw the tower, their faces lit up.

The Leaning Tower of Pisa gives people so much pleasure. Although considerable money and thought has gone into trying to correct its famous lean over a period of some eight centuries, the fact that it tilts shows something of man's inability to always get it perfect, and I think that's a lovely reminder to us all.

OF THE many things I love about Europe's small cities, my favorite is that they place all transportation terminals near the town. Exhibit A is Pisa's airport. In North America you have to drive at least an hour and a half to get to a major airport that always seems to be located in some godforsaken industrial hinterland where the terminal then has apparent free rein to stretch and expand and generally throw its weight around like a teenager going through puberty.

Not Pisa. It was the most stress-free visit to an airport I've experienced. It was a quick ten-minute drive from the not-so Grand Hotel—we probably could have walked it if we had to—and soon we were driving into the delightfully named Aeroporto Galileo Galilei, which practically begs you to break into a round of "Bohemian Rhapsody." I later learned that the train stops at the airport before continuing to downtown Pisa. Well, what a concept. It makes me apoplectic to think of the unnecessarily complicated and bloated designs of North American airports.

Well-marked signs guided us to a passenger drop-off area, where we showered Colin with farewell hugs and kisses.

"Thanks so much for coming," I said. "Sorry about…"

"No, let's forget it," he smiled. "It was a lot of fun. I'm glad I came."

That's how the Brits are: You can have a near-nuclear row with them one day, and the next they are saying what a grand time they had. I never did find out what had been bugging him when he first arrived, but by the time he left things between us had settled back to normal. We had not shared a room—my mother disapproves of conjugal relations between unmarried people—and this was a sore point for me. I did not raise this with her, and Colin accepted the room arrangements without question, but I was peeved at my own lack of gumption—I'm in my fifties, for God's sake!—and how I continue to kowtow to my mother's preferences rather than to my own.

Mom and I carried on to Florence, about an hour away from Pisa unless you get snarled in the morning rush-hour traffic, which we did.

"What's Freezie?" Mom asked as we inched along the highway.

"Firenze," I corrected her. "Firenze is Italian for Florence."

"Well, it looks like Freezie," she said determinedly.

We were both looking forward to Florence, having heard so much about this treasure trove of art and architecture. Mom and I agreed we would need at least three days to soak it all in.

Naturally our first order of business was to find a hotel. We breached the law that forbids cars in the *centro storico* and came to a stop in front of the Piazza della Repubblica. I put the car in park and took off on foot to find accommodation in one of the handful of *pensiones* whose signs were visible from the square.

The first was full, so I ran back to confer with Mom. Then I sprinted off to resume the search. This is an exercise that lacks the adventurous appeal it has at, say, age thirty.

I scaled the Hotel Olimpia, which was located on an upper floor, in an old-fashioned cagelike lift, the kind you see in movies from the 1940s. There was nothing fancy or charming about this establishment, but the desk clerk was very polite and showed me a large corner room with huge windows facing the piazza. I felt it would be perfect for Mom and me.

"It is good you check in now," he said in broken English. "There are security cameras everywhere. They watch and record all cars that come into the center of town. You would have got a ticket, but now that you have a hotel reservation, which I can verify to them, they will withdraw the ticket."

The clerk said he would call an attendant, who would take our car to be parked in some unknown lot or sold for parts on the black market—I wasn't quite sure which.

I returned to the car puffed with pride at having scored a room.

"What about the Savoy?" said Mom. "It's just over there."

"We won't be able to afford it," I said prudently, undoing her seat belt.

"Why not?" she cried.

"This hotel will be fine," I assured her.

"What if I don't like it?" she whined.

I struggled on the sidewalk with umpteen bags and suitcases, plus the red walker, plus my recalcitrant mother. I handed the car keys to a glum, grease-smeared man. When he left I realized I had forgotten to ask him if he was indeed the person the hotel had called. What the hell, I thought, as I struggled to grip the handle of another suitcase with three already attached to various parts of my body.

I managed to squeeze both us and our luggage into the tiny lift, and out of it when it arrived at the hotel level.

"This is our room?" said Mom when I opened the door to our room.

"Yes, isn't it great? Corner room, high ceilings. Look at all those tall windows; they all open onto the square. We can people-watch!"

"This looks like a slum," she countered.

It was not a slum. The room was open and airy and sure, it could have used the services of an interior decorator to haul it from the '50s to the present, but it was no worse than the room in which we had stayed in Taormina. I was in no mood to get into a fight, so I changed the subject.

"Are you up for some sightseeing?" I said with feigned brightness.

"Don't change the subject," she said. "I don't like this."

"Well, it's too late now. We've signed in, and the car has been taken away."

"Then ask for it back."

"Mom, be reasonable. This will be fine. Let's go out."

We left the hotel and made our way slowly down the Via Roma. We passed several plaques denoting B&Bs. At every one Mom urged me to check it out. She even asked me to check the Savoy, which was fully booked.

"We already have a place," I reiterated.

"But we're not happy with it," she shot back.

"We?"

"Oh, Jane, admit it; you don't like it, either. It's the worst hotel we've stayed in."

"How is it the worst?" I said. "It's on one level, it has enough room for you and your walker to do wheelies together, it's bright, it's close to the elevator and the dining room. It's central. For the three days we'll be spending here, it will be fine," I said. "Besides, do you know the hassle it would be to change hotels now? I'd have to lug all our gear by myself down the street."

"That's OK," she said. "I'll help."

I gave her a look of disbelief. Who was she kidding? She could barely walk, let alone drag luggage.

"No!" I said firmly. Then, in yet another attempt to distract her, "Isn't that a church?"

I drew her by the hand across the Piazza del Duomo toward the cathedral of Santa Maria del Fiore.

"I don't like it, Jane," she insisted. "Did you hear me?"

"Yes, I heard you, and the answer is still No! We are staying where we are," I hissed to her as we passed beneath a poster of the Madonna and Child.

There were scads of people about and no sign indicating where the entrance was except an enormous line-up that curled around the side of the cathedral. I knew Mom would not tolerate that. I helped her mount the stairs, which she did with great difficulty, and we walked toward the cathedral's small wooden door where a cluster of people had begun to file in.

I pushed Mom ahead with a nod to the man at the door and a *"Mia madre è disabile."*

Our eyes adjusted to the dark coolness of the interior of Santa Maria del Fiore.

"Now, let's talk about that room," said Mom. "You know I'm not happy with it. I want it changed."

I wandered away from her to keep my temper in check.

The interior of the cathedral was a vacuous space, completely devoid of character, certainly far more austere than its marble facade. In fact the most compelling attraction was the sight of tourists walking around with their digital cameras poised, trying to find something, anything, worth shooting. Even the high altar was a letdown, though, to be fair, the dome was beautifully painted and the inlaid marble floor was exquisite.

After a respectful period of time—and frankly, five minutes in there seemed an eternity—I indicated to Mom that I had had enough. We were about to exit when I saw a small sign off to one side that explained that all the artwork—paintings, statues, treasures—had been removed from the Cathedral of Santa Maria del Fiore and transferred down the road to the Museo dell'Opera di Santa Maria del Fiore.

Well, that just made me angry. I can certainly appreciate
that there is a responsibility to exhibit the vast richness and
surfeit of Florence's religious art rather than having it lan-
guish in some basement storehouse (and I'll grant you that
there are pieces that have suffered from disintegration over
the years and would be better maintained off-site in a place
like the Museo dell'Opera), but to entirely eviscerate a cathedral and relocate its contents down the road is to partake of a
kind of desecration—is there such a word as "articide"?—that
defies comprehension.

We left the cathedral and plodded toward the Museo
dell'Opera di Santa Maria del Fiore. There was no lineup,
but there was a ticket person only too happy to take six euros
from each of us. We did, however, receive a brochure in return
and learned from it that the building had been in constant use
as a construction office for the cathedral ever since the first
stone was laid in 1296. It had also served as a studio to many
Renaissance masters over the centuries. Donatello painted
here, Brunelleschi toiled over the plans for the cathedral's
dome and its facade here, and Michelangelo carved his *David*
in the courtyard.

It was strange to see pieces out of context with their original purpose or their original place in the cathedral. For
instance, the *cantorie* (singing galleries), created by Luca
della Robbia and Donatello in the 1430s are lovely to look at,
but they make no sense hanging on a white wall when they
were sculpted to fit over the doors to the two sacristies of the
Cathedral.

My first thought when my eyes alighted on a life-size
wooden statue of Mary Magdalene was, "Well, now they've
really done it; they've brought modern art into the joint." But

as I edged closer, I learned from a description attached to it that it was not new; it was sculpted by Donatello in 1455. Artists throughout the centuries have portrayed Mary Magdalene as a voluptuous woman clothed in billowing taffeta and a hint of ironic innocence. This is nothing like that. It is the most heartbreaking statue I have ever gazed upon: a gaunt, ragged, sunken-eyed, emotionally and physically spent Mary Magdalene clinging to her faith with bony hands pressed together in desperate prayer.

WE LEFT the museum and shuffled back along the Via Roma toward the Piazza della Repubblica, where we stopped at an awning-covered café for refreshment.

While waiting to be served, we struck up a conversation with a young woman at the next table. She was from New Orleans and introduced herself as Deborah—heavyset, raven haired, and scarlet lipped. She had just been laid off from her job in the hospitality business, she said, and being at loose ends she figured, "Hey, I might as well visit Florence."

She was spunky and straightforward, a refreshing change after weeks of the more formal Italians.

"Well, if you're in the hospitality business you must adore the food here," I said, bracing myself for her glowing assessment.

She sat back in her chair and took a deep breath. "Well, the wine I'm drinking right now tastes bitter, and I'm guessing that's because the bottle's been open for some time. Trust me, I worked in food and beverage for twenty years—I know. And this lasagna? Chef Boyardee must be in the kitchen. I do better Bolognese than these guys. Granted, I've only been in Italy a week, but so far the food has been seriously mediocre.

The Italians have done a good marketing job on their mythical haute *cucina*—ha! I just thought of that! Clever, huh?"

I began to wonder whether a support group existed for all the people who had visited Italy and found the food so utterly lacking. (I feel compelled at this point to add an aside: I returned to southern Italy with Colin a year and a half later—it was September—and we had some spectacular meals. All were in restaurants not easily accessible to those with a physical disability.)

Tea had revived Mom, and when we returned to our hotel room, she continued her rant about our accommodation.

"It's only for three nights," I insisted again. "You're always telling me to 'roll with the punches,' but it seems that only applies when the punches are acceptable to you."

I looked at the scuffed dark wood furniture, the worn but clean brown bedspread, the deflated-looking pillows, the bare tiled floors. There was no TV and no radio, but who cares about those things on holiday? Sure, the room's walls were a dull beige, but it was clean, and as I had pointed out to her earlier, the location was great.

"This is a dump," she countered. "And the bathroom—it has a step-up, you might have noticed. You know how bad I am on steps—and it's small and badly laid out. What sort of place allows a toilet to share the same space as the shower? I can hardly get in that bathroom, let alone use it. Plus, the water pressure is almost nil, and the toilet barely flushes."

She was right, of course. I was going to add that the hotel's Internet connection constantly crashed, but I didn't feel this was the time.

"But look, we're right in the center of the city; our windows open up on to the square!" I enthused.

"What's so great about that?" she said, marching determinedly toward the window. "It will be noisy, and who wants to look at all those people anyway? No, I don't like this one bit. You did not consider my needs when you picked this place. I think we've had enough of Florence. Let's leave."

"What? We just got here! Look, I think you need a nap"—a very long nap, I was tempted to add. "Why don't you have a lie-down, and I'll go out and look around?"

"Yes, you do that; and find us a new place to stay."

Jesus Christ. Do seniors get PMS?

One thing was certain: I was not leaving Florence without a visit to the Uffizi.

I left the hotel and followed a small road to the Piazza della Signoria, where the place was positively abuzz with humanity in all its glorious chaos. There were colossal statues everywhere, including a replica of Michelangelo's *David*. I strode confidently over to admire it, only to discover how ridiculously uncomfortable it is to be gazing up at a man's testicles and at a penis so tiny—has anyone else noticed this?—for a young man with such large hands and feet. Perhaps Michelangelo was running out of marble.

Around the perimeter of the piazza, cafés were clogged with people enjoying a late-afternoon aperitif and watching the passing parade. There did not appear to be a lineup at the Uffizi—hurrah!—but it was not until I reached its front doors that I understood why. It was Monday, and the Uffizi was closed on Mondays. I was disappointed, but as I walked back to the hotel, an idea popped into my head.

"I found the most amazing place," I said to Mom as I entered our hotel room. "You have to see it. It's not far, and there are cafés around and we can have dinner there."

She looked unsure of this idea—after all, I was the one who had chosen the hotel—but she grudgingly got herself ready.

Off we went. Mom and her ever-present red walker rumbled over the uneven cobblestones. At least the red walker looked more excited about the excursion than Mom. When the street finally ended and opened onto the Piazza della Signoria, I watched for her reaction.

Nothing.

"Isn't this incredible?" I enthused.

"I need to sit down," she said. "How about dinner?"

I looked down at the walker to see if I could elicit a more favorable reaction, but it always stayed loyal to its mistress.

We settled into a ringside table at the first café we came to and ordered outrageously priced G&Ts and dinner. Our waiter tried to slip an extra item onto our bill, but I was now wise to the practice.

Mom and I were enjoying the last drops of our coffee when two Italian men sat down at a table next to us. One of them began chatting with me. His name was Raphael, and he owned a leather shop in town. When he learned that I was from Canada, he mentioned that he had family in Toronto. We had a pleasant chat, and then Raphael gave me his business card and said he would be only too happy to help me pick out a nice leather coat. I had heard that Florence was the place to buy a leather coat, but I wasn't in the market for one.

"That seemed like a shifty deal," Mom said, eyeing me. "You didn't make plans to go out with him later, did you?"

"Are you mad? Of course not! What do you think I am?"

"Well, you never know," she said. "He seemed rather persistent."

AT SEVEN o'clock the next morning I hit the cobblestones and made tracks for the Uffizi. The air was cool, and the sun was rising through light clouds. The cobblestones had been cleansed of their daily grime by an overnight drizzle and were still damp. All was silent except for my footsteps echoing off the buildings. Morning is my favorite time of day. I love hearing and seeing a town wake up, and I am fascinated by the people who stoke the day and get the activity started.

At the Uffizi I took my place in the thick lineup, about four abreast, that had already begun to form, curling like a swollen python beneath the museum's long U-shaped colonnaded porch.

It was a restless group, and everyone wore the same anxious look of concern about whether they would gain entrance to the famed museum—the fresh-scrubbed family of four wearing varying shades of fluorescent-colored Crocs; seniors in Tilley hats; svelte, smartly dressed middle-aged couples trying not to look like tourists despite the Rick Steeves books nosing out of the wives' leather handbags. Each new arrival to the lineup was greeted warily. You didn't dare jump the queue with this crowd.

Visiting cultural highlights in cities takes on the air of an extreme sport. Those who joined the queue were armed with bottles of water, food, and blankets, some with folding stools, newspapers, handheld devices that play games, and the ubiquitous cell phone. Some also come with strategies, such as the couple ahead of me who were conveniently spelled off by their newly arrived travelling companions for a tea-and-pee break. Oh, the benefits of travelling with spry, able-bodied companions.

How can there be so many people and not one of them

with a physical disability? I hoped they realized how lucky they were, though more likely than not—as is the case for all of us able-bodied people—they took their health and mobility for granted.

Having nothing whatsoever with which to amuse myself while I stood in line, I eavesdropped on the conversation of the couple in front of me. They were young and, based on what I overheard, from California. The woman was a pretty and perkily chatty woman of Asian heritage with long, glossy hair; her non-Asian boyfriend was the glum and silent type. The girlfriend—oh, I have seen this, I have done this so many times with men—was gamely trying to keep the patter going with her partner with conversational games and idle gossip. So many women really do work hard to bring life to their relationships.

"Would you rather watch a movie on a boat or on a plane?" the Asian gal asked her man. I could not hear his mumbled response.

"Would you rather see a play or a rock concert?"

Another mumbled reply.

"Let's see. Would you rather be eaten by a shark or swallowed by a whale?"

When she tired of this game she tried another.

"Guess what I'm thinking now."

"Guess what I'm looking at right now."

And then she moved to gossip.

"Do you know how she's wearing her hair now? It's like chopped to here with bangs, and it's white!"

And so it went.

I tried to find a way to join the conversation because, while the conversation itself was more than a few brain cells short of a Mensa meeting, at least the woman was animated. By this point I had begun to ponder rather seriously whether I would rather be eaten by a shark or swallowed by a whale.

After an hour or so a slight murmur arose from the crowd when the Uffizi's mammoth doors were pushed open. The line began to surge and shuffle toward the entrance.

When my turn finally came at the ticket wicket, I was told I could not buy tickets in advance except on the Internet. Also, I could not buy tickets for someone who was not accompanying me.

Well, there was an hour and a half of my life that I won't get back.

I ran back to the hotel, rushed Mom into some clothes, and hustled her against her will out of the hotel and across the cobblestone streets and the vast piazza and back to the Uffizi. This time, however, I walked her boldly to the front of the line and asked a young ticket taker about wheelchairs, invoking my practiced, *"Mia madre è disabile."*

He immediately let us through the doors. Once inside, I feigned shock and horror that we did not have tickets.

"Momento," he said, and dashed off.

A minute later he returned with our tickets. There was no charge, he said.

"I must take you places more often," I smiled at Mom.

I fetched a wheelchair for her and parked the red walker behind a customer service desk.

A crush of people attempted to surge as one through the turnstiles.

"This is madness!" a teenaged Brit cried out to no one in particular. The British find disorder a very grave and distressing offense. I believe it was the British-Hungarian author

George Mikes who once said that an Englishman, even if he is alone, will always form an orderly queue of one.

We wandered the sprawling Uffizi for no other reason than it seemed it was required of us as visitors to Florence.

We waded through the throng clustered around Botticelli's *The Birth of Venus* and the master's other crowd-pleaser, *La Primavera;* we turned a corner and came face-to-face with Piero della Francesca's famous profile of Federico da Montefelto sporting a red, flat-topped, felt hat above an almost comically impassive face. He has a nose so hooked you could hang laundry on it. The painting is actually a diptych (I did not know that), and in the second panel is the less famous but gentler profile of Battista Sforza (I later learned that she was Mrs. Montefelto).

There was Caravaggio's grimacing, decapitated *Medusa,* an image that still induces nightmares in one of my grown children. And over there, wasn't that, yes, of course, it was Leonardo da Vinci's *Annunciation*!

So familiar were many of the paintings—endlessly reproduced over the centuries in art books and on tote bags, tea cozies, fridge magnets, bookmarks—that I reflexively greeted each with a nod and a smile of recognition, as if I were bumping into a long-lost friend at a party. But there my fascination with the Uffizi ended.

The Uffizi is undeniably huge and grand, and its collection is certainly impressive, but the place has the same effect on one's system as gorging on a box of chocolates.

Since I have already committed heresy by panning Italy's food, allow me to hang myself further by saying this: Unless you have a craving to stand two feet away from *The Birth of Venus* (and it's behind glass now, by the way) or you possess

268

a fetish that involves looking at art while standing on your tiptoes and subjecting your neck to the hot, stale breath of strangers, skip the Uffizi.

IT IS impossible to escape the leather-hawkers in Florence. Casually inquire about an item at one of the numerous stalls that populate the piazzas, and its keeper will hound you relentlessly, maybe even grab you by the hand and drag you through a series of dark back alleys to his supplier, who will then show the full line of wares. Even Houdini would be stymied by the experience. If you so much as venture in to a leather shop or showroom, prepare to surrender your wallet on the spot. Don't even try to leave without buying anything.

Mom and I were picking our way slowly along a semi-deserted street a block or so away from the hustle and hucksters of the Via Roma. She was pushing her red walker; I was trying not to go insane from walking at a pace I can only describe as slower than a death march.

"There's a nice coat for you," said Mom, gesturing toward a shop window.

I often wonder what my mother imagines my life is like when she suggests items of clothing for me. The coat she pointed out was truly beautiful: a below-the-calf length of soft, tawny suede. The skirt of the coat was slightly gored to produce an elegant flare. The collar, cuffs, and hem were trimmed with an uncertain species of rich-looking fur. It was the sort of coat that would raise the ire of a PETA supporter. I slipped it on to appease my mother; it fit like a glove.

"That is definitely you!" she gushed as her eyes lit up. "Look, since you've done all the driving on this trip let me buy you the coat as a gift."

I began to protest, but my mom's words had already reached the ears of the owner, who had been unpacking bags of coats at the rear of the shop. He sprang to our side to assist in the seduction, quickly launching into a heady combination of flattery and fibbing. When he started fawning over my "lean figure"—a point so patently false—I had no choice but to put us both out of our misery.

Had I been a movie star, a call girl, or the arm candy of a jet-setting tycoon I just might have let them talk me into the coat. Instead I opted for a practical, knee-length trench-style coat in black leather. I've regretted my choice ever since.

I wore my new coat that night as Mom and I tucked into yet another dull meal near our hotel. The air was cool and damp, and a few cafés with patios had turned on their outdoor heat lamps and were handing out fleece blankets to their patrons.

To avoid being ripped off again, Mom and I kept the order simple: half a bottle of wine, soup, and spaghetti. There was no cover charge, but the menu announced that an outrageous sixteen percent service charge would be applied to all bills.

I was lifting a forkful of spaghetti to my mouth when who should approach our table but Raphael, the leather guy from the previous night. He stopped and bowed slightly, but instead of being warm and pleasant, as he had been the night before, he was tense and terse. His eyes darkened when he saw my new coat; he grabbed a fold of the sleeve and gave it a quick feel between his fingers.

"Hmm, very nice," he said in a sarcastic tone, and then turned on his heel and stomped off, turning his head to shoot me his best wounded-beast look.

Mom and I were dumbstruck.

"I can't believe that!" exclaimed Mom. "How did he know we were here?"

Then she leaned over her soup and said in a loud whisper, "I hate Florence. There's something dirty about the place. I think we've had enough. Let's leave."

There was so much in Florence I wanted to see: Dante's home, the Palazzo Pitti, the Galleria del Costume, Fort Belvedere, and the Ferragamo shoe museum. But I was not loving Florence, either. It was rushed and rude. Earlier that day, at a café on Via dei Castellani located outside the rear exit of the Uffizi, a short, snotty little waiter had kicked—kicked!—Mom's little red walker and snarled at us in contempt. And this was *before* we placed our order! Out of sympathy I stroked the walker's handlebars.

Witness to this was an elegant couple polishing off their sandwiches at the next table.

"Do you want me to hold him down while you kill him?" the man deadpanned in an American drawl.

"Is it just me, or are the waiters in this city unbelievably arrogant and rude?" I asked.

"It's not you," he said. "We travel all over the world and this is the worst place we've experienced. Are you going to Venice?"

I gave a shrug of uncertainty.

"Go to Venice," said the man. "It's a gentler place, and the waiters are lovely."

That night, I packed up my soiled, ugly clothing and gazed enviously through the tall slim windows of our hotel room at the steady stream of customers shopping for new duds at Zara across the road. I could have popped over but I dislike crowds and my aversion to them is amplified in stores. Florence was a

271

nonstop shopping mecca; it seemed there wasn't much more to Florence than lining up for art or at a cash register.

I looked over at Mom, who had taken a break from packing and was staring dreamily out onto the piazza. She was dressed in a silky taupe nightgown, her elbows resting on the marble windowsill, her hands propping up her chin. Below her swarms of people strolled along the sidewalk for the evening *passeggiata*.

I wondered what Mom was thinking about, whether she was imaging a younger version of herself among all those people, or perhaps wishing she could have experienced Florence with my father. Maybe she was asking herself why they had kept putting off many of their trips in order to stay home and toil at work or on the latest renovation of their home. Save it for a special occasion, my parents used to say. My father saved bottles of champagne and wine, and when he died, we had to throw most of it out because, like him, it had had an expiration date. Unlike my parents, I do not save for a rainy day or a special occasion. The future is too uncertain. To me, every day is a special occasion.

I moved toward a window to observe the passing parade for myself. Down the Via Roma, toward the Savoy Hotel, another wave of humanity surged along the sidewalk. In its midst was a little girl about five or six years old dressed in a pale pink sweater and patterned pale pink skirt. She was skipping while holding the hand of her mother, who was dressed in a cream-and-white linen top and trousers and smart black leather flats. The sight of them made me think of my daughter.

Long ago we too had held hands: Zoë skipping beside me free of self-consciousness; me full of maternal devotion. I would hold her hand for all the practical and protective reasons, but really I just loved the feel of her soft little hand in mine. It made me want to scream with joy, "I have a daughter!" Although I had been holding hands out of duty with my mother during this trip, I could not ever recall holding her hand out of pure love.

"What are you looking at?" asked Mom as she waddled over beside me.

"Look at that mother and her little girl, skipping along so happily. Did we ever do that?"

"No," she said curtly, waving her arms dramatically. "You never wanted anything to do with me. You were always off doing your own thing. That woman does have a lovely outfit though, don't you think? You'd look good in that." She turned away and resumed packing.

More than any other Italian city we visited, Florence was the city of mothers and daughters. It is a shopper's haven, and shopping is, regrettably for those of us who are not shoppers, the preferred activity of mothers and daughters.

I watched how they interacted with each other, the mother always conscious of her proximity to her daughter, the daughter more conscious of her proximity to the clothing racks. You could see in the mothers that they adored their grown daughters, were breathless with awe at how their once chubby, clumsy child—not so long ago sprung from the womb—had been transformed into a sleek, poised, self-possessed beauty.

That night in bed I was lulled into sleep by the gentle sounds of a bass cellist, a keyboardist, and a soprano serenading people in the piazza below. Italy is wonderful for moments such as this. And yet the longing for home returned once again.

There comes a time when the thrill of travelling wanes for me—when I can't stand packing and repacking my suitcase or hauling it everywhere, when I get so sick of my travel wardrobe that I want to burn it, when my moisturizer and toothpaste run out, when my bank card is rejected by the ATM, when restaurant food starts making me ill and I start craving my own bland cooking, when I pine for the comforts of my own bathroom and my own bedsheets, when I start anticipating a return to my routine, the very one I wanted to escape just weeks earlier.

I also wanted to go home while I still liked my mom. We were entering the fourth week of our trip and the fourth cycle of repetitive stories and anecdotes (if I heard the one about the uncle and his affection for hot dogs one more time I was no longer going to hold myself responsible for my actions). The sound of her cane clicking on the tiled floors sounded like a tongue clucking disapproval; I resented the way she hogged the extra pillows and ninety percent of the bathroom towels.

"I wish I could make the clock go faster," Mom said as we both waited for sleep to overcome us. "I can't wait to leave."

She was talking about Florence; I had the same thought about Italy.

16

Rome

EASTER WEEKEND in Rome. It never occurred to me to book a hotel room in advance of our arrival in the Eternal City. My punishment for this oversight was eternal fretting.

After the debacle over our hotel in Florence, I was concerned about the fact that we had snagged the last available hotel room in Rome, or so the reservation clerk had told me. My worry was compounded when I telephoned the hotel in Rome from Florence and they easily accommodated my request to check in a day earlier than originally planned. All I could think of was, How bad is the last available hotel room in Rome? I prayed all the way to Rome that it would be something acceptable to She Who Insists on Perfect Accommodation. Mom was already grilling me about it and questioning my booking abilities.

Only when we rolled up to the white pillared, portico entrance of the Hotel Aldrovandi was I able to relax slightly.

"Well, it didn't have to be *this* grand," gasped Mom.

"Oh yes it did," I muttered to myself.

The doorman greeted us with a low bow and gently guided me away when I attempted to unload our luggage from the car. At the front desk, the clerk informed us that we had been upgraded to a suite. Things were looking up! Did I also mention that the sun was shining, and we had not seen rain for two whole days?

The bellhop took us to our room, and I ended up pressing into his hand the last three euros I had. He tossed them into his pocket without even looking at them.

When Mom steered her walker into our room, she was positively beaming at the soft yellow walls, furniture upholstered in sumptuous pale yellow, sage, and white, and walnut side tables. The large gleaming-white marble bathroom was stocked with loads of complimentary swag. While she did wheelies in the living room, I dumped our bags in the bedroom and spread out the road map by the telephone to figure out the last leg of our trip.

We were spending five nights in Rome and then driving north again, this time to Venice for two nights, before flying out of Treviso to begin our journey back to Canada. Yes, I know I had initially vowed not to go to Venice, but by this stage I thought, what the hell, we're in the neighborhood.

The trip to Venice was also a trade-off to my mother for my decision to end our trip a week earlier than planned. Mom was fraying physically, and I was fraying emotionally. Nearly five weeks on the road together had taken its toll. Selfishly, I just couldn't cope with her anymore. I needed a break, and

I yearned for the small and irreplaceable comforts of home. I was counting the days.

We could have visited Rome at any time during our holiday, but Mom had scored tickets from Catholic HQ in Canada granting us seats in the enclosure at Saint Peter's Square for Easter Sunday Mass. Our entire trip had been planned around this event.

"I am going to bring my walker," Mom intoned solemnly as we prepared to set off for a pre-Sunday visit to the Vatican. She looked at me when she mentioned the walker, knowing how much I hated it. I looked down at the red walker contemptuously so that it understood how much I resented it and that it better behave. It shuddered a bit and stuck close to Mom's skirt.

Forget Satan, forget the seven deadly sins, nothing confounds the Eternal City like a walker. The cab driver who arrived at our hotel to take us to Saint Peter's was stymied when confronted with it. He scratched his head and with help from the doorman tried stuffing in to the trunk, to no avail. They let it sit on the hotel driveway and stared at it as they pondered various solutions. Eventually the walker wound up in the front seat of the cab and Mom and I in the backseat.

Saint Peter's Square is a vast and daunting plain of cobblestones. You might as well have asked Mom to walk across the Prairies. There were no directions and no signs of assistance for anyone with physical limitations.

Web sites will tell you that Saint Peter's is "accessible," but that's a lie unless "accessible" means that there is room for people to push a walker or wheel themselves in a wheelchair. It is a lot to ask of a disabled person to cross that square without assistance, especially over rough cobblestones.

Police officers and the Papal Swiss Guardsmen in their smart gold, blue, and red pantaloons and matching spats were out in full force that day making sure we didn't have bombs strapped to our bodies. Aside from that they were useless. They saw my Mom huffing and puffing, her face red with distress, but they showed not a smidgeon of concern.

We wandered into Saint Peter's Basilica only because we saw threads of people scurrying in and it seemed the right thing to do at the time. I nearly tripped over myself while trying to take in the scale of the interior: columns twice the size of tree trunks, mammoth marble statues hanging off the walls or suspended from the ceiling, paintings the size of small homes adorning the walls. The treads on the steps were the depth of a pantry.

"There must be a Mass," I said to Mom as the pews began filling up.

"Oh goody," she replied. "It is Maundy Thursday, you know."

We stuffed ourselves into a crowded pew as a posse of priests assembled around the altar. Out of their midst came none other than Pope Benedict XVI.

When he started chanting the first few lines of the *Gloria,* I thought Tom Waits had hijacked the microphone. It appears His Holiness is, like the rest of us, groggy of voice first thing in the morning.

Benedict may lack the natural charisma of his predecessor, but there's something about a man in white robes that makes the girls crazy. A gaggle of nubile and not-so-nubile nuns were jumping up and down in front of us, flashing their cell phone cameras at their idol while being restrained by the Vatican guards in their silver, centurion-type helmets.

278

Mom nudged me.

"See, even the nuns have cell phones," she nodded approvingly.

"SISTINE CHAPEL?"

I nodded affirmatively to the young security guard in the Vatican Museum.

"All the way to the end and turn left," he said.

I stared at the dot on the horizon and calculated that the distance might reasonably require overnight accommodation or at the very least a meal stop. Mom had taken to using museum wheelchairs as walkers rather than riding in them, but I convinced her to let me wheel her this time.

After a long journey we were standing in the middle of the Sistine Chapel, shoehorned in with a percentage of the three million people who visit the chapel each year, a number of them walking around with their heads tilted up, oblivious to the fact that they were bumping into others. People squeezed closer. I felt myself poked and groped and grazed. I couldn't tell whether I was being shoved or assaulted. It took all my self-restraint not to snap, "Will you kindly fuck off?" to everyone who invaded my personal space. There was a creepy guy with short dark hair, dressed in a plaid, short-sleeved shirt and khakis, walking around with an air of innocence. I was certain he had intentionally copped a feel.

These are not the conditions under which I enjoy appreciating art and culture. It was guerilla tourism of the worst kind.

"What did you think of it?" Mom asked me as we barrelled through the crowd to escape.

"No roaring hell," I said. "Michelangelo strikes me as an angry man with obsessive-compulsive disorder. You?"

"I can't see what the fuss is all about," she said. "I expected better."

ONE AFTERNOON I was surprised to find myself with nothing to do. Zippo.

Mom was napping, the sun was bright, and I had a good three hours to do as I pleased. I cast about for a destination.

I wanted something removed from the hordes, something that would encourage quiet reflection. Not quite certain where I was going, I slipped out of our luxurious Alcatraz and sauntered down a virtually empty Via Ulisse Aldrovandi beneath a hot sun. I crossed into the Borghese Gardens, attracted by the shade of soaring trees, and followed a long, narrow, quiet path that disappointingly delivered me to a wide, chaotic street of blaring horns and busy people.

I took one look at the mayhem and was about to turn my back on it when I noticed a gypsy mother in a long, tattered, rose-colored skirt cradling a sleeping baby and approaching people with her hand outstretched. We had been warned about the gypsies—by Rome's cab drivers, by the hotel concierge, by newspaper articles, by anyone who we told we were going to Rome—and I had seen a number of them, especially around the Vatican.

I knew gypsies were considered a huge problem all over Europe, but I was unprepared for the hostility directed at them. Passersby literally swatted the young mother away. One well-dressed man came up to her and cursed her loudly just inches from her face—I could hear his bellowing across the street from where I stood. The gypsy mom did nothing, oblivious or simply inured to the abuse.

I returned to the gentility of the Borghese Gardens. The

scent of Spring was in the air, and the soft colors of the early flowers—pale pinks, lavenders, and buttercup-yellows—bestowed a cheerful, innocent serenity.

I walked the narrow crushed-gravel paths pondering the gypsy mother, and those thoughts led me to think about myself as a mother. There was a time when I lost my job and had thought that it would be only a matter of time before my life resembled that of the gypsy mom. But I refused to let that happen, and today my resilience is my most hard-won and satisfying achievement.

281

Then, as ever, my mind flipped back to my mother. She had been a model of resilience and self-sufficiency. Those traits alone were reason enough to be grateful for having been born to such a woman. And yet I could not quell the quiet anger that sporadically rose in me whenever my thoughts moved toward the relationship I had with her. I still wanted to broach the three grievances that she had not allowed me to share that night in Viterbo. I was fearful about bringing them up myself because as much as I wanted an honest relationship with her, I was too exhausted to argue with her anymore. Maybe she felt the same way. Still, my mind continued to scream for resolution. How much longer did I have to carry this crap around with me? Why was it always me having to bring it up?

Along the path, with my hands stuffed in my pockets and my head bowed in thought, I came across an elderly woman in a wheelchair. A dull, thick blanket covered her legs; a little wool cap sat on her head, which hung to one side; and her face wore an expression that could charitably be described as checked out. Beside her, seated on a wooden park bench and staring ahead, lost in thought, was, I assumed, the woman's adult daughter, about my age. She jolted slightly out of her reverie as I approached. I smiled a greeting of solidarity to her. Caring for elderly parents is a lonely, solitary labor of love, duty, and perhaps guilt.

The path I was on eventually led me back to Via Ulisse Aldrovandi. Across the road was the Galleria Nazionale d'Arte Moderna, a stark white, classical-looking edifice that I had passed numerous times during our stay in Rome. Unlike the Uffizi and other famous art galleries, the Galleria Nazionale d'Arte Moderna did not appear to get many visitors, so I seized the opportunity to take a look. Modern art, by Italian definition, refers to anything produced from 1850 to the present, and soon after purchasing my ticket, I was lost in the simple delight of conducting a lazy, random gander through the gallery's many bright, arresting, and blissfully crowd-free rooms.

Across one of the galleries, in an adjoining room, a life-size statue of ghostly white marble caught my eye. I made a beeline for it, as if drawn by a magnetic force. As I stood in front of it, tears gathered in my eyes.

La Vedova, sculpted in 1888 by Ernesto Bazzaro, depicts a girl of perhaps six or eight years of age and her young mother. The girl looks as if she wants to play or at least get a moment of face time with her mother—her small hand is on her mother's chin, as if trying to physically turn her mother's face toward her. The mother, however, is lost in a long gaze of worried distraction—Bills? Domestic strife? Loss? How to be smarter? More stylish? How to get ahead? Or perhaps how to get to the end of the week without slitting her wrists? The looks on the faces of both mother and daughter were achingly familiar.

My mother had been distracted during my childhood— distracted by her weight gain, by the need to be her own person and develop her own talents, by her commitments to various volunteer organizations. I was the little girl in that statue, always trying to get her to notice me, to listen to me. Even then, when her hearing was perfect, I had to repeat things two or three times to get her attention.

But hadn't I also been a distracted mother? Are we all distracted during early marriage and motherhood at some point? Don't we all stress about how to make ends meet, how to make our children's lives easier and richer, how to maintain the other relationships in our lives—with spouses, in-laws, parents, friends, bosses—how to keep from losing ourselves? In the process we let slide the relationships we take for granted, the relationships that are in fact most important to us.

My mind rewound to ten years earlier, when my daughter would come out of school at the end of the day and scan the crowd of waiting parents. When her eyes landed on me, she would shoot me a thousand-watt smile, yelp happily, and race across the school yard into my waiting arms. So swamped was I with the pressing matters of daily life that I often did not return the same devoted attention to my daughter or my sons at the very moment they offered it. I would hear them excitedly spill out the events of their day and about their happy discoveries, but I didn't always listen. Why does it take us so long—and until so much later in life—to realize the value of our undivided attention?

As mother and child age, the balance shifts. The mother's time is freed up from myriad responsibilities; the child's time becomes dominated by social interests outside the home. Eventually it is the mother who is begging the child for face time and undivided attention. Funny how that happens.

The therapeutic discussion I had hoped to have with Mom in Viterbo was one-sided, and not once since then had she asked about my grievances. Was she scared of what she would hear? Were her regrets as a mother the same as my regrets, but she was simply unwilling to be put on the defensive? I guess if I were a different person, I could have challenged her brazenly.

284 But the hour of our lives was late, and looking at that statue, I understood that I no longer wanted to be controlled by the past. As much as I wanted to have it out with my mother, I also wanted a happy peace between us. And you simply can't have it both ways. I had wasted so many years hanging on to old hurts, coaxing them along like tender plants so that the bitterness would continue to bloom, watering them with my resentments.

Standing in front of Bazzaro's statue, I began to see the work I had to do to correct *my* behavior and to make peace at *my* end. How she chose to deal with the past was her business; I had a responsibility only to mine. What's more, I understood that for better or for worse, I was my mother's daughter. And I accepted that.

Perhaps that was the only lesson I needed to learn on this trip.

I reached into my purse, withdrew the small sheet of lined, white paper on which I had jotted down my three grievances, ripped it up, and tossed the pieces in a nearby bin.

EASTER SUNDAY. The day of redemption and rebirth. How perfect, how apropos. Mom and I were sitting in an enclosure in Saint Peter's Square waiting for Easter Sunday Mass to begin. We had arrived two hours before it was to start. Elderly people have a compulsion about arriving early. Not that I minded in this case; the sky was bright blue, and the cheerful sunlight warmed my spirit.

A pretty young nun—wearing foundation and lip gloss, no less—was scurrying to secure seats for anyone who belonged to a religious order. Occasionally she held her cell phone above the throngs and snapped photos.

"She has a cell phone," Mom said, in case I hadn't already noticed. "Should I get one?"

Everyone around us seemed to have a cell phone, using it as a camera or a phone. Some used them as GPS devices to locate friends and relatives lost in the crowd. A person would stand on their chair, barking instructions into their cell phone while waving frantically so that the person on the receiving end of the call could see them. I have a recurring nightmare about a not-too-distant future where people of my generation, most by then with acute hearing loss, are yelling into their cell phones, or worse, putting their devices on speaker mode.

In a crowd of this size locating people seemed beyond futile. But people don't give up, bless their hearts, and so they barked and waved with abandon.

"Where are you? OK, turn around and face the Basilica. Now look to your right. Do you see a man waving a striped umbrella? That's me! Yes!"

An hour before the start of the service Mom leaned over and asked, "Do you know where the washrooms are?"

"You're joking," I said. "You can't go to the washroom here. Have you looked behind us to see how many people are here? There must be a million. Why didn't you just wear a diaper?"

"I'd rather use a washroom," she sniffed proudly. And then, "Maybe I should have worn dark pants." Those are words I do not like to hear.

"I cannot believe you're doing this," I chided her as she prepared to set off with her red walker. I had visions of her evacuating in Vatican Square.

"I'll be fine. You stay here and guard our seats," she said.

I can only describe the moment as akin to bidding farewell to someone who is about to embark on the expedition of a life-time and whose return cannot be guaranteed. Frankly, I did not expect to see her again.

Miraculously—and on an Easter Sunday in Saint Peter's Square this counts as a true miracle—she returned about forty minutes later.

"Have I got a story for you," she smiled triumphantly as she pushed her walker into our row. I folded it up and placed it beside me.

"The women's washrooms are so overcrowded that the women have taken over the men's washroom!" she said, taking her seat. "The men sure aren't happy about it, either. When my turn came for a stall, a man pushed me out of line. Imag-ine the nerve! So I left and went to the Red Cross office. It's over there." She pointed out the location of the office, a dis-tance from our seats roughly equal to that between Venus and Mercury. "I asked to use their washroom, and they said they didn't have one. But I persisted, and eventually a nun inter-vened and led me to the washrooms reserved for nuns."

When my mother tells me stories like this, I don't always believe what she says. I suspect she embellishes her stories and I tend to regard them as more metaphor than fact.

Nevertheless, I play along.

"Wow! What an ordeal!" I said gamely, still amazed that she had found her way back on her own. "But you're OK?"

"Oh, I'm fine," she smiled. "You gotta be pushy around here you know."

A young seminary student—the spitting image of Tom Cruise—asked in Italian if the seat beside Mom was free. I nodded and moved my knees and the walker out of the way to let him pass.

He turned out to be an American, from northeast Texas, he said, introducing himself as Nolan. He had spent five years in seminary and had three left to go until he was ordained.

"This is my first year in Rome," he gushed.

"They make you spend eight years in school before you get ordained?" I asked.

I believe you can get through law school faster than you can get into the priesthood.

A nun abruptly stood up in the row in front of us and began shooting random photos with her cell phone. It's a sad day when a nun has more technical literacy than someone like me.

"I can't get over all the nuns with cell phones," I said to Nolan.

"Just wait," he said. "I heard there's a hand-held gadget— like a BlackBerry—being considered by the Vatican that contains the entire missal, prayers and all."

Mass began in all its low-tech Latin glory. It was hard not to be awestruck. Sitting on your folding chair twenty rows from the Pope, it hits you that, wow, this is Saint Peter's Square and I'm sitting here on Easter Sunday and that's the Pope talking. Even for a non-Catholic like me it brings on goosebumps.

"This must be pretty exciting for you," I said, leaning over to Mom.

"Oh, yes," she replied excitedly, and then promptly nodded off.

17

Venice

THE NEXT morning we checked out of our luxury hotel and sped off to Venice. The air was fresh from a sprinkling of rain the night before as we scooted through the quiet Easter Monday streets of Rome. The sun was out, and it felt as if the temperature would easily surpass the expected high of sixty-eight degrees.

The A24 spit us east clear across to the Adriatic, through three regions, each with distinct landscapes—the gently rolling hills of Lazio, the drier soil of Abruzzo, and the soaring, snow-capped Gran Sasso mountains, through which a portion of the A24 has been breathtakingly tunnelled. One tunnel was six miles long, and I had never been so glad to see daylight at the end of it.

At the Adriatic the road splits north and south, and the terrain flattens. We turned north. It must have been Public Urination Day; I counted no fewer than six men at various points relieving themselves at the side of the road. They seemed unconcerned with issues of modesty or manners. They stood with legs brazenly akimbo, some with hands resting on the back of their heads or on their hips ("Look ma, no hands!") and pelvises thrust forward. Surely there's an international law being drafted somewhere to prohibit such behavior once and for all.

Farther up the coast, in the Emilia-Romagna region, the scenery became more industrial and urban the closer we got to Bologna. By the time we entered Veneto, with its flat, fertile land and abundant canal system, we thought we were in Holland.

Mom and I had initially agreed that this would be a leisurely drive. I had wanted to spend the night in San Marino, for no other reason than to say that I had slept in one of the world's smallest and oldest principalities. But as the day progressed, Mom changed her mind and ordered me to press on to Venice. The "leisurely" drive turned into a nine-hour, four-hundred-mile slog with barely a break.

Even then she was not satisfied. "Why is this taking so long?" she nagged. "I think you've taken the slowest route."

"Look," I said, showing her the map. "This is the most direct route there is. And we're on the autostrada. It doesn't get any faster than this."

She refused to believe me and kept insisting that there was a faster way. At one point she complained because the landscape was boring. I clenched my teeth and gripped the steering wheel tighter. Yes, it was a good thing we were going home early. Another week of this and I could envision the sort of scene that makes the six o'clock news and then gets optioned for a movie of the week.

By the time we arrived in Venice, both of us had ground our molars to dust. We parked the car in one of the usurious lots at the edge of the city, purchased a pair of twenty-four-hour transit passes, and stepped aboard a vaporetto, one of Venice's floating buses, to be taken to our hotel.

"Oh dear, I left my cane in the car," said Mom as the vaporetto merged into the busy traffic on the Grand Canal.

"Too late now," I said. I glanced at the red walker and murmured: "Don't let me down, buddy."

Say what you will about its pollution problems and crumbling architecture; the blend of water, hazy light, and Renaissance dishabille makes Venice the dreamiest place on the planet.

"I think this is my favorite city," Mom gushed. "Aren't you glad I talked you into coming here?"

I sure was. And I wished it were for more than twenty-four hours. A part of me wished I were spending it with someone mobile, someone other than my mother.

"I've already picked out four places where I'd like to live," Mom beamed as we sailed beneath the Rialto Bridge. "How about you?"

Maybe I was here with exactly the right person, after all.

I was as smitten as her by all of it: the Moorish-inspired architecture of the palazzos; the water gently lapping at everyone's doorstep—How fabulous would it be to step out of your home and into a boat rather than a car?—the elaborate domes of the churches, whose oxidized copper streaked like mascara across the stone facades; the small arched stone bridges on the side canals; the tall, slightly tilted wooden poles of the piers; the hunky but indolent gondoliers in their tight black-and-white-striped T-shirts, catnapping on the sumptuous scarlet cushions of their glossy black gondolas or drawing seductively on a cigarette as they wait for the tourists to descend. Truman Capote once said, "Venice is like eating an entire box of chocolate liqueurs in one go." I know exactly what he meant.

The Hotel Locanda San Barnaba was a short distance from the Ca' Rezzonico stop, down a lane that barely accommodated Mom's walker but that mercifully had no steps or bridges. We had arrived early in the day, about 11:00 AM, but our room had already been prepared, and the front desk clerk had thoughtfully placed us in the only main-floor bedroom that was both wheelchair accessible and handily located near the front door. The breakfast room was located on the other side of the front desk and had a walkout to a courtyard garden that bordered a side canal.

We graciously accepted a welcome cup of tea and croissant that were offered to us.

"Come on," I said to Mom, hurriedly brushing croissant crumbs off the front of her shirt and dabbing a napkin at the corners of her mouth. "We only have twenty-four hours here."

I dragged her back to the vaporetto stop, and we caught a boat to Piazza San Marco and then transferred onto another vaporetto bound for the island of Murano. The light breeze we had enjoyed on shore had switched to a brisker version on the water, but the sun was sparkling and I was lost in the enchantment of Venice's beauty.

Standing next to me were two teenagers, English girls with those nasal voices and high-pitched whinnies that hint of upper-class breeding. The taller of the two kept absent-mindedly tossing her long blond hair into my face, and one of her elbows kept jabbing me in the breast. Occasionally the boat's jerky motion would cause her to lose her balance, and she would stumble into me. She never bothered to apologize. Another case of middle-age invisibility, I thought. I aimed my inner death-ray laser at the back of her head.

While I was busy applying vitriol to enemy targets, Mom fell into conversation with two elderly English ladies. They were sisters; one lived in Bristol, the other in London. There was no mistaking which one lived where: one had the hardy, ruddy complexion of a life spent enjoying the outdoors; the other looked like she was on her way to lunch at a Kensington High Street restaurant.

They were a jolly pair, and gradually I migrated into their conversation. We were trading stories about the rudeness we had encountered from both natives and tourists, and I was just about to remark on the insolence of the teenage girls next to me when one of the women mentioned that the reason they were in Venice was that they were treating their great-niece and her friend to a brief holiday. The great-niece, they confided—the one who had been assaulting me with her hair and body parts—had lost her mother to cancer a few months earlier. I withdrew the death-ray lasers.

We made a cursory visit of Murano and its canalside glass shops, then took the two English sisters' advice and visited the Basilica of Santi Maria e Donato, a small 7th-century church, to admire its intricately designed mosaic floor.

On the vaporetto back to Venice Mom, despite her sore legs, decided she wanted to see the Doge's Palace.

You can't miss the Doge's Palace. Its pink-and-white mosaic brickwork and two-tiered arcade and gallery make it look like an enormous wedding cake with stiff white royal icing piped on in the shape of columns and tracery, arches, finials, and statues. The other feature you can't miss—the non-architectural one—is the ribbon of humanity lined up beneath the palace's colonnaded arcade waiting to gain admission. Lineups, schlineups, I smiled smugly.

I guided Mom to the front of the queue and uttered the magic words to the ticket taker: *"Mia madre è disabile."* The large doors swung open immediately. That phrase worked like "abracadabra."

It was afternoon by the time we got back to our hotel, and Mom needed a nap.

I took off to explore the winding maze of walled lanes that is Venice, over minibridges and across small piazzas.

The work day had just ended, and so the lanes and bridges and cafés were crammed with people scuttling home from work, meeting up with a friend for a quick drink, or dashing into a shop for last-minute items for the evening meal. This was what a pedestrian rush hour looks like, and I embraced it immediately.

A poster announced an evening concert of Vivaldi, Mozart, Pachelbel, and Rossini farther up the Grand Canal; a young woman handed me a brochure for a performance of *Così fan tutte* and *The Barber of Seville;* yet another brochure that I had picked up earlier outlined a string program of Vivaldi, Corelli, and Bach. So much music! So little time!

I studied the map to locate La Fenice, Venice's famed opera house. It was on the other side of the Grand Canal. I regarded the quickly fading light and decided it would not be prudent to go searching for it now. Another time, I told myself.

I took the long way back to the hotel—the back streets—and dallied on the small jaunty bridges that grace the quieter side canals, watching the water pass beneath me, listening for the silence that comes when the tourists have retreated to their rooms.

Twilight fluttered over Venice. On a side canal an incandescent glow formed an aura around a shuttered window, and I wondered if the person living in the apartment behind it was still enamored of Venice despite the incessant warnings of impending environmental disaster.

THE NEXT morning it was time to take our leave of Venice. It hardly seemed fair.

"You go out and take another look around," said Mom as we finished our breakfast. "I'm going to take my walker up the street and window-shop. Let's meet back in an hour. If you see something that interests you, go in and look around. Don't worry about me."

The bright morning air was sprinkled with the sounds of people scurrying along the narrow lanes and of metal café chairs and tables being untangled from their neat stacks and scraped across the stone piazza of Campo San Barnaba.

I crossed a tiny bridge and saw a woman opening the shuttered windows of her apartment and preparing to hang laundry on her small balcony that jutted over the canal. The Ca' Rezzonico museum was just down the lane, and that's where I was headed, on the recommendation of the two English sisters.

This palazzo-turned-museum-and-art-gallery was everything I had hoped to see in a museum, and more. A repository for early Venetian art, Ca' Rezzonico is a stunning masterpiece—historically, architecturally, culturally. If I ever did a tour of Italy again, I would dispense with every gallery and museum except for Rome's Galleria Nazionale d'Arte Moderna and Venice's Ca' Rezzonico.

I purchased my ticket on the ground level and immediately became distracted by a black-lacquered gondola that had been used by the family who once lived in the villa. I had no idea that gondolas were built from eight different types of wood or that one side of the craft is longer than the other to counteract the weight of the gondolier.

On the next level I passed through a series of reception rooms sparingly decorated with antique chairs and tables. The scene-stealers were the ceilings. A series of artists had been employed by the Bon and Rezzonico families when the palace was under their ownership, from the mid-16th century through the 17th century.

In one room with crimson, cloth-covered walls two masters—Gerolamo Mengozzi and Giovanni Tiepolo—had created the Nuptial Allegory, Mengozzi had painted a trompe l'oeil balustrade around an architectural fantasy of plasterwork and richly carved "wood" architraves. Inside this faux frame Tiepolo had painted an airy skyscape with chubby cherubs frolicking among clouds that were so light you felt you could move them with your breath.

Tiepolo's characters are always voluptuous creatures with rosy, dimpled bottoms and gently imploring eyes. His skies are dreamy and ethereal; the taffeta on his subjects shimmers, and their skin looks softer, less chiselled than the stern perfection wrought by Michelangelo.

I moved from room to room, my head tilted back and my mouth open in awe. I had never seen such beautiful art in my life.

Again I found myself asking the question, How does this stuff get relegated to second- or third-banana status? How come people are waiting eons to get into the Uffizi or

the Vatican Museum while work of this caliber—the Tiepo-
los, Guardis, Longhis, Molinaris (equal if not superior in my
humble opinion) goes largely unnoticed by tourists? And may
I just add this fact: There are no lineups at Ca' Rezzonico.

Figuring I had seen everything there was to see in the
museum, I was about to take the stairs back to the main floor
when I spied an arrow pointing up a small set of stairs. I followed it and came upon the top two floors of the palazzo,
which now serve as a comprehensive exhibit of Venetian
painting from the 15th to the 18th century. Oh my God! I fell
into artistic ecstasy.

I glanced at my watch. Damn, I had already spent an hour
and a half there and had only managed the briefest tour. I
did an embarrassingly quick trot through the galleries before
forcing myself back to the main floor and scurrying back to
the hotel.

"Where on Earth have you been?" Mom demanded.

"You wouldn't believe the palace I've just been through. It
was incredible. So much better than the Doge's Palace."

"You went through it and you didn't bother to come back
and get me?" she scolded.

"You told me that if I saw something that caught my eye to
go in and not bother coming back to get you!"

"Well, you should have. Really, you're impossible. Come
on. We'd better check out."

THREE HOURS later we were holed up in an unappetizing
Best Western on the fringes of Treviso. I stood, deflated, on
a small hotel balcony looking down at a gas station and a tree-
less, dusty suburban wasteland where a long lineup of cars
waited impatiently at a traffic light. I pined for Venice and the

splendors of the Ca' Rezzonico, for the small stone bridges and narrow, winding lanes.

I returned to the stultifying blandness of our room to resume the business of repacking. Our luggage was straining the zippers, and I could barely lift any of our suitcases.

At the airport ticket counter the next morning we faced a clerk who informed me that our luggage was severely over-weight. We were frog-marched to a Ryanair kiosk to pay the penalty.

We were then directed back to the ticket-counter lineup and told by the same clerk that no wheelchair had been ordered for Mom. (I had triple-checked this detail when changing the reservation only a few days earlier.) She said the printout with our amended flight information, the one I held in my hand, was insufficient, and insisted on seeing the original reservation.

Luckily I still had that piece of paper, but it was buried in the farthest reaches of my suitcase.

"Open your suitcase here," the counter clerk demanded.

"But...isn't there somewhere more...private?" I asked. Behind me was a line of grim travellers, their arms crossed and their feet tapping with impatience.

"Right here is fine," said the clerk. "Hurry up, please."

I hate strangers looking in my suitcase. It's creepy. When I have found myself witnessing other passengers opening their suitcase I have to look away. I just think the contents of one's suitcase are too personal for public viewing.

Reluctantly, I crouched down and upzipped my suitcase. It sprang open like a jack-in-the-box.

The red walker, which Mom and I had bound with pack-ing tape, suddenly toppled over with a crash. This drew even more attention to us. People spun around and stared as if I had set off the fire alarm. A few people wandered over and stood just beyond my personal space, peering into my suitcase as if I were about to set up a flea-market stall. I shooed them away angrily.

My hair flopped in my face as I plunged my hands into every corner of my suitcase, searching for the missing flight document while simultaneously keeping tabs on five bags—well, six, if you count my mother. I could feel perspiration gathering on my brow and around my nose.

Mom shuffled to my side.

"There's no wheelchair," she said in an agitated voice. "How could this happen? What are we going to do about that? You're going to have to ask them to find one. Otherwise, they'll have to carry me. Oh, and I need to find a washroom. Do you know where it is?"

Tears began to squirt from my eyes. The toetapping behind me grew louder.

I kept my head down—achieved a small victory when I located the documents—and proceeded to stuff the contents of my exploded suitcase back in place with one hand and force the suitcase top shut with the other.

Never again, I muttered to myself, my lower lip quivering. Never again will I take a trip like this.

18

Making the Effort

"LET'S GO to Italy again," said Mom.

It was not the first time she had suggested the idea shortly after our return home. I chuckled politely and hoped she would drop the subject.

"Well, why not?" she pouted, clearly not pleased with my dismissive response. "I'm ready to go again."

She said this after having just wheezed out an account of how exhausting her day had been—a day spent picking up a few groceries and playing bridge.

"Mom, you can't get around," I said evenly. "Don't you remember the pain you were in? How you barely made it up a flight of stairs? How out of breath you were?"

"Oh, that was then. I'm fine now," she said brightly.

The woman is infuriatingly indomitable.

"I'm sure you're fine," I answered. "But I haven't fully recovered. I don't think I could handle it again."

She might very well want to take on Italy again, but deep down we both know the possibility is unlikely.

I wouldn't say that out loud to her. If there is anything I have learned from our trip it is that the elderly cling to hope. It's their last resource and their prime motivator. Making plans, voicing possibilities, launching ideas is what keeps them—all of us, when you think about it—feeling vital and in the game. When you're held hostage by your body's limitations, hope is all you've got.

"I just can't seem to get into Christmas this year," she said one evening when I arrived to help her string some lights on the artificial trees in her home. "But I want it to look as if I'm at least making an effort."

That's what life comes down to eventually—making the effort.

Since our return from Italy I have become more conscious of my mother's health, more appreciative of what she has to struggle with daily. Her frequent episodes of dozing off during our trip, for example, were actually an early warning signal of unhealthy levels of carbon dioxide in her system. I am hyperaware of signs of her regression, and I'm also forgiving of them. The best I can do for my mother is, well, mother her. It's still a learning process for me, but better late than never, as they say.

She doesn't come to the door to greet me anymore when I visit her, and I take no offense to that. I know I'll find her in the den, sitting in her favorite chair, her trusty red walker by her side like a faithful pet.

Once I've taken off my coat and slipped off my shoes, and we've given each other a warm hug or a cool air-kiss, depending on our mood, she will eventually pull herself up out of her chair and with shaky, arthritic hands grab hold of the handlebars of her walker, and shuffle slowly toward the kitchen to stir something in a pot on the stove or check on what she's got in the oven.

Her dark brown eyes have paled and become watery over the years. The once feisty twinkle is dimming, as if the bulb is sputtering. She can still be defiant, but on closer examination the look in her eyes is wary, unsure, a little frightened.

Years ago, when she and I fought bitterly, I thought the only thing that could bring her down was a silver bullet and a wooden stake. Now I see that it will take much less. The thought of her dying makes me gasp for air. I love her—her quirky, impatient, irritating, food-drooling, incontinent self. Well, maybe not the incontinent part.

I have come close to losing her a few times since our return from Italy—one night in Guelph General Hospital she was given just hours to live—but she's a tough old gal, and each time she bounced back. During one stay in the hospital she actually said "I love you" to me without me saying it first to her. I've always known she does, but I need it said to me to make it real. It was when I saw her with a ventilator strapped to her face, surrounded by enough tubing and cable to dial in a planet, and with the staccato beep of the heart monitor marking time, that I realized I truly loved her, and that the sparkle of my own life will diminish when hers is over.

My relationship with my own daughter is one that I have come to appreciate more and more, too. I never want her to regard me as an adversary, and I don't want her to think that a bond between people just happens, especially among family members; it has to be nurtured.

During the holidays I took Zoë to Toronto for a matinee performance of the National Ballet of Canada's *Nutcracker*. We were the oldest mother-daughter duo there. All around us little girls bounced excitedly or pirouetted in their fancy red velvet Christmas dresses while their mothers fumbled with ticket stubs and tried to locate their seats.

The outing was something I had put on my mother-daughter to-do list the moment I learned that I was pregnant with my daughter. It took seventeen years for the stars of Opportunity, Time, and Money to align. Or maybe it was Desperation: The following year, Zoë would leave for university.

302

The Nutcracker provides a magical subtext that I doubt Tchaikovsky realized when he composed it. It is the mother-daughter dance. The young leads in the ballet, who fight constantly, as brothers and sisters do, could easily be replaced by a mother and daughter whose day-to-day bickering gets suspended at times by moments of awe and shared hopes for fantasy and exoticism. The reason we fight is that we are so much the same and we want the same things.

I told Zoë that this outing to *The Nutcracker* was much more than a chance to go to the ballet—I told her from my heart what it meant to me and what she meant to me. Such candor makes teenagers cringe. I didn't care. I continued to tell her so that she would never forget. Eventually, she was reduced to rolling her eyes and yelling, "I KNOW HOW IMPORTANT THIS IS!" But in the car on the way to the performance she glanced at me and said with a quiet smile, "I'm really excited, too."

That was all I needed.

I telephoned Mom a few days later and told her about my outing with Zoë. "I don't suppose you remember when I took you to *The Nutcracker?*" Mom asked tentatively, almost resigned to the fact that I would not remember it because, as she so often has said, "You only remember the unpleasant things from your childhood."

But she was wrong this time. "Yes, I do," I replied excitedly. "It was at Eaton Auditorium on College Street. I can even picture us in our seats and what I was wearing—a red wool coat and matching hat. I remember us watching people come into the hall."

I detected a smile and a sigh of relief at the other end of the phone.

And then, "Remember Italy?" she said, her voice softening. "Wasn't that fun! What was it that you said to the gas station attendants about playing piano for a whore?"

We both broke into laughter.

She fell silent for a moment, and I pictured her with a faraway look in her eyes, flipping through her memory reel and reliving moments of our road trip—Alberobello's countryside woven with ribbons of drystone fences and studded with little *trulli,* the cargo-ferry ride to Sicily, the caves of Matera, Easter Sunday with the Pope, the thrill of sailing down Venice's Grand Canal past endless renovation possibilities.

Perhaps she was thinking back to when she paused at the massive windows of a disappointing hotel room and gazed down onto a bustling Florentine piazza, imagining herself—the version of her that is young, carefree, and able to move her limbs freely—striding confidently across the piazza, twirling coquettishly, arms outstretched, and filled with the joy of simply being alive and being in Italy.

From the sidelines, a grown daughter wonders whether she has glimpsed herself twenty-five years hence.

Acknowledgments

FRANK MAINOLFI, the owner of Bar Michelangelo in Hamilton, Canada, first suggested I take an extended trip to Italy (I think he meant this in a nice way), and I am grateful for his push.

Thanks also to Tony and Sofia Verna for their kind hospitality and invaluable research assistance, and to Mary Lou Atkinson for serving as creative midwife for the title of this book.

I'd like to express my deep gratitude to the folks at Greystone Books, particularly Rob Sanders, Corina Eberle, and Emiko Morita for their ongoing encouragement and behind-the-scenes magic. Many extra gold stars go to my editor, Nancy Flight, who guided this project from start to finish. Her wise suggestions helped me tell a story that was, at times, difficult to articulate.

Finally, to those nearest and dearest to me, a heartfelt *grazie mille*.

What the Psychic Told the Pilgrim

Whoa! what the hell are you doing in May?"

Thus spaketh the psychic, definitely not the type who holds her tarot cards close to her vest.

She had done a couple of readings for me in the past, and I decided to visit her just weeks before my pilgrimage—part due diligence and part perverse desire to see whether her psychic powers were still sharp.

Lori is a youthful, slim, pretty woman with long brown hair and green eyes that freak you out a bit because they look like lizard eyes. She wears faded jeans, a pink off-the-shoulder sweatshirt, and bare feet. She looks more like a pole dancer than a psychic.

Tarot may well be her specialty, but subtlety is not her strong suit. "Whoa!" was the tip-off.

So, just what was I doing in May?

"Well," I began tentatively, "I'm going to Spain in May. I'm walking the Camino de Santiago de Compostela. It's an ancient pilgrimage route that runs through northern Spain. About eight hundred kilometers long."

My speech began to speed up, gaining momentum like a horse off the rein. I was excited about the Camino, and I wanted her to be excited, too.

"It's not an organized trip," I continued. "You have maps, and you just follow the signs and arrows along the way. You start off crossing the Pyrenees; that's the mountain range that divides France from Spain. You carry a pilgrim passport with you, and it gets stamped in each town you stop at the end of the day. When you reach the end—in Santiago—you present your pilgrim passport and receive a parchment certifying that you completed the journey."

Lori stared at me. Her lizard eyes flashed. I half expected a tongue to fly out and slap me.

"But you're not going alone," she said matter-of-factly. Her brow furrowed as she puzzled over the tarot cards laid out before her.

"No," I replied brightly. "I'm leading a group of fourteen other women."

Lori raised her head and gave me a look of profound incredulity. "*Fourteen* other women?" She said this in a tone of voice that indicated that I should know better. She rolled her lizard eyes and let out an exasperated sigh. I sat chastened, my eyes downcast.

"*No!*" the Little Voice Inside urged. "*Don't you dare shrink. Don't let anyone screw your dreams.*"

I raised my eyes and looked defiantly at Lori. Come on, Lizard Eyes, I dared her. I can take it. I leaned in a little to show her I was unafraid of what she had to dish about the fourteen women.

Instead, she gathered up her cards and changed the subject.

"How much hiking have you done?" she asked tauntingly, glancing at my long skirt and pointy-toed stilettos. I might not look like a hiker, but, damn it, she didn't look like a psychic either. I refused to let her stare me down.

"Actually, I've been hiking the Bruce Trail and the Hamilton Waterfront Trail," I answered haughtily. "Been hiking for, oh, let's see, about seven months."

A sarcastic smile crept over her lips. Now it was her turn to lean toward me. "Have you ever been camping?"

The word "camping" caused my body to jerk.

"No, I haven't camped," I said, stiffening my resolve. "We won't be camping anyway; we'll be staying in *refugios*—pilgrim hostels."

Lori shuffled the deck and peeled off one card at a time, dramatically snapping each one face up against the shiny surface of her dining room table.

"You might find that this experience is a bit more... *rustic* than you want," she said with forced diplomacy. She began flipping the cards faster. I watched her and wondered whether I had wasted my money coming here just to be scolded.

"Watch your money," she blurted. "There's the possibility you may overspend."

I'm paying fifty dollars to hear *that*? There's *always* the possibility of my overspending. It's in my DNA.

"Be frugal," she added, narrowing her eyes on me. My cheeks flushed; I hoped she wasn't a mind reader.

She arranged a new round of cards in a semicircle, studied them, gathered them up, and reshuffled.

"Don't take jewelry."

Reflexively, I fingered my necklace that held a few personal totems—a silver cross, a gold pendant in the shape of Pelee Island, a small filigreed gold heart with the words "#1 Mom" (a gift from one of my sons), and a tiny gold shell, the Camino's universal emblem, given by a friend as a token of pre-Camino courage.

"I wear this everywhere," I told Lori. "I almost never take it off. And these earrings"—my hands moved to touch the gold hoops and diamond studs that decorated my ears. The hoops were a gift to myself when I was downsized out of a job and barely had money for groceries; the studs were a gift from a man who later downsized our relationship.

"If they're important, don't take them. You'll definitely lose something."

Lori dealt the cards again and pondered their message. I could almost hear the wheels turning in her brain.

Finally, she exhaled audibly. "Well, this trip may not be awful, but it won't be fabulous. You might write a book about it. You'll meet two celebrities."

My ears pricked up. "Like Harrison Ford?" I asked eagerly. "Or Robert Redford?" I hastily added Redford's name because in my excitement I forgot that I had removed Ford from my Hot Men list when he dumped his wife and kids for Calista Stickwoman. Now visions of hiking with movie stars raced into my mind. There I was with Redford, walking along a moonlit path as we murmured to each other about spiritual destinies...

"Not men," said Lori, interrupting my reverie. "Two women."

Crap.

"It won't be the trip you hoped it would be," she continued, "but oddly enough..."—she paused to double check her dog-eared cards as if disbelieving their message—"yup, looks like you'll do this sort of thing again."